WESTERN AND HARD-BOILED DETECTIVE FICTION IN AMERICA

Western and Hard-Boiled Detective Fiction in America

From High Noon to Midnight

Cynthia S. Hamilton

**MACMILLAN
PRESS**

First published 1987

Published by
THE MACMILLAN PRESS LTD
Houndmills, Basingstoke, Hampshire RG21 2XS
and London
Companies and representatives
throughout the world

Printed in Hong Kong

British Library Cataloguing in Publication Data
Hamilton, Cynthia S.
Western and hard-boiled detective fiction
in America: from high noon to midnight.
1. Detective and mystery stories, American
– History and criticism
I. Title
813'.0872'09   PS374.D4
ISBN 0-333-40495-5

For my family
who kept wanting to know when it would be finished

Contents

Preface

There are a number of people I should like to thank. My husband has undoubtedly contributed more to the successful completion of this project than anyone else. He has acted as sounding-board, typist, and on occasion as research assistant. He has also done the dishes. Marcus Cunliffe supervised the initial stages of my research and writing on the American adventure formula, and has continued to take an active interest in my work. Rupert Wilkinson's meticulous reading of my dissertation was invaluable. I am grateful for his time and patience, as well as for the discomforting accuracy of his criticisms.

Cindy Pateras has provided a great deal of bad coffee and good advice on the craft of writing. John Whitley and Geoffrey Hemstedt have taken a helpful interest in my project, for which I am grateful. My daughter contributed a great deal of eager interest, both in whatever I happened to be working on at the moment, and in the timing of her supper. My editor, Frances Arnold, has been both helpful and patient.

Although I had formulated my own approach to formula literature before reading John G. Cawelti's work, his *The Six-Gun Mystique* and *Adventure, Mystery, and Romance* have certainly helped to shape my own thinking. Although I admire his work, I have reservations about his theoretical framework. Richard Bridgman's notion of colloquial style, and Philip Durham's identification of the concept and components of the objective technique have provided the framework for my discussions of style, though the insights on individual writers made possible by their groundwork are my own. John Paterson's fine essay on the private eye had the effect of immediately crystallising what had previously been nebulous. Robert Edenbaum and Steven Marcus did me a similar service for Hammett's work. I have relied heavily on a number of biographies, mainly for facts, but occasionally for some insight:

White on Wister, Gruber on Grey, Easton on Faust, Layman on Hammett, and MacShane on Chandler. While this book covers much of the same ground as my doctoral dissertation, 'American Dreaming: The American Adventure Formula in the Western and Hard-Boiled Detective Novel, 1890–1940' (1984), the reader may wish to refer to the dissertation for a fuller discussion of Owen Wister. The dissertation also contains a more detailed assessment of the approaches and issues which emerge from a survey of critical studies on the Western and hard-boiled detective formulas.

In the Introduction and the chapters that follow, I have used the following format for referencing: (a: b); 'a' refers the reader to the numbered bibliography, where full particulars of the work cited can be found, and 'b' identifies the page(s), or volume and page(s), in question.

C. S. H.

Acknowledgements

The author and publishers wish to thank the following who have kindly given permission for the use of copyright-material:

Dodd, Mead and Co. Inc., for the extracts from *The Notebooks and Poems of 'Max Brand'*, copyright © 1957 by Dorothy Faust, copyright renewed 1985 by Judith Faust, Jane F. Easton and John Frederick Faust;

Zane Grey Inc., for the extracts from *The Border Legion, The Lone Star Ranger* and *The Wanderer of the Wasteland* by Zane Grey;

the University of Oklahoma Press, for the extracts from *Max Brand: The Big 'Westerner'* by Robert Easton, copyright © 1970 by the University of Oklahoma Press;

Alfred A. Knopf Inc., for the extracts from *The Maltese Falcon* and *Red Harvest* by Dashiell Hammett;

the late Mrs Helga Greene, College Trustees Ltd and Alfred A. Knopf Inc., for the extracts from *The Big Sleep* and *Farewell, My Lovely* by Raymond Chandler;

the late Mrs Helga Greene and College Trustees Ltd, for the extracts from *Raymond Chandler Speaking*, edited by Dorothy Gardiner and Kathrine Sorley Walker.

Introduction

This is an analysis of the dynamics of one generic traditio. the American adventure formula. It is a study of its development and change during the half century from the purported closing of the frontier in 1890 to the eve of US involvement in The Second World War in 1941.

The book focuses on two subgenres, the Western and the hard-boiled detective novel, both of which are structured on variants of the basic formula. Both are built around the testing and confirmation of key American values, especially individualism, and are closely tied to the myth of the American dream.

Formula itself is a much maligned and misunderstood phenomenon. Although many studies of formula literature have been done recently, no one has reached the very nub of the matter and explored the dynamics of formula. This is due to a generally held assumption: that formula is essentially static. Formula has been dissected as a corpse, to the accompanying disbelief that such an organism could ever have lived. What I propose is a delicate operation which leaves the heart still beating, and traces the paths of the life force as the organism reacts to the irritations of history and adjusts to the discipline of individual authors.

Once one understands that the complexities of formula come from its dynamic nature rather than from any complicated constructional elements, it becomes plain that a little common sense and a very few definitions can replace a multitude of jargon terms, lists of alternate patterns and pieces, diagrams, and other devices of critical obfuscation.

Formula is in fact merely a set of interrelated conventional elements found in a large number of individual works. Such conventions spring from an agreement between writers and readers which allows the artist to simplify his material and to control, through concentration, the reader's connotative associations. A group of literary works which all adhere to the same

1

formula belong to the same genre. Thus we can speak of the Western and hard-boiled detective novels as 'subgenres', for both can be subsumed under the American adventure formula, or 'master formula'. From this it follows that a number of 'levels of generalisation' are possible: the individual author's interpretation of formula, the subgenre, the master formula, and the archetypal story pattern.

The formula itself is defined by the particulars of its 'setting', 'hero', 'plot', 'style' and 'theme'. It is the combination of these elements taken as a whole that makes the formula unique; singly and in lesser combinations they can be found in numerous genre outside the American adventure formula. There are two crucial elements in the setting of the master formula: lawlessness and the maximum opportunity for personal enrichment. These two characteristics make the setting the best possible proving-ground for the individualistic values of the American ideology. The hero is the best man; he demonstrates what it is possible for the individual to accomplish. The plot in which he is presented involves some form of the chase. The story is told using a colloquial style of narration, characterised by the literary imitation of everyday speech. The theme which permeates every aspect of the master formula is the primacy of the individual; he is seen to be the key unit of society.

The time span I have chosen to scrutinise is, from the standpoint of most genre studies, very narrow. There are good reasons for going against the conventional wisdom in this respect. The specificity of a definition framed within a narrow time span is likely to prove a subtler critical tool, more useful in explicating the dynamics of particular works than one which relies on broadly defined attributes or categories. It is also more likely to provide useful insights into the links between a generic tradition and the intellectual history contemporaneous with specific developments. A narrow time frame also allows one to give individual authors and their works the detailed attention they deserve.

I have chosen the period from 1890 to 1940 because it allows me to trace developments in the American adventure formula at a time when historical and institutional pressures were shaping it decisively into recognisably new patterns. It is always difficult to confirm specific connections between historical events or trends and changing literary modes. One would not wish to posit a simplistic cause-effect relationship, but current attitudes, preoccupations, and worries do find their way into the literature of a period. During the decades under study, the individualistic ethic, the very cornerstone of American values, was under attack. At the very least one can say that the innovations in the American adventure formula seem an appropriate response to the fears which surfaced during these tumultuous years.

In the paragraphs above, I have endeavoured to set myself apart from other critics of formula fiction. There is one other important difference which should be underscored: I do not agree with the conventional wisdom concerning the nature of the field of popular culture. The conventional view rests on a hierarchical notion of culture which divides cultural products into such categories as 'high-brow' and 'low-brow', or 'high art', 'popular culture', 'mass culture' and 'folk art'. As one ascends from mass culture to high art – folk art is usually treated separately with the indulgence due a noble savage – one is not climbing a simple aesthetic hierarchy. If works were categorised on the basis of artistic success or merit, this approach would not pose problems for formula literature. Such is not the case. The hierarchical notion of culture is laden with preconceptions about the inherent limitations of formula.

To begin with, while high art is defined in terms of its most successful examples, popular culture is defined in terms of its lowest common denominator. While high art is defined as an individual phenomenon, popular and mass art are defined as social phenomena. When one looks, for example, at the hierarchical approach developed by Stuart Hall and Paddy Whannel in *The Popular Arts*, one finds that the descent from high to mass art is associated with an assumed progressive loss of control by the author over his work. Accordingly, the high-art novelist is more concerned with his material than with his audience. High art is less conventional, and is said to be judged by its ability to challenge and disturb the reader, whereas popular and mass art offer confirmation and reassurance (19: 58ff).

While such categories are not entirely incorrect, they are certainly dishonest. The critic pretends to provide a basis on which to judge popular culture 'in its own terms' while handicapping, through definitional limitations, potential artistic achievement; he then condemns pieces by the standards of high art. The concept of conventionality is particularly telling in this regard. Popular culture is not exclusive in its use of conventions; if high art did not employ them it would be both less accessible and less rich on a metaphoric level. The issue should be the artistic skill with which conventions are employed, not the limitations of conventions themselves. Hall and Whannel acknowledge this, but another issue weighs rather heavily in their considerations; the kind of conventions employed:

> As the cinema begins to move towards high art, it caters more naturally for the educated, middle class audience familiar with the more traditional forms. This development is good, in so far as it brings the cinema in touch with the standards of high art, and makes it a medium of complex and subtle communications: but it can help to stratify the audience, and affect adversely the quality of its more popular work.   (19: 76)

The distinction made here is the kind we make when calling a sonnet highly conventional while labelling a Western rigidly formulaic. The worst sonnet appears superior to the worst Western; it may even be superior to the best Western. This intellectual snobbery is accompanied by its social equivalent which assumes that the educated middle class will appreciate the forms of high art, while the great unwashed must be fed formula pieces.

Such preconceptions muddy the thinking of many who attempt to formulate a methodology for dealing with formula literature. In *Adventure, Mystery, and Romance: Formula Stories as Art and Popular Culture*, John G. Cawelti begins by setting up two sets of important distinctions. The first is between cultural and universal conceptions of story types, and is not problematical. The second, between descriptive and aesthetic modes of generalisation, creates problems for him from the start; he blurs the distinction even as he defines it. Cawelti speaks of two related, but distinguishable, objectives: the study of large groups of literary works 'for the purpose of tracing historical trends or relating literary production to other cultural patterns', and the use of literary classes 'as a means of defining and evaluating the unique qualities of individual works' (14: 7). The categories he sets up to accommodate these different aims are basically the same category under different names:

> When we turn from the cultural or historical use of the concept of formula to a consideration of the artistic limitations and possibilities of particular formulaic patterns, we are treating these

formulas as a basis for aesthetic judgments of various sorts. In these cases, we might say that our generalized definition of a formula has become a conception of a genre. (14: 7)

In other words, when you wish to be descriptive, you call formula 'formula'; when you wish to make aesthetic judgements, you call formula 'genre'. The problem with this is that Cawelti has already made it clear that he is not thinking solely in terms of neutral definitional elements; he is using the concept of genre 'not simply as generalized descriptions of a number of individual works but *as a set of artistic limitations and potentials*' (14: 7, emphasis added). It is clear, then, that his view of individual works will be hampered by expectations based on the lowest common denominator to be found.

It seems to me that the time has come to take a fresh look at the hierarchical notion of culture and its correlative, the study of popular culture, for they create a false issue – a falsely complicated issue. Formula literature is not a special case: one needs the same skills to write it well as for any other form of literature; one needs the same skills to criticise it; and one should take into account the same kinds of social factors in both cases.

The present study is an attempt to create a different kind of methodological framework for the study of popular literature: a framework which allows for both a broad perspective and the detailed, subtle analysis of individual works. I have in mind a framework which allows one to trace historical trends in the development of genre literature. It must facilitate the detailed study of interconnections between a generic tradition and the intellectual history contemporaneous with specific formulaic developments. I have in mind a framework which shows the interweaving of generic traditions. It must explain new offshoots and cross-breeds which result from this entwinement. It must display the layering of generic traditions, and show the effects of layering within individual formula pieces. Finally, I have in mind a framework which recognises the artistic prerogatives of the individual author, and the aesthetic integrity of individual works.

These aims will help to explain something of the organisation of this book. Part One sets out the kinds of relationships which my methodology is designed to study. Chapter 1 places the formula within its historical frame. Chapter 2 shows the layering-process in which different generic patterns are superimposed one on the other, resulting in richness where one layer reinforces another, or tension where there is conflict. Chapter 3 discusses the formula in relation to the marketplace. It deals with the way the material aspects of production shape not only the formula itself, but also the reception accorded to formula literature by audience and critic.

Part Two focuses on individual authors and their work, displaying the potential of my methodology as a critical tool for unlocking the richness and variety of formula writing. I have chosen to concentrate my study on two authors of Westerns and two hard-boiled detective novelists. Each is well known within his field and all have achieved a considerable measure of popularity. Though some have been more prolific than others, each has had an important impact on the development of the formula. Some have achieved recognition and praise, others have attracted only sneers. Together they display the remarkable versatility of the formula. Zane Grey and Frederick Faust ('Max Brand' *et al.*) are both synonymous with the term 'Western'. Dashiell Hammett and Raymond Chandler are highly acclaimed writers of the hard-boiled detective novel.

I have devoted a considerable amount of space to the interpretation of biographical material. Such an approach is necessary to obtain insights into an author's values, interests, preoccupations and thought patterns. This information then serves as a useful point of reference for the critical examination of the fiction itself. The full import of patterns or seeming contradictions within a particular novel often becomes understandable only when viewed within a larger context: that of the author's background and the general body of his writings. The continuity and malleability of formula becomes more impressive when such diversity is recognised, while the contributions of individual authors to a formula tradition stand out more clearly. Such territory is just beginning to be explored. My approach has, I believe, allowed greater depth and detail than previous studies.

Part One
The Study of Formula Literature

1

The Historical Frame

The values and assumptions built into the American adventure formula are also central to the ideological tradition of the United States; to that body of ideas which form the basis for its political, economic and social system, and which often take the form of unstated and untested assumptions underlying thought and expression. 'Individualism' is a main constituent of American ideology: it postulates that the individual is the foundation of society and that his interests and rights should have priority over those of the society. Ideally, the individual surrenders as few rights as possible to the domain of societal control. Though individualism may take on more socially benign forms of self-realisation, one very important product of individualism can be 'possessive individualism', as C. B. Macpherson has pointed out:

> The individual, it was thought, is free inasmuch as he is proprietor of his person and capacities. The human essence is freedom from dependence on the wills of others, and freedom is a function of possession. Society becomes a lot of free equal individuals related to each other as proprietors of their own capacities and of what they have acquired by their exercise. Society consists of relations of exchange between proprietors. Political society becomes a calculated device for the protection of this property and for the maintenance of an orderly relation of exchange.   (57: 3)

The self-aggrandisement implicit in the notion of possessive individualism is necessarily competitive where self-interests conflict, and so we have its correlate, 'competitive individualism'.

This last has some disquieting implications. Society becomes a false concept, for, when an individual's first duty is to himself, social responsibility is ignored, and group needs and collective responsibilities are not considered when they clash with an indi-

9

vidual's needs of the moment. Indeed, group action comes to be seen as devious, as a contravention of the code, for it circumvents the duty of *self*-reliance and *self*-protection.

Disavowal of the group and impatience toward restraints make the ideal society one without law. Lawlessness is a double-edged blessing, however. No assurance is provided that the contest will be fair; the winner may well be the man least troubled by self-restraining ethics. Justice becomes a contest of strength, devoid of abstract notions of guilt, responsibility or compensation. And the weak are left to perish.

The setting of the American adventure formula is an idealised environment which allows competitive individualism free reign. The two crucial attributes of the formula's setting are lawlessness and the maximum opportunity for personal enrichment. Lawlessness grants perfect freedom in the pursuit of self-aggrandisement, but the resulting contest is often brutal. Women and the aged are particularly at risk. Not surprisingly, the lawlessness is often viewed with ambivalence: detrimental to society in general, it tests a man's true worth, both morally and competitively. The result is a contradictory impulse to perpetuate lawlessness while eliminating it; to take the law into one's own hands, meting out extra-legal revenge to reassert the importance of virtue.

The second element of the setting is equally important in the formula: provision must be made for material accumulation, with wealth both abundant and accessible. Property functions as an emblem of power and badge of success, just as it does within the American ideology. This emblematic significance hinges on the correlation between the difficulty of the contest and the value of the compensation. Wealth is also meant to function as a lasting reward. These two symbolic functions conflict, for the former requires the maintenance of free competition, jeopardising the reward by making it impossible to retire from the fray.

Wealth is always present, but material accumulation is not always portrayed favourably. The lawlessness can taint the reward with the sordidness of the contest. Legitimate wealth is the result of an individual's endeavours in a fair contest. The burden of defending even legitimately acquired property may also make its possession less attractive.

The ideology of the American dream shapes other aspects of the master formula. The hero is the archetypal individualist, the 'best man'. The style reflects a democratic insistence that one man's language is as good as another's. The plot allows the hero to demonstrate his superiority. Thematically, a problem is put forward which challenges the viability or universal applicability of American values, then demonstrates that the problem is more apparent than real. American individualism reigns supreme. The reassurance implicit in this formula's covert argument must have seemed deeply reassuring in 1902 when Owen Wister's *The Virginian* appeared, setting the mould for a new form of Western adventure writing. The decade preceding the book's publication had been one of acute social, economic and political upheaval aggravated by the worst depression before the 1930s. The schisms within American society became alarmingly apparent.

The violence of Homestead, Pennsylvania, in 1892 and the Pullman Strike of 1893 showed the bitter antagonism that had developed between capital and labour. Racial tension rose as discrimination became institutionalised through a series of court cases and legislative ploys designed to strip blacks of their voting and civil rights. The lynching of blacks increased. Friction between immigrants and members of the established community became acute in a society which had more than tripled in population in the space of fifty years. Russian Jews fleeing pogroms were greeted with the virulent anti-semitic rhetoric of the Populists. The Reverend Josiah Strong railed against the dangers of alien Roman Catholic traditions.

Sectional interests also clashed. Indebted farmers, squeezed by falling prices and monetary deflation, raged bitterly against the money interests of the industrial East. The tariff provided another forum for controversy. It was higher than it had ever been before, benefiting the East. The South and West, both largely agricultural, complained of the inflated prices on manufactured goods which resulted.

America's very image of itself was threatened. A frontier nation saw its free land broken into to such an extent that the frontier was deemed closed, a rural people had to recognise the economic and political dominance of the city and the flow of its population into urban areas, and a predominantly WASP culture had to acknowledge the impact of massive immigration by those with alien traditions. The city political machine, urban poverty, the domination of the economy by huge corporations and corporate trusts, and the antagonism between capital and labour presented new problems which were inconceivable within the old notions of American identity.

Against this background, the master formula argued for the universality of core American values. Confronted with a rapidly diminishing frontier and deeply felt sectional hostilities, the Western subgenre reasserted a continuity of values between East and West, echoing the arguments of a contemporary historian, Frederick Jackson Turner, who saw the frontier as a certain kind of environment which encouraged especially 'American' character traits.

Turner's thesis was itself part of a larger debate initiated by the 1890 census report, which declared the frontier line an outdated concept. The wilderness had been conquered; the free land which Jefferson, upon the purchase of the Louisiana Territory, had declared adequate for 'a thousand years' had given way to newer frontiers, themselves conquered.

The attention given to the purported closure of the frontier reflected a sense of ending and loss which had little to do with the actual needs of the society at the time for free land. The loss was felt on a deeper level, and it was this symbolic dimension which Turner addressed when he discussed the relationship of the West to the American icons of individualism, self-reliance and the self-made man. 'The West, at bottom, is a form of society, rather than an area', he said in 'The Problem of the West' (1896) (150: 205).

The form of society he describes is one where competitive individualism has free reign:

> It followed from the lack of organized political life, from the atomic conditions of the backwoods society, that the individual was exalted and given free play. The West was another name for opportunity. . . . The self-made man was the Western man's ideal, was the kind of man that all men might become. Out of his wilderness experience, out of the freedom of his opportunities, he fashioned a formula for social regeneration, – the freedom of the individual to seek his own.   (150: 212–13)

Turner even goes part way toward acknowledging the essential lawlessness of such a society, but does not admit that it is the strong who are apt to secure 'Justice': 'The frontiersman was impatient of restraints. . . . There was a reproduction of the primitive idea of the personality of the law, a crime was more an offense against the victim than a violation of the law of the land' (150: 212).

The shaping of society by frontier conditions, Turner argued, had given the United States its unique identity and special strength. Although the frontier had been conquered, the character traits it inspired were still important. He discussed the relevance of frontier virtues to capitalism in a later essay, 'Contributions of the West to American Democracy' (1903): 'Long after the frontier period of a particular region of the United States has passed away, the conception of society, the ideals and aspirations which it produced, persist in the minds of the people' (150: 264). The transition to an industrial economy, he says, was encouraged by frontier values:

> The old democratic admiration for the self-made man, its old deference to the rights of competitive individual development, together with the stupendous natural resources that opened to the conquest of the keenest and the strongest, gave such conditions of mobility as enabled the development of the large corporate industries which in our own decade have marked the West. (150: 258)

One can see how Turner's picture of the West would offer a theoretical defence of the key American values given deference in the East, providing an ideal environment for displaying the efficacy of these values while simultaneously arguing for their importance in the development of the American nation. Ironically, as Turner himself recognised, the socio-economic mobility his argument assumed was losing ground in the face of ever-growing conglomerations of wealth. 'The Owners of the United States' had assessed this situation in 1889, concluding, 'The United States of America are practically owned by less than 250,000 persons, constituting less than one in sixty of its adult male population' (62: 273). The Sherman Anti-Trust Act of 1890 and President Theodore Roosevelt's later rhetoric attempted to soothe public fears and to reassert the importance of individual competition.

The Western formula reflects this crisis, offering further reassurance on the importance of the individual. It also downplays the significance of sectional rivalries, for thematically, the Western demonstrates that competitive individualism is central to both East and West, civilisation and nature. This demonstration is implicit in the initiation process undergone by hero and heroine. The hero is 'civilised': he accepts the responsibilities and limitations represented by a wife and family, and may even hang up his guns and pursue a more conventional career. Meanwhile, the heroine learns to accept Western ways, making the transition from East to West, civilisation to nature, in terms of the values she accepts as workable. She is likely to discover that lawless individualism is preparing the way for her more civilised, but impractical, values.

Such transitions argue for a revitalisation of American values; for the rebirth of Western zeal, boldness and toughness in the Eastern drawing-room. East and West are easily bridged because they are essentially the same, with differences only a matter of degree: individualism is the predominant social philosophy of both. In the East, where the struggle is more muted, man is seen to have lost his toughness, however. The Western seeks to underscore the continuing need for tough competitiveness. Clearly, the West of the Western is an Eastern creation, wished for within the frustrations and restraints of the East, and located in a theoretical place innocent of these restrictions.

The core of the Western's setting is a society much like the one Turner depicts, with instantly recognisable historical and geographical costuming. The landscape, dress and architecture are close enough to old photographs and to a cultural memory fed by various media to be recognisable as 'the American heritage'. While such historical and geographical attributes are metaphorically important, they are not enough. The focus of attention is a society in the first stages of development. The land is rich with untapped resources, but alien and treacherous, dominated by space and silence.

Space is absence, the civilisation that isn't there; the gap that must be bridged. Space isolates towns, ranches and individuals; it makes the necessity of self-reliance pictorially apparent. Silence is the auditory equivalent of space, and it works in much the same way. Both intensify the presence of anything which holds the foreground, contributing to the drama of the action.

Though the Western is set in a beleaguered, remote place, there is a tendency, especially during this time span, to portray the setting as a virgin land of untapped natural resources abounding in possibilities for exploitation. The land may yield rich mineral deposits, prove fertile farmland or provide lush grazing for cattle. Though rich and starkly beautiful, the landscape is wild, alien, testing seekers of wealth with difficult terrain, vast emptiness and silence.

The settlers are relative newcomers, and their hold on both the land and their own lives is tenuous. A society is just beginning to form, and the Lockean social contract has not yet been endorsed; the institutions which regulate behaviour and protect members' rights are still either non-existent or ineffective. Accordingly, every individual has perfect freedom and absolute responsibility for his own protection. Once the social contract is endorsed, the participant loses a portion of his freedom in return for protection, but this has not yet happened. The individual must prove himself superior to both the hardships of the land and the strength and cunning of others. If he emerges victorious, he is likely to secure material well-being, the esteem of his fellows, and 'get the girl'.

Owen Wister provided the model for this setting in *The Virginian*, which he described as 'a colonial romance'. 'For Wyoming between 1874 and 1890 was a colony as wild as was Virginia one hundred years earlier. As wild, with a scantier population, and the same primitive joys and dangers' (197: vii). In this Wyoming, the ideal conditions for mobility are re-established:

> We had seen little men artificially held up in high places, and great men artificially held down in low places, and our own justice-loving hearts abhorred this violence to human nature. . . . Let the best man win! That is America's word. That is true democracy. And true democracy and true aristocracy are one and the same thing.   (197: 147)

Not surprisingly, the best man does win. The Virginian is tested against a series of adversaries, and is found to be a natural gentleman and an able businessman, the match of any man, Eastern or Western. His victories against all those of suspect integrity give the book a 'high moral tone' and a rather simplistic duality between good and evil. The term 'best man' retains a certain ambiguity, however. A balance is achieved where the moral dimension submerges awareness of the precarious position of the weak, while the practical dimension discourages the enquiry, 'What if the best man morally does not win?'

Moral transgressions emerge as a question of skill: 'You've got to deal cyards *well*; you've got to steal *well*; and if you claim to be quick with your gun, you must be quick. . . . You must break all the Commandments *well* in this Western country. . . .' (197: 399). Indeed, transgressors are treated more sympathetically than their hapless victims. When captured outlaws and vigilantes breakfast together at the Cottonwoods before the lynching, discussion centres on the failure of the rustlers to outwit their pursuers rather than on their misdeeds.

The link between lawlessness and deprivation is underplayed while the ineptitude of the victimised is emphasised. The Virginian tells Shorty that as a reckless youth he often made, then lost, large sums at cards: 'The money I made easy that I *wasn't* worth, it went like it came. I strained myself none gettin' or spendin' it. But the money I made hard that I *was* worth, why I began to feel right careful about that' (197: 272–3). In part, this represents a moralistic distinction between rightful earnings and the ill-gotten gains of speculation, but Wister's failure to distinguish between the practical problem of defending property and the moral justification for possession also provides a useful sleight-of-hand. Existing property-holdings are justified, the impartiality of tenuous ownership is affirmed, and the illusion of fluid distribution is retained.

The Western also pays homage to the need for progress. It seems to have its eye firmly upon the glorious future toward which it is inevitably moving: after the lawlessness is crushed, after this land is tamed and its riches are realised, the glorious future will dawn. Hence the general note of optimism which characterises the Western of this period.

The euphoria is in fact generated by ignored contradictions and a retrogressive notion of progress. Once society is fully formed, material holdings are no longer an infallible indicator of individual worth. When, for example, unearned wealth can be inherited with the protection of the law, competitive individualism is circumvented. The ideal society exists only in a moment of transition. What follows is anti-climactic, a world dominated by social institutions rather than by individuals. The epic movement of the Western, its great thrust toward progress, is really the illusory movement of running in place. This is the irony of the Western setting, and, as Marcus Cunliffe has pointed out, it threatens to make the whole exercise ridiculous.

Wister manages to turn the transitory nature of the Western setting to good advantage by using it to emphasise the continuity of American values. East and West, past and future, become hopelessly ensnarled. The East is what the West will become, but is itself an older West. The West represents a living past and emerging future. These interconnections help to emphasise continuity, as do the movements of characters between East and West. The Virginian, the keystone of unity, is seen finally as a man in the American mould, transcending differences between East and West.

He makes the transition from Western cowpuncher to Eastern-style capitalist, becoming 'an important man, with a strong grip on many various enterprises, and able to give his wife all and more than she asked or desired' (197: 503). By the end of the book, he is esteemed in both Bear Creek and Dunbarton.

Molly Wood, the young Eastern schoolmarm, undergoes a parallel transformation, learning Western ways. Superficial differences are easily accepted, but acquiescing to competitive individualism in its balder forms requires a sterner choice. Indeed, Molly Wood's initiation differs in kind from the Virginian's; in accepting her hero, she denies herself and her conscience. When she throws her arms around this dusty victor, she accepts him as husband, but also as killer.

The narrator is also initiated into the ways of the West; his wary fascination with the picturesque gives way to admiration for the hero's skills and respect for the egalitarianism of the West. He comes to realise that the West is purer in its regard for American values than the East. Although the narrator attains a degree of self-sufficiency, he never becomes fully integrated into Western ways, for he cannot accept vigilante justice.

For Wister, a member of the Philadelphia Bar Association and one-time practising lawyer, this 'rough justice' was difficult to accept. Wister evinces little sympathy for the underdog, however. The losers, the weak, are simply dismissed as unimportant. It is disturbing that such callous indifference has been preserved in such a popular formulaic construct.

Wister's personal indifference is more understandable. His sympathies and attitudes are those of the upper-class Eastern establishment. He was born into an upper-class Pennsylvania family of distinguished ancestry. His private schooling in Switzerland, England and the United States, his Harvard degree, and his membership in the prestigious university clubs, the Dickey and the Porcellian, provided him with further credentials appropriate to his family's social sphere. Wister was known to Theodore

Roosevelt as 'Dear Dan' throughout a long correspondence, and was a member of the inner circle of the President's friends, a group which included Associate Justice of the Supreme Court Oliver Wendell Holmes, Jr; writer Henry Adams; Senator Henry Cabot Lodge; and Elihu Root, then Secretary of State. It is no wonder that, when Wister caught a glimpse of Coxey's army of unemployed marchers, the sight merely amused him, for, as he explained later, 'I did not live in coal mines or railroad yards; the talk I commonly heard was the talk of powerful people, well-to-do, sheltered by their own ability and the success which it had brought them . . .' (194: 200). He was much less amused by the Pullman Strike of 1894, which caused him considerable personal inconvenience. While he could forgive a capitalist such as Averill Harriman, whose offences were 'those of his era', he considered the labour-leader Bill Haywood to be 'a malignant public enemy' (194: 235). One sees these attitudes in Wister's comments about the West, as when he says of the cowboys, 'They are of the manly, simple, humorous, American type which I hold to be the best and bravest we possess and our hope in the future. They work hard, they play hard, and they don't go on strikes' (183: 246).

The contempt Wister shows for the weak was enshrined in the social theories of his day, especially in social Darwinism. As popularised in the United States, this creed provided a justification for the brutality of competitive individualism. It could readily embrace the reality of slums and urban poverty and the brutality of capitalistic competition: 'We accept and welcome . . . as conditions to which we must accommodate ourselves', wrote Andrew Carnegie in 1889, 'great inequality of environment; the concentration of business, industrial and commercial, in the hands of a few; and the law of competition between these, as being not only beneficial, but essential to the future progress of the race' (37: 16–17). These conditions, while 'sometimes hard for the individual', were 'best for the race', because they ensured 'the survival of the fittest in every department' (37: 16).

This struggle for survival was seen as both inevitable – evolution being an in-built principle of the universe – and desirable, in that improvement over time was assumed. Competition was not merely justified, but promoted as a positive good. As Richard Hofstadter has pointed out, social Darwinism, especially in its American forms, was a body of belief 'whose chief conclusion was that the positive functions of the state should be kept to the barest minimum, it was almost anarchical, and it was devoid of that center of reverence and authority which the state provides in so many conservative systems' (48: 7).

Such was the particularly American synthesis of the ideas of Charles Darwin and Herbert Spencer which Carnegie helped to popularise during the last quarter of the nineteenth century. The appeal of the notion is not surprising. It justified the poverty and misery which were becoming increasingly visible in the industrial labour pools of American cities, and provided a seemingly scientific basis for the old-style individualism which was increasingly under attack. Furthermore, it was able to subsume very neatly the older icon of the 'self-made man', whose fortunes were dependent not on the prior advantages of inherited position or wealth, but on his character, skills and ability. The success of the self-made man demonstrated the fairness of the contest, and served to highlight the more positive aspects of social mobility by espousing 'self-improvement'. Horatio Alger's hugely successful juvenile stories, from *Ragged Dick* (1868) to *A New York Boy* (1898), helped to fix the image of the self-made hero in the American consciousness.

Social Darwinism, in concert with the Turner thesis, eased Eastern fears, and each doctrine helped to bolster the other. Projecting the brutality of current social conditions backwards onto a frontier setting demonstrated the universality of social Darwinism, while the applicability of social Darwinism to current conditions provided further evidence of continuity. The Western formula embraced both constructs, together with the ideal of the self-made man.

The prototype for the self-made Western hero is to be found in *The Virginian*. His triumph may be interpreted in social Darwinist terms, but Wister did not advocate this philosophy directly. That advocacy was left to Zane Grey. In Grey's work one plainly hears the echo of Darwin rather than Jefferson: 'Here at last was revealed the deepest secret of the desert, the eternal law men read in its lonely, naked face – self preservation and reproduction. The individual lived and fought and perished but the species survived' (222: 220).

For Grey the focus is no longer triumph, but survival. What Wister developed as social doctrine, Grey acknowledges as universal law. To a degree, this inflation makes the brutality of the principle more acceptable because it seems inescapable. But

Grey also makes it clear that the individual is apt to regress to instinct and bestiality when the battle reaches its highest pitch. In *Wanderer of the Wasteland* (1923), the starving hero battles with a snake, hoping to kill it for food. Grey's description dramatises the atavistic streak in man:

> Adam let out a hoarse yell. Something burst in him – a consummation of the instinct to kill and the instinct to survive. There was no difference between them. Hot, and mad and weak, he staggered after the crippled snake. The chase had transformed the whole internal order of him. He was starving to death, and he smelled the blood of fresh meat.   (222: 79–80)

The confrontation ends when Adam falls and lies spent on the sand, literally face to face with the rattlesnake. Waiting for the snake to strike him, Adam is 'only a fearful animal, fascinated by another, dreading death by instinct' (222: 80).

This is a danger of the desert, the West. The strife by which the fittest survive tests the individual spiritually as well as physically: only those who acknowledge some form of idealism survive as men:

> When the desert claims men it makes most of them beasts. They sink to that fierce level in order to live. They are trained by the eternal strife that surrounds them. A man of evil nature survivin' in the desert becomes more terrible than a beast. He is a vulture. . . . On the other hand, there are men whom the desert makes like it. . . . I've met a few such men, an' if it's possible for the divinity of God to walk abroad on earth in the shape of mankind, it was invested in them. The reason must be that in the development by the desert, in [the] case of these few men who did not retrograde, the spiritual kept pace with the physical. (222: 64)

Here Grey carefully separates physical strength from spiritual worth, raising the disquieting possibilities Wister submerged by blending the two. The distinction allows Grey to insist on the claims of a higher morality, however. He attempts to combine social Darwinism with a more compassionate philosophy, that of 'Christian humanism'. In doing so he attempts to bridge a rift within American values themselves.

At first, Christian humanism seems to provide an antidote to the disquieting implications of competitive individualism and the harsher aspects of social Darwinism. Divine law provides guidance in a lawless state. Social responsibility is reasserted as a positive good. The identity crisis is assuaged by following one's 'calling'. The professional ethics implicit in the notion of calling replace the amorality of the main chance. Social status is shown to be illusory, unimportant when viewed beside the salvation of the worthy.

Unfortunately, while this value set provides answers to many of the objectionable features of social Darwinism, it raises more problems than it solves. Although both doctrines spring from an individualistic outlook, they are incompatible. In so far as Christian humanism promotes the virtues of mercy, charity, fellowship and humility, it is diametrically opposed to the aggression of social Darwinism. Since Christian humanism emphasises the importance of every person's soul equally and stresses a common humanity, social Darwinism appears selfish and brutal when viewed from its vantage point. Looking the other way, Christian humanism seems impractical if not suicidal. Social Darwinism demands freedom from restraints, while Christian humanism pleads for equality of circumstances.

The gap between the two can be seen most clearly where Grey attempts synthesis. For example, *The Heritage of the Desert* (1910) raises the problem of the strong, virtuous man, Hare, who will not fight to defend his rights because he believes that it is wrong to use violence. The book makes it clear that no one can escape from the struggle to survive.

Hare knows a special trick that makes him very fast on the draw, but hangs up his guns to avoid bloodshed when trouble comes. He is shot for his scruples. As a result, he learns that 'he had come to the somber line of choice. Either he must deliberately back away, and show his unfitness to survive in the desert, or he must step across into its dark wilds' (207: 193). In the course of the same book, Augustus Naab learns a similar lesson. His reluctance to use his formidable strength is demonstrated in his confrontation with Dene, an outlaw gunman. Naab displays his fast draw, then shows Dene a huge fist: 'One blow would crack your skull like an egg-shell', Naab declares. 'Why don't I deal it? Because, you mindless hell-hound, because there's a higher law than man's – God's law – Thou shalt not kill!' (207: 30). Augustus Naab follows the dictates of his conscience, hoping that his enemies will be satisfied with what they have already taken, but they are not. He gives up one range with a valuable spring, then another complete with stock. Finally the rustlers attack his home, kill his son, and carry off his adopted daughter. The final outrage is too much; he denounces his creed and prepares to fight back, but Hare, out of gratitude for Naab's many kindnesses, takes the burden of revenge upon himself. Naab rides into town to find his enemy already dead:

> 'Eighteen years I prayed for wicked men', he rolled out. 'One by one I buried my sons. I gave my springs and my cattle. Then I yielded to the lust for blood. I renounced my religion. I paid my soul to everlasting hell for the life of my foe. But he's dead! Killed by a wild boy! I sold myself to the devil for nothing!'
>
> (207: 291)

Here in all its starkness is the contradiction involved in pairing social Darwinism with Christian morality. The last chapter of *The Heritage of the Desert* is an attempt to reverse the pessimism, to cover over the hollowness of Naab's victory with the happy ending of Hare's and Mescal's honeymoon. But Grey cannot easily submerge the issues he has raised, for he has introduced a problem central to both the Western formula and the ideology that stands behind it.

In this as in other respects, Grey is an almost perfect mirror of the contradictions of his society. He came from the Midwest, from the middle class, and grew up on baseball, adventure tales and small-town shenanigans. He absorbed the values of conservative, small-town America completely and uncritically, and swallowed the myths of his culture whole. Grey's fiction is an attempt to put forward a simplified version of life, a reconstruction better able to support his self-image and values. Grey escaped from the complexities of life into fiction, but he could not evade the contradictory tendencies within his small-town values. These he worries at and exposes, seemingly unaware of their true nature.

In *The Heritage of the Desert*, Grey uncovered the value rift between social Darwinism and Christian humanism. Later books display a solution typical of his culture: he assigns the seemingly passive moral perspective to women, the moral guardians of society, while allowing men to be active, aggressive and 'practical'. Structurally, this solution is built into the formula itself. The plot conventions of the Western, as established in *The Virginian*, 'marry' the two by bringing hero and heroine together. This marriage requires the heroine to surrender her conscience in the name of practicality. In *The Virginian* this is obscured by the greater prominence given to the hero's less problematic initiation. Grey explores the dilemma of the heroine more explicitly. In the process he necessarily exposes the gulf between the value sets she must bridge: 'If you go deliberately to kill Beasley – and do it – that will be murder. . . . It's against my religion. . . .', pleads Helen in *Man of the Forest* (1920). 'But, *child*, you'll be ruined all your life if Beasley is not dealt with – as men of his breed are always dealt with in the West', Dale replies (212: 351, emphasis added).

Helen, like Molly Wood, must deny her self, but in Helen's case this surrender is worked through in a series of interior monologues. Discussion of the 'forces' at work on her personality is intermixed with the acknowledgement of newly perceived marital inclinations, making her thinking conveniently cloudy: 'Helen did not analyze that strange thought. She was as afraid of it as she was of the stir in her blood when she visualized Dale' (212: 222–3).

Even before she falls in love, Helen feels the impact of her new environment, and wonders whether she might succumb and drift toward primitivism. Dale, her hero, provides Grey's answer: 'There must be a great change in either you or me, accordin' to the other's influence. An' can't you see that change must come in you, not because of anythin' superior in me – I'm really inferior to you – but because of our environment?' (212: 158–9).

Grey's heroines must not sink too far, however. They are civilisation's missionaries, pointing the way toward a more humane society which it is men's duty to fight to establish. Women provide the rationale for men's violence. The proper feminine role is a projection of male needs, just as the West is a projection of Eastern needs. In the end, the heroine becomes a housewife. Helen accepts this, her true role, and with it her husband's superior wisdom: 'How full and perfect her trust, her happiness in the realization that her love and her future, her children, and perhaps grandchildren, would come under the guidance of such a man!' (212: 382). Helen is revealed as a male-ego prop on a number of different levels.

This ideologically convenient definition of sex role implies severe social constraints. Grey accepted these wholeheartedly: the 'modern woman' seemed vulgar and unfeminine to him, and he was shocked by the loosening social and sexual mores of the inter-war years. The Tahitian girls were more to his taste: 'They wore their hair in braids down their backs, like American schoolgirls of long ago when something of America still survived in our girls', he noted wistfully (229: 171).

Grey's stance is always essentially conservative. He was baffled and repelled by many aspects of twentieth-century America. His books were written in conscious opposition to the literary standards of the day, to counter realism:

> In this materialistic age, this hard, practical, swift, greedy age of realism, it seems there is no place for writers of romance, no place for romance itself. For many years all the events leading up to the great war were realistic, and the war itself was horribly realistic, and the aftermath is likewise. Romance is only another name for idealism; and I contend that life without ideals is not worth living. Never in the history of the world were ideals needed so terribly as now.   (218: Foreword)

Had Grey been a true believer in social Darwinism, realism would have been his narrative mode of choice as the stance best able to cope with the Darwinian struggle descriptively. Grey's championship of the philosophy was decidedly ambivalent. He took it in as part of his intellectual heritage, welcomed the excitement which nature 'red in tooth and claw' could produce, but was troubled by the spiritual vacuum at its centre. Social Darwinism could provide no aura of heroism, nor could it support the old morality of small-town America.

Like the segment of society whose views he reflects, Grey rejected the amoral perspective. His answer to the decadence and corruption of the present, as sketched in such books as *Majesty's Rancho* (1942) and *The Code of the West* (1934), was to return to the simple virtues of the past. Whether his books pose the contrast between the scatter-brained college youth and the noble cowboy, between the immoral flapper and the true heroine of the West, directly or not, almost all of them are an attempt to turn the clock back, and to place before the reader the nobility of a former time. In this sense, Grey's revolt was essentially conservative, though Grey himself would no doubt have preferred to see it as idealistic.

Grey acknowledged that he was a romantic, an idealist, a dreamer; indeed he dignified his idealism as a generalised human need: 'I have yet to know anyone who has not some secret dream, some hope, however dim, some storied wall to look at in the dusk . . .', he wrote in the Foreword of *To the Last Man* (1922), 'We are all dreamers, if not in the heavy lidded wasting of time, then in the meaning of life that makes us work on.'

Grey's longing to return to a simpler time and less complex society, his distrust of the new-fangled, his sentimental idealism and his compassion for the victims of life's struggle all reflected his deep links with small-town, middle-class America around the turn of the century. His unease with the current direction of American social and economic trends was also typical, as was his faith in the essential goodness of the American way of life and his optimistic view of the future.

Up until the end of the First World War, much of American society, including the social theorists, shared this optimism. Progress was assured. The utopian writers of the 1890s, the turn-of-the-century muckrakers and the Progressive reformers all assumed that America's current problems were growing pains which could and should be overcome. By the end of the First World War the mood of the country had changed. The extent of the reversal can be judged by contrasting the difference in stance of the Western, forged at the turn of the century, and the hard-boiled detective novel, developed in the 1920s. The latter typifies the big-city weariness and wariness of this post-war period; tired of idealism, cynical of reform, it mingles acceptance with outrage as it looks around at a world brutalised and morally bankrupt from a dirty, unheroic war and widespread corruption. This new cynicism was largely an urban phenomenon. Grey, like many of his readers, kept the faith long after it had become unfashionable to be sentimental, idealistic or optimistic; and he continued to enjoy a wide readership.

The size and sympathies of rural, small-town America, even during the 1920s, should not be underestimated as they affected the attitudes of the city dwellers themselves, many of whom had grown up in a less urban environment. The uncomplimentary portrait of the city in hard-boiled fiction reflected this continuing agrarian bias, as George Grella has pointed out (296: 11). The same bias gave the Western its aura of impending well-being.

By 1920 the intrusion of the city on American life could not be ignored: less than half of the population lived in small villages or on farms (53: 225). While cities were becoming more important politically and economically, they often seemed the repository of all that was evil. The city housed many of the vast wave of foreign immigrants who threatened, in the eyes of many, to dilute true Americanness. This was also the world of the flapper, the gangster and the party machine – each a travesty of some aspect of American values. The flapper was an assault on traditional concepts of sex role, especially on the notion of women as the moral guardians of society. The gangster's illicit success sullied the character of the self-made man, while the party machine stood as a contradiction of America's democratic self-image. The hard-boiled detective novel comes to terms with these troubling urban phenomena; its violence is an act of exorcism.

The urban setting of the hard-boiled detective formula stands in stark contrast to that of the Western. Resources and space are limited. The inhabitants are dwarfed by the buildings which block their horizons and intrude, drab and ugly, on their lives. The streets are labyrinthine and menacing, a world of shadows; indeed, the argot term 'to shadow' connotes this aura of unknown danger.

The city is a conglomeration of individuals without a sense of community, where people become lost or lose themselves among the faceless. The rich and the slum-dweller coexist; the majority compete to 'get by'. Even women have joined the fray. The fastest, easiest road to wealth is an illegitimate one: the wealthy mobster demonstrates the contrast between the relative stasis of the socio-economic structure as a whole and the booming extra-legal economy. Hence the temptation to which everyone, including the guardians of law, is exposed. Almost everyone crosses the line at some point, but there are many gradations of self-indulgent criminality, from drinking or selling illegal whisky to killing for personal gain. This vast spectrum of law-breaking contributes an aura of corruption which pervades the hard-boiled novel. The deference paid to success, however achieved, makes this lawlessness provocatively troublesome. Societal values appear hypocritical at best.

The impetus toward progress which characterised the Western is lost; the city is a world locked into the present, without a sense of future. If the perspective is not ahistorical, it is nostalgic. A loss of certainty is manifest, and, for many, wealth fills the vacuum left by less tangible values. Wealth allows one to buy things, people, power, and often dispensation from justice. The tie between material well-being and happiness is broken, as is the connection between riches and worth.

The more critical attitude to wealth and the wealthy found in the hard-boiled formula mirrored changing social attitudes. Before the turn of the century, the great industrialists had been national heroes celebrated at length in the popular periodicals of the day. The muckraking years dethroned them, exposing much greed, dishonesty and corruption, as well as highlighting the poverty and misery caused by business policy and practice. The behaviour of the Harding administration seemed to confirm this view of the dirty dollar, as did, in later years, the findings of the Pecora committee on unethical Wall Street practices. The speculative fever, conspicuous consumption and tawdry materialism of the twenties, especially when viewed in retrospect from the Depression, further discredited the notion of wealth as an indicator of worth.

The private eye's refusal to accept a monetary reward reflects this awareness of the corrupting power of the dollar. The generally unsympathetic portrayal of the wealthy in the hard-boiled novel also reflects this view: they are empty souls who hide behind a showy façade, or manipulative brokers ready to consider any commodity as a medium of exchange, or they are outright hoodlums.

Dashiell Hammett's depiction of Personville in *Red Harvest* (1929) is an extreme example of this physical and moral squalor. The narrator's first impressions set the scene: 'The city wasn't pretty. Most of its builders had gone in for gaudiness. . . . Since then the smelters whose brick stacks stuck up tall against a gloomy mountain to the south had yellow-smoked everything into uniform dinginess.' The inhabitants are equally shabby: 'The first policeman I saw needed a shave. The second had a couple of buttons off his shabby uniform. The third stood in the centre of the city's main intersection – Broadway and Union Street – directing traffic, with a cigar in one corner of his mouth. After that I stopped checking them up' (352: 1). It does not take Hammett's nameless detective hero, the Op, long to learn why Personville has become known as Poisonville. Rival gangs battle for control of the town, which had been owned, mayor, police force, patronage and party machine, by a local industrialist. Not surprisingly, the police force is corrupt and partisan. The townspeople are a villainous lot. The bank clerk embezzles from his employer and kills his ex-girlfriend; the boxer has orders to throw his fight, but is forced to win because he is blackmailed; and both the town prostitute and the local lawyer indulge in extortion to supplement their incomes. The cleansing of Poisonville produces a bloodbath notorious in detective fiction, and in the end what is left is a city as essentially corrupt as when the Op started.

Personville is an extreme case, a concentration almost to absurdity of the horrors of the city. Through magnification, *Red Harvest* attacked the present directly, describing a social mileu recognisably close to that of the tumultuous cities. In doing so it represented a response which was different in kind to that of the Western, where the social mileu depicted was already an anachronism. The Western spoke to the present through the mythical past it created, providing a reassuring ideological framework for interpreting the bewildering problems of the present.

The ostensible realism of the hard-boiled detective formula provided a means of mythologising the present directly, as Hammett quickly realised. Conscious of the instant credibility awarded him as an ex-Pinkerton operative, Hammett took full advantage of public gullibility in this respect. His work displays his awareness of the re-formation – the alteration and intensification of meaning – of the 'real' detail reproduced in an arbitrarily ordered fictional framework. J. Edgar Hoover came to a similar realisation from a slightly different perspective when, during the 1930s, he used the fictional detective formula to remake his life: 'Hoover managed to persuade the public that the FBI agent was a real life version of the fictional detective hero Americans idolized in their magazines, comic strips and radio shows. Therefore as the head of the G-Men Hoover must be the greatest of them all, the archetypal detective' (315: 218).

Richard Gid Powers describes the way Hoover used the realistic social costuming of the hard-boiled detective formula as a bridge between life and fiction. On the one hand, Hoover made himself look the part of the heroic fictional detective by having himself photographed in 'typical action poses', and by drawing parallels between the exploits of his men and those of fictional detectives. On the other, he encouraged writers to take details from life, using the FBI and Hoover as heroes in works of popular culture (315: 218).

The private-eye hero of the hard-boiled detective formula is a much more marginal figure than Hoover's exploitation of the image would imply. The much-admired toughness of the hero is not what it initially seems to be. Far from being swaggering bravado, it indicates vulnerability, and is the tight-lipped response of the potential victim. The private eye lives in jeopardy, physically, socially and metaphysically. In part, the hero's marginality is a product of his loss of faith. Unable to trust society, he must look to his own resources. The detective, a man of conscience, becomes judge and executioner, upholding his personal vision of justice in much the same way as the Western hero, but for very different reasons. As John Paterson has pointed out in his fine essay 'A Cosmic View of the Private Eye', this role, with its 'dangerous power and terrible kind of freedom' reflects the individual's isolation, disillusionment and uncertainty (313: 31). This situation can produce two very different types of hero: the man aware of the existential ambiguities in which he must survive (Hammett) and the hero who rejects uncertainty and becomes a crusader (Chandler):

> Dashiell Hammett is, I think, with so many of his literary contemporaries, protesting the horrors of a savagely competitive society, the horrors of an urban-industrial civilisation. For when we scrape away the tough exterior of his hero we find not heart of stone and nerves of steel but the tortured sensibility of the Nineteen Twenties, its romantic isolation and its pessimism, its inability to find grounds for action. With Chandler's Philip Marlowe, however, we pass into another world, the world of the Depression. . . . For he represents the moral and social ardor of the Depression years, the impulse toward reform; and he is frequently prone to feelings of boyish optimism.   (313: 32)

Paterson does not address the central irony of the situation: that both responses represent an individualistic response to a crisis in competitive individualism. One can no longer gain nobility and mobility by pitting oneself against a hostile wilderness. As a result, the focus is shifted to the conflict between persons, and this struggle is often brutal, cruel and stealthily dishonest. Success is problematical: one cannot win a loyal wife, wealth is suspect, and the participants are tarnished by the combat. However, even at its bleakest, the hard-boiled detective formula does not utterly abandon the individualistic ethic. The same ideological assumptions are defended by it as were supported by the Western; only the focus of the thematic argument has shifted.

The hard-boiled detective formula deals with the problem of corruption and criminal conspiracy, an interest created, to some extent, by the national press's lurid reporting of 'the crime problem'. Public concern for this 'new' problem developed in the 1890s when a fledgling network of nationwide news media publicised local offences, and when their search for the sensational meant that demand for crime exceeded the local supply (315: 206). The virulent nationalism of the war years, the Red Scare of 1919 and the union-bashing of both Harding's administration and Coolidge's fuelled a public concern with criminal conspiracy. The machinations of big-city politics and the scandals of the Harding administration, most notably Teapot Dome, made it clear that corruption and hypocrisy had penetrated to the very core of American government.

Prohibition merely added to the problem, much to the dismay of those who had expected it to improve public morality. Public awareness and concern over crime, especially over the violence and corruption associate with Prohibition, became so great that Herbert Hoover's acknowledgement of the problem in his inaugural address was the aspect of his speech which made headlines. Not only did Prohibition create a violent, but booming, extra-legal economy, it also defined a large new class of criminals who had little respect for the law they broke when purchasing bootleg whisky, thus giving America's traditionally ambivalent regard for law a new twist. The hard-boiled detective formula met the threat of criminal conspiracy and punished political corruption while maintaining this ambivalence.

In attacking the issue of criminal conspiracy, the hard-boiled detective novel also dealt covertly with the threat of collective action. Socialism and trade unionism had long acted as bogeys within American society. Both were despised as vices imported by a subversive alien community. After the First World War the distrust of foreigners and foreign ideas was heightened by the feeling that European machinations had drawn Americans into the mire of the trenches. The foreigners whom America had sheltered were not to be trusted. Zane Grey used the 'Wobblies', the International Workers of the World, as a villainous force in *The Desert of Wheat* (1919), hinting darkly that they had worked for the enemy throughout the war. 'Shall We Let the Cuckoos Crowd Us

Out of Our Nest?' asked Owen Wister in a 1921 article in the *American Magazine*: 'They tell each other that private property is highway robbery. That is merely because they haven't any, and want yours and mine without working for it' (195: 47).

The hard-boiled detective novel tackled the problem of collective action by placing the conflict between an individual and a conspiracy at the centre of its plot. Collective action is discredited at the outset; group action is defined as criminal. The hero's demonstrable ability to deal with a collective adversary despite the unequal nature of the contest defends the efficacy and desirability of the individualistic ethic. Sleights of hand are employed here, as in the Western: the conspiracy sometimes dissolves on closer examination, or falls apart into its component individuals due to infighting or mutual suspicion. The unequivocal success of the Western hero is not enjoyed by the private eye. The detective cannot enjoy the personal benefits of his success, and his victory is at best temporary.

Even with these provisos, the strength of the individualistic bias is impressive. Hammett, the avowed Communist and perceptive critic of competitive individualism could not rid the formula of this premiss. His heroes are isolated despite the presence of associates. In *Red Harvest*, the Op dismisses one aide because he can not trust him; the other complains, 'Don't tell me anything that's going on – I'm only working with you' (352: 153). The unreliability of Effie Perine's woman's intuition becomes a running joke in *The Maltese Falcon* (1930). And it is Nick's wife who, out of boredom, gets him involved in a dangerous murder case. The need for self-reliance is emphasised by the failure of these allies. The individual is shown to be the only source of positive social action.

At first sight, the criminal conspiracies appear to provide more successful examples of group action. While they last, they circumvent the competitive code and subjugate the individual to a group outside his control. Each of Hammett's novels has such a conspiracy: there are the warlords of Personville in *Red Harvest*, Fitzstephan's web of criminal alliances in *The Dain Curse* (1929), the rather shaky Cairo-Gutman-O'Shaughnessy partnership in *The Maltese Falcon*, the political camps of *The Glass Key* (1931) and the Macaulay–Wolf conspiracy in *The Thin Man* (1934). These alliances are short-lived, however; they disintegrate as much from the strains placed on them by greed, distrust, and ambition as from the actions of the hero. As the conspiracies dissolve, the basic social unit of the competitive individual comes to the fore.

Hammett appears to be caught in a philosophical 'Catch-22': competitive individualism is bad because it is divisive, but collective action is impossible because individuals are competitive. Hammett cannot get past the basic ideological assumption of the primacy of the individual, and can pose no alternative. In this respect, the later condemnation of Hammett's work as subversively Marxist must be considered wryly ironic.

Competitive individualism triumphed in the formula, but within American society the plight of the individual provoked increasing anxiety. Such social theorists as Herbert Croly and Richard T. Ely attempted to reconcile individualism with the needs of an increasingly complex society. The Progressive movement as a whole reflected anxiety over the endangered autonomy of the individual. 'At bottom', notes Richard Hofstadter, 'the central fear was fear of power, and the greater the strength of an organised interest, the greater the anxiety it aroused' (46: 241). In the political sphere it was the party machine which threatened to disenfranchise the individual. Within the economy, it was the swollen power of the corporate interests.

The brute power of the trusts was not the only aspect of the developing industrial organisations which threatened the integrity of the individual. Henry Ford's introduction of the first assembly line in 1914 made the individual attendant to the productive machinery. The continuing trend toward rationalisation within industrial management made employees keenly aware of their subordination to the corporate structure.

The First World War undercut the position of the individual further. It justified more centralised political control, and accelerated changes in the industrial sphere. The scale of operations within a global theatre dwarfed individual ambitions. And on the battlefields the individual soldier was gassed or mortared by an unseen hand, undistinguished and indistinguishable from his fellows. John Dos Passos's tribute to the unknown soldier in *1919* powerfully captured this terrifying anonymity.

As if these attacks on the male model of the competitive individualist were not enough, the changing social ambitions of women threatened to undermine their ideological role of moral guardianship. Although women had used this very concept of inherent moral superiority to argue for the ratification of the Nineteenth Amendment, and had succeeded in gaining the vote in 1920, the suffragettes had shown a militancy which was not soon to be forgiven them. Women had sinned in other ways as well. They had been active in the trade-union movement, and now public sentiment had shifted away from the unions. Having joined the workforce in increasing numbers, entering new fields of employment during the war, women were now viewed as usurpers. Women's organisations had been active in pushing for reforms during the Progressive era, but with the campaign for Prohibition successfully concluded, reform was in disrepute. The increased personal freedom enjoyed by women, including the much announced new sexual freedom of the 1920s, also stirred resentment; their search for personal fulfilment socially, sexually and intellectually was seen as a direct abdication of their guardianship of Christian humanism.

The hard-boiled detective novel reflects the changing status of women as well as this reservoir of resentment, often portraying them as competitive, devious, wily and morally degenerate. This changed image conveys the impression of a society fragmented and embattled, and invites a pornography of violence which was not exploited until after the Second World War. Women's changing role, as reflected in the hard-boiled detective novel, raises problems not found in the Western. Women not only compete, but prove to be dangerous contenders, able to use their sexuality to trap and weaken men. Even the detective is at risk; his need for love and sexual fulfilment leaves him vulnerable to their allure. Women become adversaries, and are often among the criminals the detective seeks.

A particularly jaundiced view of the 'new woman' can be found in Raymond Chandler's work, where old concepts of sex role meet the new social reality head on. Chandler's detective hero Philip Marlowe approaches women with an outmoded chivalry, treating them with an elaborate courtesy and protective attentions. Marlowe's, and Chandler's, image of the proper feminine role is not far removed from that of the Zane Grey heroine. The virtues of the traditional homemaker–helpmate are expected: chastity, cloistered unworldliness and moral purity, ultimate obedience, and the abnegation of an independent self in the service of husband and family.

Such expectations contrast sharply with the social realities of *The Big Sleep* (1939). Carmen Sternwood stands as the nightmare version of the new woman: she is a psychopath, selfish and self-willed enough to murder men who refuse her sexual advances. She is the exact inversion of old-style femininity; instead of servicing men, she is serviced by them. Where the myth demands wholesomeness, she is physically degenerate; where it seeks homely wisdom, she is intellectually blighted; where it asks for guidance, she is morally abhorrent; where it requires providence, she is profligate.

Carmen Sternwood is an extreme example, however. Anne Riordan, the good girl of *Farewell, My Lovely* (1940) shows just how narrow the acceptable limits of female behaviour are. Anne's attempts to compete with Marlowe intellectually meet with resentment, as do her attempts to direct his behaviour. What Marlowe approves of wholeheartedly is her domesticity. It is when she provides a comfortable, peaceful refuge for him, when she acts the part of homemaker that she awakens in him an alluring vision of peaceful and supportive comfort: 'She came back with the glass and her fingers cold from holding the cold glass touched mine and I held them for a moment and then let them go slowly as you let go of a dream when you wake with the sun in your face and you have been in an enchanted valley' (379: 162). Woman's place, clearly, was still in the home.

The image of proper feminine behaviour displayed in Chandler's work is a projection of both masculine wish fulfilment and cultural utility. It represents a reaction against newly won rights, opportunities and freedoms, and is particularly critical of the active, competitive woman who would presume to take advantage of them. However, Chandler's portrayal of women has a vehemence which can not be fully explained by current social attitudes and anxieties; it shows a terror of sexuality which is characteristically his own. Even this has a wider significance, for it is expressed in terms of the conventional image of woman as a temptress.

Mrs Grayle's portrayal in *Farewell, My Lovely* is an exploration of the allure and terror inspired by the female as sex object. Mrs Grayle's picture leads Marlowe to see her as the ultimate temptress: 'A blonde to make a bishop kick a hole in a stained-glass window. She was wearing street clothes that looked black and white, and a hat to match and she was a little haughty, but not too much. Whatever you needed, whatever you happened to be – she had it' (379: 84). She is the sought-after vessel, both black and white. Her allure is associated with her moral ambiguity. On the one hand, she is Eve, weak and ready to fall; on the other, she is the keeper of the faith. She is a temptress whose allure is related to her weakness and a saint by virtue of her mortification to the needs of society.

Such a role requires a fine balance which is virtually impossible to maintain. Mrs Grayle's progress traces her fall. By the time Marlowe confronts her with the full range of her crimes, she is no longer even pretty: 'She looked merely like a woman who would have been dangerous a hundred years ago, and twenty years ago daring, but who to-day was just Grade B Hollywood' (379: 242). It is not until she sacrifices her life for the man who loves her that her essential ambiguity, and her allure, are restored.

The image of womanhood in Chandler's fiction shows how much had changed, and how much had stayed the same, over the four decades from the publication of *The Virginian* to that of *Farewell, My Lovely*. Molly Wood and Mrs Grayle are at first unrecognisable as sisters, but the ideological genes are there. Over these decades expectations had lowered significantly, while the ideal remained, perhaps honoured in the breach rather than in the observance, but recognisably the same. The Virginian and Philip Marlowe are more easily discernible as brothers, though the easy confidence and optimism of the former have clearly been ground out of the detective. Forty years had taken their toll, but the self-made individualist and his idealised, humble helpmate remained central to America's dreamscape.

2
The Layering of Contexts

The need to recognise different, coexistent layers of formula is implicit in the argument of the last chapter. Thus in *The Virginian* Wister uses the archetypal adventure setting, that of a dangerous landscape. More specifically, he follows the pattern of the American adventure formula: lawlessness allows the individual maximum opportunity for personal enrichment. Like other Westerns, *The Virginian* features an even more particularised setting: an embryonic society struggles in a wilderness environment. All these layers are present in Wister's setting.

Each carries with it metaphoric baggage, the memory of associated works. The adventure setting brings to mind the Africa of H. Rider Haggard, while the specifically Western elements call forth Cooper's Leatherstocking tales, and the West of numerous dime novels. Some associations are highlighted, others supressed. Wister underscores the ideological importance of his setting, and the connections with African adventures fade into the background. He allows one layer to reinforce another, but dulls the unwanted connotations by highlighting the more particularised attributes of the subgenre.

A self-conscious author can take advantage of the dynamics of this interplay, as Hammett does in his thematic argument. Hammett accepts the expectations engendered by the archetypal level, with its implicit plea for the triumph of virtue. His work fits within the scope of both the master formula, which argues for the vitality and continuity of American values, and the hard-boiled subgenre, which explores the problem of conspiracy. But Hammett undermines all these levels. His virtuous heroes are identified by their role within the formula rather than by their personal qualities, and their victories are tenuous. Hammett's irony cuts straight through the implicit optimism and moral certainty as he pits his existential vision against the absolutes built into the formula. The layered contexts become his foil; he takes advantage of the

36

strength produced by layer upon layer of reinforced reassurance, while deftly cutting away at the assumed objectivity and moral absolutism.

Interplay between the layers of formula can be seen once the fact of layered contexts is recognised. When the layers are in accord, as they are in *The Virginian*, the associations combine to impart an echoing depth of connotation, but, when one layer pulls the formula toward a different philosophical perspective, tries to shift the focus of concern markedly, or requires a radically different kind of emotional engagement, there is bound to be tension. Particular attributes may be redefined in a way which holds to the letter of the formula, but pulls in a different direction, as with Hammett's redefinition of 'virtue' and 'triumph'. Here the tension is of the author's making, but discontinuities may be built into the layers themselves, creating inherent obstacles for the formula writer, who is pulled first in one direction, then in another. This in-built conflict is visible in the emotional appeal made by the style of the master formula, as against that in the Western subgenre.

The master formula uses a colloquial style of narration. The vernacular appropriate to the characters and their mileu is featured. The vernacular's most disreputable relatives, slang, cant and argot, play a prominent role. Insistently nationalistic, the language boldly sets itself apart from proper English: 'When we Americans are through with the English language,' says Mr Dooley, 'it will look as if it had been run over by a musical comedy' (59: 96). Such a style proclaims a linguistic democracy where all are equal, and upholds democratic informality. The colloquial voice does this assertively, in the best brash American tradition. The penchant for linguistic shortcuts which colloquialisms exhibit also displays the American infatuation with speed and efficiency. Further insights into the national character can be culled from colloquialisms, as H. L. Mencken contends:

> Such a term as *rubberneck* is almost a complete treatise on American psychology; it reveals the national habit of mind more clearly than any labored inquiry could ever reveal it. It has in it precisely the boldness and contempt for ordered forms that are so characteristically American, and it has too the grotesque humor of the country, and the delight in devastating opprobriums, and the acute feeling for the succinct and savory.
>
> (59: 92)

Such picturesque usage makes for a lively and often humorous style, tending on the one hand toward vulgarity and on the other toward the condensation and striking imagery of the poetic: 'Slang', says Mencken, 'originates in the effort of ingenious individuals to make the language more pungent and picturesque – to increase the store of terse and striking words, to widen the boundaries of metaphor, and to provide a vocabulary for new shades of difference in meaning' (59: 563).

This delight in colourful language is clearly visible in the Western subgenre, where a man meets his 'pardner', rides his 'hoss', and 'drills' his enemies. Such expressions are placed within their natural habitat; the speech patterns of individual characters are reproduced, complete with slurred words and dropped endings:

> 'Queen Elizabeth would have played a mighty pow'ful game,' was his next remark.
> 'Poker?' said I.
> 'Yes, seh, Do you expaict Europe has got any queen equal to her at present?'
> I doubted it.
> 'Victoria'd get pretty nigh slain sliding chips out agaynst Elizabeth. Only mos' prob'ly Victoria she'd insist on a half-cent limit. . . .' (197: 154–5)

In this passage from *The Virginian*, Owen Wister makes good use of the naïveté of the colloquial style. It allows him to contrast the unconventioanlity of the expression with the shrewdness of the insights expressed. He achieves the condensation, the unexpected juxtaposition and the grain of truth which go into good humorous writing.

Unfortunately, few Westerns display the artistic potential of the colloquial style. Most flourish their dialect writing with a mixture of embarrassment over its vulgarity and triumph over its boldness, using it as an object for attention rather than as an artistic medium. Grey is particularly prone to do this.

This failure is understandable, for the Western-writer views his material sentimentally. His stance is almost elegiac. The Western slides over the controversial, conceals the problematic, and bridges the contradictory; it hands out praise with one eye shut, but not with a wink. The emotional tone of the colloquial style is of a very different timbre; it is deflationary and starkly unsentimental, as an ostensibly elegiac piece of doggerel shows:

> When men lived raw in the desert's maw,
> And Hell was nothing to shun.
> When they buried 'em neat
>   without preacher or sheet,
> And writ on their headboards
>   crude but sweet,
> 'This jasper was slow with a gun.'
>
> (123: 95)

There is delight in exposing contradictions, hypocrisy and pomposity, and often a sting, a wry twist intended to shock the reader or listener. Let loose, such raucous echoes could give the Western-author 'more troubles than a rat-tailed hoss tied short in fly-time'.

None the less, the discontinuities these different voices introduce need not be deleterious to individual formula works. In *The Virginian*, Owen Wister comes to terms with the contrary tendencies of these levels while using the style to convey his own particular point of view. His style is easily recognisable as within the parameters of the formula:

> ' . . . Brown the wheat!' he commanded, through the hole to the cook, for someone had ordered hot cakes.
> 'I'll have fried aiggs,' said the Virginian. 'Cooked both sides.'
> 'White wings!' sang the colonel through the hole. 'Let 'em fly up and down.'
> 'Coffee an' no milk,' said the Virginian.
> 'Draw one in the dark!' the colonel roared.
> 'And beefsteak, rare.'
> 'One slaughtered in the pan, and let the blood drip!'
> 'I should like a glass of water, please,' said I.
> The colonel threw me a look of pity.   (197: 150)

Despite the evident relish for colourful colloquialisms, Wister is careful to distance himself from the vulgar medium by using the narrator's more literary style as both foil and frame.

His awareness of the expressive potential of vulgar colloquialisms conflicts with his need to assert cultured superiority. He compromises, using two stylistic perspectives simultaneously. The book benefits from this distaste of cultural egalitarianism, for he is able to overcome the tension between the levels of formula by channelling opposing tendencies into his characterisations of the narrator and the Virginian. The elegiac stance is maintained by the narrator while the Virginian is allowed a rowdy, deflationary, even irreverent commentary:

> It [the American climate] was a potent drug, I said, for millions to be swallowing every day.
> 'Yes,' said he, wiping the damp from his Winchester rifle.
> Our American climate, I said, had worked remarkable changes, at least.
> 'Yes,' he said; and did not ask what they were.
> So I had to tell him. 'It has made successful politicians of the Irish. That's one. And it has given our whole race the habit of poker.'
> Bang went his Winchester. The bullet struck close to my left. I sat up angrily.
> 'That's the first foolish thing I ever saw you do!' I said.
> 'Yes,' he drawled slowly, 'I'd ought to have done it sooner. He was pretty near lively again.' And then he picked up a [dead] rattlesnake six feet behind me.   (197: 209)

Ironically, it is not the drawling Virginian who suffers in juxtaposition. The narrator's prose seems unnecessarily verbose and pretentious.

Wister makes his style work hard. Not only does the dual perspective reconcile differing layers of formula; it also reinforces the continuity of values between East and West. By setting the speech of the Virginian against the more literary language of the Eastern narrator, Wister begins by underscoring the gulf between East and West. Stylistically, the book then moves from the opposition of East and West, or the literary and the colloquial, to a merging of the two on ground more Eastern than Western as the Virginian's rising education and ambitions move his perspective closer to that of the narrator.

The Virginian who replies to the 'dude' narrator's enquiry, 'Find many oddities out here like Uncle Hughey?', with 'Yes, seh, there is a right smart of oddities around. They come in on every train' (197: 10), has changed greatly by the end of the book. When asked about the future of the cattle business, the Virginian replies, 'we'll have big pastures fenced, and hay and shelter ready for winter. What we'll spend in improvements, we'll more than save in wages. I am well fixed for the new conditions' (197: 502).

The tonal lesions which Wister managed to use so successfully plagued other writers who took up the Western formula, but those working in the hard-boiled genre did not have to overcome this tonal discontinuity. In the hard-boiled detective novel the vulgarity of the language is appropriate to the tawdry world portrayed, and the tendency of the colloquial style to deflate pomposity and unmask hypocrisy provides a welcome tool.

This conflict between master formula and Western subgenre is the most blatant form of in-built tension; other varieties are more easily overlooked. For example, the progressive restrictiveness of the layers of formula means that material is continually being put aside as the definitional attributes became more particularised. Faust's treatment of the Western hero provides an interesting case study in the reactivation of latent material from a more generalised level. His heroes draw heavily on the folk tradition of the archetypal hero, that of the virtuous survivor, and in doing so bring in elements of an alien ideology.

Three basic types of virtuous survivor are common: the conquering hero, the clever hero and the unpromising hero. Orrin Klapp describes the attributes of these three types. The conquering hero is a man of strength and consummate skill. He vanquishes his foes in fair contests, executes feats of daunting proportions, and exhibits courage and tenacity when undergoing trials. Ultimately, he emerges victorious. The clever hero, who triumphs by his wits, and the unpromising hero, whose hidden potential allows him to prevail, are both underdog heroes.

Because all three patterns emphasise the success of the individual, the master formula should be able to draw on any without complications, though the hero of the master formula does tend to be moulded on the conquering hero. The hero of the American adventure formula is self-reliant, independent, competent, strong, and has his own internalised code of behaviour. He is honest. He does not take advantage of his superior strength, nor use it without considerable provocation, and then only in a fair competition. Weaker individuals are granted protection, if worthy, and he is chivalrous to women. His code separates him from the bully, and his self-restraint justifies the violent acts he performs.

The Western hero represents a further differentiation, but still tends to draw heavily on the prototype of the conquering hero. In scale with the vastness of his setting, he is oversize physically or presents an overbearing presence, or both. The stereotyped Western hero is the cowboy gunman, whose skill with a six-shooter is unsurpassed, but this role is only one of many open to the hero. Pre-eminence can be attained by outwitting the hero's opponent, or out-lying him. Strength may lie in the hero's arm, nerves or reputation. He may be a cattleman, miner, lawman or vagabond. Whatever his vocation, the hero is the 'best man', and as such he has tremendous power over his fellows. Without self-restraint, he could become a despotic villain, for no one else is capable of restraining him, but his code makes him a sympathetic figure. Most characteristically, this is the code of the gunman: he will not draw first, or shoot an enemy from ambush; he goes to meet a single enemy alone, and shows mercy to his opponent.

Faust's heroes fit the 'letter' of the Western formula, but are rarely patterned on the conquering hero. He reverts instead to the folk patterns of the underdog hero, redefining the concept of 'the best man'. His heroes are equalisers who gain stature by dethroning those in power, either by the nimble use of native wit or by activating some hidden strength, the discovery of which surprises even the possessor. These unusual 'best men' clearly indicate that Fuast's concerns are far removed from the standard idealogical underpinnings of the genre. Where Grey or Wister justify the existing social hierarchy by depicting the 'natural' ascendancy of the man of competence, strength and skill, Faust deals with the magical ascendancy of the weak over the strong. Faust's heroes engage him in issues which concerned him personally; his heroes look up at society from the bottom. The son of a poor man dogged by failure, Faust needed to justify his affection for his father. Orphaned in his early teens and left to the kindness of relatives, Faust sought to unburden himself of the humiliating dependency of his youth. A highly competitive man afflicted with heart trouble from an early age, Faust needed to come to terms with his own weakness.

The traits Faust's heroes display are common in the folktales and fables which, like the Uncle Remus stories, teach survival to the victims of oppression. As with these tales, Faust views the social hierarchy as a measure of power, not worth. If one must bluff to reach the top, so be it. For Wister or Grey, bluffing is an

inadmissible projection of false competence. Their villains bluff;
the hero's superior competence does not require such deception.
Like trickster figures, Faust's underdog heroes learn to discover
and attack any points of vulnerability, to exploit any vanities their
adversaries possess, and to use their opponent's size and power
to their own advantage. Most notably they learn a relentless watch-
fulness, and prastise cunning. Orrin Klapp's description of the
clever hero is apt:

> He is supreme for wit, resourcefulness, nimbleness, elusiveness,
> deceit, impudence, and sense of humor. . . . He does not meet
> an opponent head-on but prefers to trick him. He is a specialist
> in triumphant but sometimes shady transactions which, on the
> whole, amuse people more than they outrage them.   (51: 23)

In *Brothers of the Trail*, Rickie's determination and quick wit
vanquish Little Charlie, who is on his yearly drunken rampage:

> the door of a saloon split open, and a jam of half a dozen men
> exploded out of it, some running right, and some running left,
> and some bolting across the street. Out behind the fleeing man
> leaped the giant, and caught the last pair, and knocked their
> heads together, and dropped them into the dust.   (252: 51–2)

It is Rickie, nicknamed 'Shorty', 'Stub', 'Stubby', who must subdue
Little Charlie and take him home.

Rickie bluffs to blind Little Charlie with rage, then turns the
giant's brute strength to his own advantage. Little Charlie charges,
taunted beyond patience, only to miss and batter himself against
walls and other obstacles while Rickie hits him as he struggles.
Though his blows do little damage, the immunity Rickie enjoys is
decisive. A subdued Little Charlie complains, 'He looks small only
when he's standin' still' (252: 63).

Perhaps the most astonishing confrontation occurs in *Larramee's
Ranch* when the crippled, slight youth Tom Holden, who wears
glasses to make himself look older and more formidable, successfully faces down a grotesque giant. Crogan's shoulders are huge
mounds of flesh, and he has immense long arms and a hideous
face. Here the power differential is so great that Tom Holden's
victory is barely credible. Tom's attitude rings true, however; it is
the underdog's view of the strong:

'You see,' he urged bitterly, 'God made me weak. I've loved strength. I've worshipped strong men. I've forgiven brutes who hurt me, just because I believed in their right to be cruel so long as they were powerful. But I was always the way you see me – something to be despised. I've despised myself more than other people could. Will you believe that? But finally I saw that in order to live, even, I had to pretend to be something that I wasn't! I had to pretend to be clever, and witty, and wise, and very, very brave!   (259: 198)

Although this has the ring of social Darwinism, Faust has changed the emphasis dramatically. Wister and Grey dwell on the material rewards of victory and on the status achieved. The hero is not allowed to savour the power he attains, for the victory must be made to look as socially benign as possible. Faust, on the other hand, takes delight in seeing the master mastered, and a rough justice achieved, and he allows Tom Holden to acknowledge the bully's pleasure.

A key problem remains: to succeed as a Western hero, Tom must achieve a credible superiority in the end. As a result, Faust must endow him with vast hidden resources and extremely good luck. Even this is not sufficient: Tom is surrounded by an aura of magic to compensate for his deficiencies. He is portrayed as a kind of enchanter. Larramee complains to Aunt Carrie about 'this young cripple, this odd devil who seems to be able to tame wolves and horses and . . . people, just as he pleases' (259: 183). Indeed, Tom's characterisation is such that the reader is left with two alternatives: either he is the weakest person in the book, or he is magically all-powerful.

Both possibilities are kept in suspension: Tom is constantly reminding the reader that he is bluffing out of weakness; that he is using the 'vague power of words' as his only weapon (259: 115). But Aunt Carrie says of him, 'That man's as strong as a giant. He can do what he wants to do, and that's as much as the best giant could do in any fairy story' (259: 193). At the end of the book both possibilities are exploded as the work, which has been pervaded by the form and terminology of the fairytale, shatters into make-believe: ' "Don't stir!" cried the witch [Aunt Carrie]. "This is a fairy tale. It isn't true. If you stir, everything will melt into thinnest air. Listen!" ' (259: 206).

The aura of magic tends to mask Tom's mental toughness,

however: he acknowledges his vulnerability and the possibility of victimisation while desperately confronting a hostile world with the resources he does possess. This brand of toughness is unusual in a Western hero, for such heroes rarely acknowledge the reversibility of their position. But it is a transitional element to the viewpoint of the private eye, who also lives a precarious existence in a hostile world.

Thus far we have traced three sources of tension which can result from the interaction of different layers of formula: authorial subversion, as with Hammett; in-built inconsistencies such as those which bedevil the stylistic stance of the Western formula; and the reactivation of latent material from a less differentiated level of formula. A fourth source may be traced to the presence of a layer with strong links to another generic tradition. The mystery plot of the hard-boiled detective novel provides an example, for, although it nests comfortably with the archetypal adventure formula and with the master formula, it also has strong ties with the generic tradition of the classical mystery.

Both the archetypal adventure plot and the American adventure formula involve some form of the chase, though the master formula often colours it with an acquisitive or crusading bent. The chase is a useful plot type, for it enables the writer to unify a number of threads in the formula. Romantic subplots fit neatly, and can be used with all the usual sentimental trappings as in the Western, or treated as a man-hunt dangerous to the hero, as in the hard-boiled subgenre. The chase also allows the hero to display his individualistic virtues, especially persistence, competence, and self-reliance, and to satisfy his acquisitive propensities.

The mystery plot fits neatly within the parameters of the chase: one wants to know 'who dunnit', to see hidden guilt revealed and punished. A crucial thread is the discernment of truth amidst lies. Often this is the theoretically simple, though practically difficult, matter of deciding who is lying when. An incisive writer can remake the issue to explore the nature of truth itself, as Wilkie Collins does within the classical tradition, in *The Moonstone* (1868). Within the hard-boiled tradition, Dashiell Hammett uses the mystery plot to explore this same territory.

Despite this common ground, the expectations engendered by the classical mystery pull in a different direction from those of the American adventure tradition which defines the hard-boiled detective story in every particular except the specificity of its central plot. The chase in the hard-boiled detective story, for example, tends to be more involved. Where the classical detective faces a fairly well-defined task, the private eye is confronted with an ambiguous one; often his assigned task is only tangentially related to the real job he finds he must do (14: 146). The difference in setting between the two genres further complicates the investigator's task. In the classical mystery, the society is portrayed as a generally stable affair where the crime or series of crimes is an aberration. The hard-boiled detective, on the other hand, is set against a society in turmoil where the crime or crimes are symptomatic of the general corruption and lawlessness. Thus the task of the detective becomes obscured by the general lawlessness.

This difference in setting means that the revelation of guilt is of a different nature in the hard-boiled detective story. While the classical mystery tends to narrow the circle of guilt from a wide range of suspects to a single culprit, the hard-boiled detective story presents an expanding concept of guilt. Although there is generally a main culprit, a wide and representative sample of characters are also implicated for their participation in the endemic lawlessness and corruption. Thus the hard-boiled detective story, unlike the classical mystery, has the potential to act as social criticism, a potential which Hammett exploits fully.

Hammett pushes the formula as far as it will go, even in the seemingly safe area of the discernment of truth. In *The Dain Curse* he neatly juxtaposes the pursuit of truth with the artificiality of the framework of the formula itself. In doing this he pits the the classical tradition, with its certainty of causation and orderly unravelling of guilt, against a confounding metaphysical lawlessness derived from the American adventure tradition. The reader feels trapped, baffled and exposed; pinned to his willing suspension of disbelief by the piercing irony which is Hammett's hallmark.

The Dain Curse implies that the history of a crime can never be fully reconstructed, an idea that threatens to explode the very basis of the mystery plot. The disparity between appearance and reality is observable in the masking of character. Mrs Leggett appears to be a rather ordinary, good-humoured housewife until she reveals the depth of her hatred when accused of two murders. Gabrielle thinks herself evil because of her 'physical marks of degeneracy', but displays magnanimity and mental toughness (339: 146). The appearance of events is equally deceptive: Edgar's suicide is really murder, the theft of the diamonds is in fact a pay-off, and the family curse is actually a plot. A certain ambiguity is essential to the suspense of the detective story, but the extent of the unreliability of appearances in *The Dain Curse* is unusually extensive, shattering the norm of identity between representation and reality.

An even more unusual aspect of the *The Dain Curse* is the extent to which the meaning of events must be reinterpreted as the frame of reference changes. This implies that meaning is variable, destroying the notional objectivity inherent in the fixed context of the usual detective story. The box-within-a-box structure of *The Dain Curse* raises the issue of context, as the explanations offered in previous sections are made inadequate by new information.

As part I winds down, the Op accuses Mrs Leggett of her husband's murder, causing her to attempt an escape which ends with her own death. In the final chapter of this part, the Op discusses the evidence behind his accusation with an old acquaintance, Fitzstephan, who complains, 'You jump around so. . . . You answered that back in the laboratory. Why don't you stick to your answer?' The Op's reply is, 'That was good enough to say then. . . . but not now, in cold blood, with more facts to fit in' (339: 60).

Part II, 'The Temple', shows how right the Op is to distrust his earlier formulations. The focus of attention shifts to Gabrielle as those close to her become the victims of murderous attacks. Although the events of part II, like those of part I, are explicable as a self-contained unit, the adequacy of both explanations is brought into question. When the Op meets with Fitzstephan to evaluate what has happened at the end of this part, he says, 'To fit in with what I saw, most of it must have happened very nearly as I've told you. If you want to believe that it did, all right. I don't. I'd rather believe I saw things that weren't there' (339: 95). When Fitzstephan protests at the 'ifs and buts' attached to the account, the Op asks, 'You actually believe what I've told you so far?' Fitzstephan replies that he thinks it a good explanation. 'What a childish mind you've got', counters the Op (339: 95). In the final part, 'Quesada', Gabrielle continues to be dogged by misfortune, raising new doubts about the adequacy of earlier interpretations. This part ends with the Op expounding a final explanation which argues that Fitzstephan had master-minded the crimes of all three parts; but this formulation may not be any more definitive than the others, as it may be equally dependent on a circumscribed viewpoint. The pattern of explication followed by doubts and contradictory evidence which was set up in parts I and II casts doubts on the final formulation as well, especially when the Op begins attaching new 'ifs and buts' to his account: 'Everybody took it for granted that he was right', he says of Fitzstephan's account of the first Dain murder, ' – everybody, including Gabrielle – though he didn't have any evidence to support what was after all only his guess' (339: 187).

The issue of context raises larger doubts as well: the self-contained nature of the novel format is made to seem highly artificial, underscoring the impression that *The Dain Curse* is a 'silly story'. The sustained dialogue between the writer Fitzstephan and the cynical Op over the nature of truth clearly shows the false posturing in which aesthetic formulation passes for true insight. Fitzstephan demands only an aesthetically pleasing design and is impatient with the Op for insisting that the adequacy of any formulation is dependent on its degree of correspondence with objective reality. What the Op accuses Fitzstephan of intellectual immaturity and begins to relate the story of Little Red Riding Hood, Fitzstephan counters that he likes that one too (339: 95). The pattern of construction, failure and reconstruction we have already examined shows the problems inherent in Fitzstephan's point of view. The Op's standard may be admirable, but it is shown to be impossible to attain: in a disordered universe any rational explanation is bound to be a distortion. The Op's world disallows the standard of objective reality; despite his efforts, his formulations can never do more than construct meaningful relationships within a small framework.

The use Hammett makes of the mystery plot within the framework of the American adventure tradition places the two generic traditions in sharp relief, exposing the complacent assumptions of the classical mystery while enriching the tradition of the American adventure formula by allowing for a many-layered plot centring on the need to apprehend the truth as well as the culprit. Hammett presents a kind of *reductio ad absurdum* of the mechanisms of the mystery plot. He has pushed definitional attributes to the point of exposure: their limitations and arbitrary conceits become glaringly apparent. Hammett can get away with this because he is working at a point of juncture; within an area of metaphoric double exposure, pitting one generic tradition against another.

Such are the dynamics of the layering-process, which critics have not even begun to explore because they have failed to recognise the fact of layering. It is not that the author may draw on material from different levels, but that he is almost forced to do so by the very connotative richness of the conventions themselves. Formula literature is not linear; it does not operate on one level. The interplay between the layers discussed in the above instances explains the both the continuity and the adaptability of formula, and shows how different generic traditions can interact to produce new patterns.

3

Formula and the Marketplace

Writers, editors, readers and critics all talk about formula, but it would be unwise to assume that all agree on the nature of the beast. For critics, formula is a necessary tool, a part of their taxonomy of literature; it allows them to classify works and to talk about the dynamics of the elements within any given work. A reader's notion of formula helps him to select works in accordance with his interests; it may also involve him in judgements about whether the author is 'playing fair' within the rules of the game. Advertisers see formula as a marketing-tool. And editors see it as a set of editorial guidelines. But what of the writer himself? Is formula merely a matter of substituting new elements for old over and over again, as is often assumed by critics and readers?

At first glance, formula writers talking about the tricks of their trade seem to have just such a ready-made pattern in mind: 'if you go after the mechanics of Western stories as such you'll find that it's a simple group of rules by which one may cut the pattern of any number of yarns', Frederick Faust admonished. 'And your bank account need never fail it you follow the rules, and clip carefully along the marked lines. And not so carefully at that. . . .' (276: 39). Frank Gruber, another pulp writer, and one who, like Faust, wrote both Westerns and detective stories, mulled over the problem of a fool-proof formula for writing detective yarns. After two years he came up with his eleven-point mystery-plot formula. 'To this day I claim that this plot formula is foolproof', Gruber writes. 'You can write a perfectly salable mystery story with perhaps only seven or eight of these elements, but get them all into a story and you cannot miss' (297: 43).

On closer scrutiny, the cut-and-paste version of formula writing which Gruber and Faust seem to espouse looks rather different.

When Faust was asked how he managed to find so many stories, he replied,

> Perhaps the best way to go about it is to ask one's self what there is about a theme that invites the writer. How much is background and how much is character, how much is action? Then you should ask yourself what kind of action develops the character most perfectly. There is a certain logic in the working out of stories, a sort of mathematical necessity in the operation of order to get the right answers, and I think you can surrender to the nature and the kind of emotion with which you are dealing. It will lead you to the right denouements.   (271: 219)

Alan R. Bosworth, who wrote Westerns for the Street and Smith publications under a variety of psuedonyms, echoes Faust's advice. The secret of writing salable pulp fiction, he says, was to use a 'narrative hook' which 'could be adapted to fit any pulp magazine, Western or otherwise'. The result of this insight was his 'All-Purpose Little Jim Dandy opening': he 'crammed a character, a setting, and a situation into one packed paragraph, and after that the plot and its unfolding took care of themselves' (1: 59).

And when Gruber begins listing his eleven elements it becomes clear that his check-list is not at all restrictive. His list runs:

1. Colorful hero
2. Theme
3. Villain
4. Background
5. Murder method
6. Motive
7. Clue
8. Trick
9. Action
10. Climax
11. Emotion   (297: 43)

Gruber goes on to elaborate, but his comments do not transform his list into a kind of algebraic prescription where one adds *a* to *b*, puts in a dash of *c* at a given point, then rounds off with *e*. On Background, for example, he says,

4. BACKGROUND. The story must be played against a colorful or unusual background. The streets of a big city are not necessarily colorful. If they're not, make them so.   (297: 44)

His discussion of Theme merely explicates his meaning. Theme is 'what the story is about in addition to, over and above, the ACTUAL MYSTERY Plot' (297: 44). So, for example, *The Lock and the Key* is about locksmiths, and *The Nine Tailors* is about bell-ringing.

These devices indicate that authors such as Gruber and Faust are using formula to generate plot line. For them, formula is a skeleton on which to flesh out a story rather than a die with which to stamp out preconceived patterns from new material. However, the finished body is also dressed to suit other people's preconceptions of the formula.

Editorial preconceptions and prejudices were undoubtedly a major influence. Stories which did not conform to an editor's conception of his readers' tastes were not published. Faust was well acquainted with his editor's preferences:

This is the sort of yarn that Blackwell laps up: A Western tale of action, without Mexicans, without women whose virtue is endangered, and concerning anything from sheepherding to lumber or mining or trapping, but preferable [*sic*] something about the old Western ranch house and a taint of cowdung early in the story. Action, action, action, is the thing. . . . There has to be a woman, but not much of one.   (276: 39)

Blackwell, the editor of *Western Story Magazine*, had once informed Faust that there were 'only two kinds of plots, "pursuit and capture", and "delayed revelation" ', and that 'delayed revelation' was merely a variant of 'pursuit and capture'. 'In the delayed revelation situation,' Blackwell added, 'the opening of the story should take place a little farther along in the course of action' (271: 76).

Captain Joseph Shaw, the most famous of the *Black Mask* editors, also had strong ideas about the kind of writing he wanted for his magazine: 'We felt obliged to stipulate our boundaries. We wanted simplicity for the sake of clarity, plausibility, and belief. We wanted action, but we held that action is meaningless unless it involves recognisable human character in three-dimensional form'

(322: vi). Frank Gruber complained of the rigours of Shaw's editorship:

> He asked you to submit stories, he suggested lengthy, detailed revisions, *urged* you to make them and you found yourself rewriting and rewriting . . . and in the end you got the most wonderful rejection. No printed rejection slip. His arm around your shoulder, his warm enthusiasm, his vast regret that this one didn't quite make it, but please, please try another one – and soon!   (297: 23)

Editorial dictates could affect a number of aspects of a writer's craft: type of story, quality of writing, and what was deemed extraneous, what crucial. Chandler complained bitterly about editorial blue-pencilling:

> A long time ago when I was writing for the pulps I put into a story a line like 'He got out of the car and walked across the sun-drenched sidewalk until the shadow of the awning over the entrance fell across his face like the touch of cool water.' They took it out when they published the story. Their readers didn't appreciate this sort of thing – just held up the action.
>
> (399: 219)

Chandler was certain that the editors were mistaken in their assessment.

Characteristically, Hammett was more circumspect in his rebellion. He derived great amusement from using the argot collected during his years with Pinkerton's, especially as the editors of *Black Mask*, who often did not know the exact meaning of these terms, but who had a strict policy against language which might be considered of questionable taste, sometimes eliminated the wrong ones.

There are tales, which may or may not be apocryphal, of much more extreme acts of editorial intervention. From the slightly earlier time of the Nickel Weeklies, there survives the story of an editorial edict that the hero of the Nick Carter stories must remain a bachelor. A tug of war between writer and editor ensued. Nick's engagement was announced, but editorial policy necessitated the demise of his fiancée in the next instalment. Finally, in defiance, Fred Dey described his hero's wedding:

Now it happened that week that the editors did not read his copy. It arrived late, and was sent directly to the linotype room. Suddenly a printer's devil came bounding upstairs with the news that Nick Carter was married. The office seethed like an angry sea. . . . Messengers were dispatched to all parts of the city in search of Fred Dey. When he appeared, he was pushed into a chair and compelled to describe the bitter death of the bride, while his own tears blotted the page.   (11: 66–67)

Clearly intervention on this scale required tame or very hungry authors, and it is unlikely that it was widespread.

Editorial intervention was often justified not on aesthetic grounds, but in terms of 'giving the reader what he wanted'. The editor had a number of ways of gauging readership response, sales being the most important. When Carroll John Daly's tough hero Race Williams was featured on the cover of *Black Mask*, for example, sales jumped dramatically. *Western Story Magazine* climbed in circulation quickly from its first issue in 12 July, 1919. By November 1920 it had become a weekly with a circulation of 300,000. The next year Faust's stories began appearing, and circulation climbed even higher.

Readership polls were also used to determine favourite authors. The progress of one such poll by *Black Mask* was reported in the February 1930 issue: Dashiell Hammett, Carroll John Daly and Erle Stanley Gardner were top favourites.

Letters sent to editors also gave some indication of readers' enthusiasms: 'Boss of the Round-Up and Folks: Just a few lines to tell you how much I like Max Brand's story, "Pleasant Jim." I couldn't think of going to bed before finishing it. What? After waiting all week fer it – "fer" as Grizzly Gallager says.' Another letter in the same issue of *Western Story Magazine* complained, 'George Owen Baxter left Thunder Moon not a bit nicely, and I think he aims to finish that later.' Ironically, both writers were Frederick Faust.

Despite editorial edicts and readership preferences, the range of stories published by editors shows that considerable scope remained for the author to manoeuvre. Lacking the direct feedback editors received from the readership of their magazines, and the self-confidence and open-mindedness this must have encouraged, critics have taken editorial pronouncements at face value. They have focused on the assessment of readership as a kind of key, but have ignored the actual readership of the magazines, instead substituting their own preconceptions about appeal. Cawelti, for example, assumes a certain readership for the Western when he discusses its appeal in terms of the Oedipus conflict:

> For blue-collar and white-collar workers at the lower echelons of the large industrial organization, or for independent farmers facing the increasing competition of large industrial organization, the corporation plays somewhat the same psychological role as the father does for the adolescent boy. . . . Couple this with the fact that the culture of working-class groups had traditionally placed a strong emphasis on masculine dominance, and it is not hard to see how the Western might fill an important psychological function for these groups.   (102: 14–15)

No attempt is made to match this against the actual readership of the Western. Had he done so, Cawelti would have been forced to wonder at the serialisation of Zane Grey's Westerns in a number of leading women's magazines. Even *Western Story* had a faithful female following: 'I want to tell you-all I have been reading WESTERN STORY for two years, and I think it is one wonderful magazine', wrote a lady from Philadelphia. Pronouncements on the restrictiveness of writing for a specific readership based on critical preconceptions are nonsense.

The inability of critics to look beyond their own preconceptions and their failure to heed contradictory evidence have encouraged a restrictive view of formula. To understand this myopia one must look at the pressures and trends within the publishing-industry at the time the American adventure formula was being shaped by and for mass-marketing. These forces shaped critical preconceptions and have since helped to perpetuate them.

Formula literature developed during a specific phase in publishing-history. The industry was expanding as population and readership increased: the population of the United States was growing rapidly, from 50,155,783 in 1880 to 105,710,620 in 1920, and illiteracy was declining dramatically from 17 per cent in 1880 to 6 per cent in 1920. Increasing urbanisation made the distribution and sale of magazines easier and more economical, while the lowering of postal rates in 1885 and the introduction of rural free delivery after 1897 made it possible for publishers to penetrate more sparsely populated areas. In an effort to court readership, publishers began to lower their prices. In 1893 general readership magazines such as *Harper's Monthly*, *Scribners'* and *Century* all cost 35¢ an issue. In July of that same year *McClure's* was introduced, priced at 15¢; in the same month *Cosmopolitan* came out for 12½¢; and *Munsey's* started publication in October at 10¢ a copy. Within two years all had dropped to 10¢. 'There never was anything deader in this world than the old idea of big profits and small volume', Munsey commented in 1898. 'Small profits and big volume have driven this antiquated theory to the wall' (7: iv,17).

Munsey set the pace in other ways as well; it was he who introduced the first pulp magazine, *Argosy*, in 1896, printed on rough wood-pulp paper in order to save on both production costs and postal charges. It took a while for the impact of this innovation to be felt, but, when it came, the expansion of pulp publishing was explosive. Barely two dozen pulps were being published at the close of the First World War, but by the middle years of the Depression over 200 pulp magazines reached 25 million readers. Outside the pulp field, expansion was also taking place; both the number of magazines and their aggregate circulation increased through 1929.

The book-publishing industry was undergoing a more modest expansion, keeping pace with the growing population, but declining as a percentage of manufactured wealth in the economy as a whole. The number of book publishers had doubled between 1859 and 1914 to number 819 by the end of the period. Book sales were also on the increase. Before 1890 a book that sold 25,000 copies was considered successful, but after the mid 1890s sales of 100,000 were common and best-sellers could top a million. Between 1901 and 1915, nineteen books surpassed the million mark.

The expanding periodical market and book trade stimulated, indeed demanded, the increased production of fiction. The 1891 copyright law, which outlawed the use of pirated British texts, further increased demand. The pulps alone consumed 200 million words a year at the height of their popularity. The prodigious output of many formula writers, with Frederick Faust as an outstanding example, is an indication of the vast appetite of the fiction industry. Complaints such as those made by Florence Kelly in a 1916 article in *The Bookman* expressed common fears: 'Quantity rather than quality seems to be the feature most admired and striven for in American fiction. The more novels an author puts out in one year and the less time he spends upon each one the surer he can be of his publisher's staunch support and the consequent winning of readers and dollars' (22: 565).

More indirectly, the expanding market may be judged by the appearance during the 1880s and 1890s of a number of periodicals intended to assist the beginning writer. Among these was *Writer*, founded by the director of a correspondence school. Other aids were also marketed. Frank Gruber remembers two he purchased, *Plotto* and *Plot Genie*, both designed to help generate usable story lines. Neither worked for him.

The expanding market, both potential and realised, provided tremendous opportunities for both writers and publishers. It also placed certain pressures on both. Book publishers constantly complained of shrinking profit margins as they were squeezed on the one side by increasing royalty and promotional costs, and on the other by price-cutting. They complained too of the public's lack of attentiveness and its tendency to squander expendable income on bicycles and other forms of recreational activities instead of buying books.

Writers had to cope with the pressures imposed by calls for increased productivity, while serialisation imposed its own demanding schedule on writers. These pressures became more widespread, though both had been felt for decades in some segments of the industry. Multiple authorship was one tried and tested way of coping. Such popular heroes as Buffalo Bill, Old Captain Collier and Nick Carter were serviced by a succession of authors. Conversely, publishers could stretch the talents of a single prolific writer to provide a bevy of salable names. *Western Story* often published more than one contribution of Faust's. Indeed, on twenty occasions, three differently attributed Faust pieces appeared in a single issue.

The forces of the marketplace influenced the way fiction was written, and ultimately shaped the literature itself. None the less, this shaping-process was not as uniformly deleterious nor as irresistible as is sometimes assumed. The pressures which encouraged writers to produce quickly, fluently, and without revision allowed them to escape the rigours of careful craftmanship, but did not prevent careful artistry. *Gunman's Gold*, one of Faust's Westerns, bears the hallmarks of hasty, sloppy execution. The reader can almost sense the line at which Faust decides he must shift the portrayal of a character to accommodate the developing story line.

At the other end of the scale we have Hammett's tight, brilliant plots.

The nature of the standard pricing-policy, payment by the word, discouraged writers from trimming excess verbage from their stories. Erle Stanley Gardner, writing Westerns at 3¢ a word, was once asked by an editor why his crack shots took all six cartridges to get their man. He replied, 'If you think I'm going to have the gun battle over while my hero has got fifteen cents worth of unexploded ammunition in the cylinders of his gun, you're nuts' (121: 62). However, not all formula writers can be accused of deliberate wordiness.

Advertising and the new marketing-mentality brought new kinds of pressures to bear, shaping the fiction and the perception of the fiction in new ways. Though advertising had been around for many years, national advertising was new. It required national distribution of both advertising and the products it helped to sell, and these circumstances did not exist until near the end of the nineteenth century. Advertising began its concerted assault on the American consumer during these years. Revenues from both newspaper and magazine advertising rose 80 per cent during the 1880s, slowed down to a growth rate of about a third in the 1890s, then increased by more than 50 per cent in the first five years of the twentieth century. Advertising-jingles and catchphrases began to insinuate themselves into the cultural consciousness: 'It floats', 'Have you a little Fairy in your home?'

The explosion in advertising had a direct impact on the marketing of literature. 'The quack-novel is a thing which looks like a book, and which is compounded, advertised, and marketed in precisely the same fashion as Castoria . . . and other patent medicines, harmful and harmless', complained Owen Wister (192: 722). Advertising-expenditures in the book trade skyrocketed despite scepticism over returns. By 1900 it was not uncommon for large publishing-houses to spend $50,000 a year on promotion. One house is reputed to have spent $250,000 in 1905, or 17 per cent of its gross proceeds; by the eve of the First World War, 10 per cent was considered an acceptable promotions budget.

The increasing preoccupation with promotion was reflected in ways other than the increasing budgets allowed for the purpose. *Publishers' Weekly*, the most influential of the trade papers, began running a 'Hints to Salesmen' column in 1891. In this and other related columns, *Publishers' Weekly* would discuss the dos and don'ts of successful marketing-practice, from the proper arrangement of shops to the making of eye-catching window displays and the design of advertising-copy and layout.

It was during this period that interest in the best-seller as a phenomenon began to agitate the industry. Best-seller lists began appearing in crude form in the *Bookman* in 1895, though the term itself was not introduced intil 1911, in *Publishers' Weekly*. The accuracy and influence of these lists were much debated, despite improvements in the sampling-technique used. In his *Economic Survey of the Book Industry, 1930–1931*, O. H. Cheney voiced his scepticism:

> Like all trade evils, the practice has developed insidiously. A bookseller, asked to report on sales, begins by trying to remember or he asks the friendly traveler what he thinks is the best-seller, Or else he sees a stack of a title which has been decreasing – and at the next step he sees a stack which he wishes would disappear – and then he remembers a title on which he ordered too many. The title becomes one of his best-sellers.   (76: 127)

Despite his scepticism over the methods used, Cheney felt the lists were influential. He agreed with such critics as Johan J. Smertenko and Frederick Lewis Allen that they stimulated the 'herd instinct' crucial to the making of a big best-seller.

There was much speculation regarding the essential components of a best-seller. Conjectures relied heavily on hindsight: Frederick Lewis Allen's 1935 article looked for trends in the best-selling books of the preceding thirty-five years (72: 3ff). George Stevens derided the humbug element in pronouncements on the making of a best-seller and suggested that no formula could be isolated. If such distillation were possible, it would be a simple matter of combining elements in order really to hit the marketing jackpot. Hence the tongue-in-cheek suggestion for a best-seller about 'Lincoln's Doctor's Dog' (93: 3ff).

The intense interest in the best-seller phenomenon and the use of the term in advertising carried a much deeper significance. Marketing books as best-sellers was one way of circumventing a central problem for the book industry. The difficulty was that of supplying the public with a uniform product identified by a brand name such as the advertisers of soap, baking-powder or sewing-

machines enjoyed. Turn-of-the-century book-advertising exhibits
a fumbling search for an effective marketing-strategy. The advertisements are often cramped, indigestible lists without white
space. Increasingly, attempts were made to highlight the most
salable aspect of a book. In the aftermath of the Spanish-American
War, for example, war books were given prominence, and any
war connection was emphasised.

Authors' names were often used to sell books. In advertisements, they were emphasised by using large, bold type. Later,
the sales potential of popular authors was more blatantly exploited:
'When They Write Books – You Make Money' announced one
advertisement to the trade in *Publishers' Weekly* in 1933. Not
surprisingly, Grey was one of the authors featured. In its advertising, the Book of the Month Club gave prominence to photographs of popular authors.

Genre-oriented marketing was another way of providing the
potential book-buyer with a reliable 'brand name': formula fiction
came as close to providing uniformity of product as it was possible
to get in the publishing-business. Ploys designed to highlight the
generic identity of mysteries were quickly developed and used.
An advertisement in the *New York Times* in late 1910 called *The
Paternoster Ruby* by Charles Edmonds Walk 'The best mystery yarn
this fall. . . .' By the mid twenties, genre advertising for mystery
stories was extensive and self-conscious. In 1928, Doubleday set
up a special subsidiary, the Crime Club, to issue large numbers
of mystery and detective stories. Its logo was a man with a gun.
Harpers ran huge double-page advertisements in the *Saturday
Review of Literature* for its Harper Sealed Mysteries, while Dutton
marketed Dutton Clue Mysteries.

Advertisers did not handle the Western with such ease. They
often seemed somewhat confused about the nature of the genre.
According to the *Oxford English Dictionary*, the first recorded use
of 'Western' as a self-sufficient noun is as late as February 1930,
when it appeared in an advertisement in *Publishers' Weekly*. Actually, my research shows that the term was used rather earlier. An
advertisement in the 15 October 1927 edition of the *Saturday Review
of Literature* describes George M. Johnson's *The Gun-Slinger* as 'A
Western with the kick of a .45.' It took a while for the new term
to catch on; a sense of improvisation lingered: 'Sell this popular
new "WESTERN" ', urged an advertisement for Ernest Haycox's
Whispering Range in December 1930, fencing off the new term with

quotation marks, and using upper-case letters to add emphasis. After 1930 advertisers began using the new label with relish: 'A Grub-stake market for prospecting and established booksellers' announced one double-page advertisement in *Publishers' Weekly* in late 1933, 'And when you feature the Morrow "brand", you're rounding up plus sales with Westerns written for intelligent men and women. . . .'

Even before the genre was labelled so handily, advertisers attempted to draw attention to a family resemblance. Line drawings of cowboys on horseback with cattle in the background often featured prominently, an appropriate counterpart to the ominous shadows often used in mystery advertisements. The 1910 advertisement for Dane Coolidge's *Hidden Water* in the *New York Times* used just such a drawing. The accompanying blurb compared the book to Wister's *The Virginian*. 'Western' was sometimes used as an adjective, as when B. M. Bower's *Skyrider* was presented to the public in 1918. 'Ever since B. M. Bower's "Chip of the Flying U"', the western novels from this author's fertile pen have been increasing in popularity.'

None the less, the treatment given to Zane Grey's work reflects the advertiser's confusion over the generic identity of Western fiction. In 1910, *The Heritage of the Desert* was marketed as a love story. Ten years later, *The Man of the Forest* was pushed as a 'best seller': 'More then half a million people (not counting those who have read library copies) have read this romance of a man and a girl and a hidden paradise. . . .' Even as late as 1930, Grey's *Sunset Pass* was advertised as 'A New Novel of the Old West'. The blurb called it 'A thrilling story of two men who fought to the death for the love of a girl when the old Southwest was frontier country.' By 1933, the advertisements had changed course. A huge advertisement in *Publishers' Weekly* for *The Hash Knife Outfit* called Grey 'America's favorite author – the ace western writer of them all.' The accompanying blurb was also different in tone: 'A galloping, breathless story of hard living and fast shooting founded upon a bloody episode in Arizona history.'

By 1934, the *Saturday Review of Literature* felt confident enough of genre awareness to use a grid system for reviews. 'The Criminal Record – The Saturday Review's Guide to Detective Fiction' used a four-column summary giving title and author; crime, place and sleuth; summing-up; and verdict. That year Hammett's *The Thin Man* was reviewed in this fashion. Crime, place and sleuth were reported as: 'Eccentric inventor vanishes, his secretary is murdered, his ex-wife calls in ex-tec Nick Charles and hell pops.' The book was summarised with the remark, 'It's the telling more than the tale that counts here, and both are even better than earlier Hammetts.' The verdict was 'extra swell'. A similar grid system was used for 'Over the Counter – The Saturday Review's Guide to Romance and Adventure'. Here the columns were headed 'Trademark', 'Label', 'Contents' and 'Flavor'. Max Brand's *The Outlaw* is labelled 'western'; its contents are described as 'Love 10%., Courage 111%, Compassion 1%; the flavour is dismissed as 'usual'.

In the magazine field, the rapid development of genre pulps from general fiction magazines, and their large and faithful following are indicative of the perspicacity of publishers and editors. *Western Story Magazine, Black Mask, Love Story Magazine,* and the later *Astounding Stories* and *Amazing Stories* were each aimed as a specific sector of the public, and all flourished. *Western Story* had an estimated average weekly circulation of 350,000 during the 1920s. Within a year of its launch, *Black Mask* had acquired a regular purchasing readership of 250,000. The circulation of *Love Story* built up to 600,000 by 1932, and within months of its founding in April 1926 *Amazing Stories* had achieved a following of over 100,000.

Editors tried to make their readers feel that they belonged to a club of like-minded fellows. *Black Mask* published a column called 'Our Readers' Private Corner: Inside Dope from Authors' in which Hammett figured prominently for a while. A letters column in *Western Story Magazine* announced, 'Miss Helen Rivers, who conducts this department, will see to it that you will be able to make friends with other readers, though thousands of miles may separate you.' Badges were offered for sale at 25¢. *Detective Story* featured a column to which handwriting could be submitted for analysis, if accompanied by the printed coupon. A puzzles column with a printed honour roll also made regular appearances.

Though each magazine had its own slant and became identified with a particular genre, a wide range of stories were published. Donald R. Arbuckle's accusation that special-interest pulps rigidified formula is therefore of questionable validity (97: 378). *Western Story* was not above bowing to seasonal interests by publishing such Christmas stories as 'The Providential Tree', a tale of the remarkable survival of a homesteader and his son who moved house to have a Christmas tree, then returned to find the location of their old homestead devastated by a tornado. 'The Gray Leader', published in the 22 November 1930 issue, stretches the 'Western' labelling in different ways. The story, set in a city, deals with a gang of thugs. It is not until the end that the hero and his girl head for open country, riding off toward the North-west wrapped in furs. The accompanying illustration is of a man wearing a Canadian Mountie hat staring in the window of a pet shop at a Husky puppy; a flapper looks on.

The range of stories published by *Black Mask* was even more varied. Indeed, it was first billed as a 'Magazine of Mystery, Romance and Adventure'. By the February 1926 edition, the emphasis had clearly changed, and the subtitle read, 'Mystery, DETECTIVE, and Adventure stories'. Only 'DETECTIVE' is in bold red capitals; the other words are in black, with only the first letter capitalised. None the less, even as late as October 1930, the cover could feature a two-fisted gun-slinger promoting a Carroll John Daly detective story: Race Williams, it turns out, is 'out of town on a gun job'. The subtitle had changed yet again by this time, to claim, 'Western, Detective, and Adventure Stories'.

Besides using genre-oriented sales tactics, pulp-publishers pushed their 'brand name' authors through the use of cover advertising and announcements of coming stories. The appearance of Race Williams on the cover described above undoubtedly boosted circulation. It has been said that covers announcing new Race Williams stories could raise sales by as much as 20 per cent. Dashiell Hammett and Erle Stanley Gardner were also heralded as sales-boosters.

The marketing-strategies of both magazine and book-publishers have had a profound effect on the critical reception of formula literature. It might even be argued that the marketplace has exerted a more profound and deleterious effect on critics than it has on the formula writers or on the literature itself. Critics have taken over market-defined categories as though these are possessed of objective reality. What is more, they have rigidified these categories with mindless fervour. The critical treatment of the hard-boiled detective formula offers an interesting case study of the use of inappropriate categories by critics suffering from a mass-marketed variety of functional fixedness.

Hard-boiled detective novels have long been marketed as mysteries, bracketing them with works in the puzzle tradition.

One Knopf advertisement for *The Maltese Falcon* used excerpts from a review by Ted Shane which compared Hammett's work directly with a contemporary mystery-writer in the classical tradition: 'Even S. S. Van Dine must lower his monocle. . . . It is everything you want.'

There were good reasons for the hard-boiled detective novel to be marketed as a mystery. It featured a detective and a crime, as did the classical variety. The firmly established generic distinctiveness of the mystery was certainly another factor. This labelling provided a handier marketing-tool than the Western with its long-amorphous generic identity. In fact, vitutally anything that resembled a mystery was marketed as such; even Eric Ambler's *A Coffin for Dimitrios* (1939) was sold as 'a mystery masterpiece'.

Once the hard-boiled detective became associated with the classical mystery it was almost inevitable that any deep links with the Western would be overlooked. The perceived distance between the mystery tradition and that of the Western was too great to encourage the recognition of generic ties. Indeed, a cartoon which appeared in the *Saturday Review* in March 1940 underscored the extent of separation. Two men are being introduced by a third. The gentleman making the introduction is attired in an ordinary business suit, as is one of the others. The third is wearing a bowler, neat vest and jacket, but also a six-gun, woolly chaps and cowboy boots. 'Mr Shipley writes both detective and western stories', reads the caption.

One can see this division reproduced in the critical treatment afforded to the hard-boiled detective story. It is alleged that this subgenre started as a reaction against the more staid puzzle-type of mystery story. Advertising of the late twenties, when both Carroll John Daly and Dashiell Hammett had their first books published, would certainly seem to support this notion. The advertisements of the period were conspicuously dominated by classical mysteries. This conveyed the impression that the hard-boiled formula was a new variant of the puzzle stories appearing in such abundance. Unfortunately, this misguided idea has been bolstered further by the impressive credentials of those supporting it. In his seminal essay 'The Simple Art of Murder' (1944), Raymond Chandler contrasts the 'traditional or classic or straight-deductive or logic-and-deduction novel of detection' with the work of Dashiell Hammett. This essay probably helped to cement the notion of the revolt of the hard-boiled writers. Joseph T. Shaw's claim, in the Introduction to *The Hard-Boiled Omnibus* (1946), that he worked with Hammett to 'create a new type of detective story differing from . . . the deductive type' (322: v) carried weight because of Shaw's position as editor of *Black Mask*. By the time Shaw took over the editorship of *Black Mask* in November 1926, however, the formula was already well developed, though Hammett's best work was yet to come. Julian Symons's important history *Bloody Murder: From the Detective Story to the Crime Novel: A History* (1972) also treats the hard-boiled novel as a rebellion against the classical pattern.

The validity of this classification is highly questionable from the standpoint of historical development, however. The adventure detective tradition had been around in the dime novels and early pulps since the time whan Allan Pinkerton began publishing accounts of the exploits of his operatives in such books as *The Expressman and the Detective* (1875) and *The Molly Maquires and the Detectives* (1877). A number of detective heroes peopled the dime novels and early pulps. Old Sleuth was one of the most popular, inspiring imitation which resulted in a highly publicised court case. He was first introduced in *The Fireside Companion* in 1872. One of his competitors was Old Captain Collier, whose detective series began running in the early 1880s with such titles as 'Old Cap Collier; or "Piping" the New Haven Mystery' (1883). By 1898 a series of novels based on this hero's exploits numbered more than 700 titles.

The adventure-detective story is a very different breed from the classical detective yarn. It is part of a tradition which grew up along side the puzzle type of story. One can see the two traditions side by side in Arthur Conan Doyle's *The Valley of Fear* (1915). The first part of the book is a classical-type Holmes story, where deduction is uppermost. The second half relates the story of an adventure detective, drawing heavily on Allan Pinkerton's *The Molly Maquires and the Detectives*. The differences between the two traditions are so great that the book effectively splits in the middle, leaving critics to complain of its 'broken-backed' character.

Mary Noel distinguishes the Old Sleuth type of story from those needing mental detective work: 'Violence rather than thought was Old Sleuth's method. He was extraordinarily handy, not so much at tracing the clues of a previous crime, as at snatching the brandished knife from the villain's own hand' (8: 165). She also suggests two reasons for Old Sleuth's popularity. The first is the urban setting, the second the unusual style, featuring slang-ridden dialogue (8: 166–7). Edmund Pearson quotes the beginning of 'Old Electricity: The Lightning Detective' by Old Sleuth (1885) in this regard:

> 'Don't wink your peepers, Larry.'
> 'What's up, cull?'
> 'That's what's up. Keep your eyelids raised for strangers.'
> 'Oh, stash it! and throw in your light, chummie. What's the "peep" now?' (9: 195)

This slang-ridden dialogue is the forerunner of the colloquial style of the hard-boiled detective formula.

The adventure-detective story, then, has a history that goes back to the 1880s, when it merges into other adventure-story patterns. Mary Noel has argued that the early detective stories 'made no fundamental change in either characterization or plot' (8: 165). She claims that these stories simply substituted a detective for a hero of another occupation. The story of Western adventure provided ample scope for such variations and it was one of the staples of the dime novel. It is not at all certain, therefore, that, when Carroll John Daly and Dashiell Hammett began to work towards a new, and highly successful, formulation of the adventurer-detective story, they were rebelling against the inadequacies of the classical pattern. Even if they were, it seems likely that the shaping of the hard-boiled formula was more positively influenced by the adventurer-detective type than it was by any negation of the classical formula.

Critical examinations of the hard-boiled detective formula which rely on the classical formula to provide a definitive framework are therefore hopelessly inadequate. John G. Cawelti's treatment of the hard-boiled formula in *Adventure, Mystery, and Romance* provides a case in point. Cawelti identifies the major elements of the hard-boiled detective formula as 'the detective', 'the crime', 'the criminal' and 'the pattern of action'. He therefore gives primacy to the plot; his formulaic elements are all defined in terms of their plot function. For Cawelti the pattern of action 'moves from the introduction of the detective and the presentation of the crime, through the investigation, to a solution and apprehension of the criminal' (14: 142). This, as Cawelti points out, is the same basic pattern of action as found in the classical mystery story. And yet, as he also points out, 'Most significantly, the creation of the hard-boiled pattern involved a shift in the underlying archetype of the detective story from the pattern of mystery to that of heroic adventure' (14: 142). As a result, he is forced to use a pattern that never really fits properly, leaving him with the compulsion continually to contrast the hard-boiled treatment of elements with the treatment given them in the classical mystery.

When one finds a critic who has written as much pioneering work as Cawelti lumbering with the burden of misinformed critical tradition, explanations must be sought. To uncover these, and to understand the misguided treatment given to formula literature generally, one must look to the impact of the marketplace. Formula literature was sold as a 'brand-name product', a sales technique which activated certain kinds of expectations and prejudices. These ranged from assumptions about the appeal of particular genre to judgements of the inherent quality limitations of work produced for mass consumption. Critics have always tended to do things backwards. Too often they make ill-founded assumptions concerning readership. Their conjectures about the artistic limitations of formula are used to create broad critical categories which have all the surgical potential of a bludgeon. It is hardly surprising that the marketing-categories for formula fiction were usurped by critics and treated as though endowed with objective reality, or that, once made, the mistake was ossified into a critical tradition.

Part Two
The Writer and the Formula

4

Zane Grey

On 31 January 1872, Pearl Zane Gray was born in the small Midwestern town of Zanesville, Ohio, a town named after Ebenezer Zane, a Revolutionary War hero and Grey's great-grandfather. Grey's unusual Christian name derived from his mother's whimsical notion of honouring Queen Victoria's fondness for pearl gray (228: 18). Although he later dropped the feminine 'Pearl' and changed the spelling of Gray to Grey, one is tempted to speculate upon the impact such a name had on his developing ego.

Grey's boyhood was filled with enough mishaps, misunderstandings and sheer impudence ⸱ ⸱n him a reputation as 'The Terror of the Terrace'. H ⸱ullied smaller boys, trampled his neighbour's tulip beds, stole dime novels from the local druggist, and was expelled from dancing-class when misquoted by another boy. There is little remarkable about his youth apart from such rebellious exploits. He attended the local school, where the course included reading, slate writing and numbers in the early grades; with geography, object lessons, drawing and Swinton's School Composition added in the third. Grey did not like schoolwork, but did enjoy adventure stories: he read Beadles's dime novels, books by Harry Castlemon, *Swiss Family Robinson, Robinson Crusoe,* Cooper's Indian tales and Charles McKnight's *Our Western Border,* published in 1876. Fishing and baseball were the activities he seems to have enjoyed most. As he grew up, Grey fought with his peers, worked Saturdays in a shoe store, played baseball in the high-school team, stood in the group by the Clarendon Hotel and watched the girls pass by, and helped out in his father's dental office.

Dr Gray was determined that his son should be a dentist. He was more than perturbed when he found a fledgling dime novel, 'Jim of the Cave', which pointed to more literary ambitions. After burning the manuscript, he gave his son a thrashing and forbade further scribbling. Grey, then fourteen, was told he must now

71

spend his Saturdays helping his father. He was compelled to continue his apprenticeship in the dental office when the family moved to Columbus, Ohio, to make a fresh start after poor investments. It was not until his freelance tooth-pulling in the rural small towns around Columbus brought the under-age Grey to the attention of the Ohio Dental Association that outside intervention allowed him to give up his 'practice'.

When he entered the University of Pennsylvania on a baseball scholarship in 1892, his father insisted that he study dentistry despite his distaste for the subject. Grey found the lectures dull and the course work difficult. He had trouble concentrating and was almost forced to withdraw in his freshman year. Though he graduated in 1896, he felt that his degree was more a measure of his baseball fame than of his academic achievement.

Not only did Grey have academic problems: he also felt uncomfortable and out of place in the social life of the university. He later recalled, 'I couldn't make many friends. I did not understand the students. Their ambitions, breeding, culture, as well as their habits of drinking, smoking, gambling, seemed to exclude me from their ranks' (238: 9). Grey was, in his own words, 'out of my element' (203: 78). Derided by his fellow students, he became a loner, independent, moody and morose, who was at home only on the baseball diamond or in the library reading adventure books and daydreaming.

After graduation, Grey faced the prospect of practising dentistry, which he hated. None the less, he rented an office at 100 West 7th Street in New York City and hung up his sign: 'Dr. P. Grey, D. D. S.' It is likely that he chose New York because of its importance in the writing and publishing-world (226: 35). He also joined the Orange Athletic Club of East Orange, New Jersey, and continued to play baseball. Although he was tempted to become a professional ballplayer as his younger brother Romer had done, he decided to pursue his literary ambitions instead.

Grey's first article, 'A Day on the Delaware', appeared in *Recreation* magazine in 1902. He began work on his first book, *Betty Zane*, that same year. No one would publish it, however, and he brought it out himself in 1903 with the financial backing of his fiancée, Lina Elise Roth. Dolly, as Grey called her, encouraged his faith in his abilities as a writer, tutored him in grammar, English and rhetoric, and edited and copied the final draft of *Betty Zane*.

Dolly became Grey's wife in 1905, and continued to play a

significant role in shaping his work. She corrected and polished nearly all his manuscripts; indeed, *The Thundering Herd* (1918), one of the few books she did not revise, was sent back by the *Ladies' Home Journal* to be rewritten (226: 119). In a letter dated 14 September 1905, she offered advice on the construction of *The Last Trail* (1906) which Grey would follow in many of his other novels as well: 'I am very anxious to read of the course of Miss Helen's love making. I suppose like the proverbial course of true love it is far from smooth. Make it as rough and exciting as possible for that stimulates interest and makes people rejoice so much more when they do get each other' (226: 54).

The book trade did not share Dolly's early faith in Grey's work. He had difficulty finding publishers for *The Spirit of the Border* (1906), *The Last Trail* (1906) and *The Last of the Plainsmen* (1908). Indeed, Mr Hitchcock of Harper and Brothers called Grey into his office after reading *The Last of the Plainsmen* to tell him, 'I don't see anything in this to convince me you can write either narrative or fiction' (203: 11). None the less, Harper published Grey's next book, *The Heritage of the Desert* (1910), and it was this work which really launched his career. *The Heritage of the Desert* was written after Grey's first trip west in 1907 in the company of C. J. 'Buffalo' Jones, a promoter of hybridisation experiments involving bison and Galloway cattle. Grey had attended a fund-raising lecture given by Jones in New York. *Riders of the Purple Sage* (1912), Grey's next Western novel, firmly established him with Harper, and brought him a wide and faithful readership.

The incidents chosen by Grey for elaboration in his autobiographical accounts cast him in the mould of the all-American hero. Grey's biographers have loyally retold these incidents, finding in them the significance which Grey has infused. A more sceptical approach is needed, for the extent to which the telling of these incidents conforms to the myths of American culture is too extraordinary to allow acceptance at face value. Grey reinterprets his youth through the popular type of the 'Good Bad Boy'. He glamorises his role of writer according to the romantic vision of the artist hero and recasts his own experiences in the West within the myth of the glorious frontier.

The recounting of Grey's youth can therefore degenerate very quickly into a Walt Disney bonanza, dripping with the saccharin of innocent bad-boyhood. Three central incidents in Grey's account illustrate this tendency: the writing of 'Jim of the Cave', the baseball game with Jacktown, and the potato-throwing episode at the University of Pennsylvania.

Grey wrote 'Jim of the Cave' at the age of fourteen. It was intended to celebrate his 'gang', their cave, and some imaginary exploits. These circumstances themselves recall the romantic idealism of Tom Sawyer's band of robbers. In retelling the incident in 'Breaking Through: The Story of My Own Life', Grey makes the act of writing the story into an adventure in itself. He sets the scene by recalling, 'I belonged to a gang of young ruffians, or, rather, I was the organizer and leader of a band of youthful desperados who were bound to secrecy by oaths and the letting of blood.' He goes on to recall their 'bad deeds': 'Once we slept in our cave all night; at least we stayed there, and each boy was supposed to have spent the night at the home of another boy.' His production is glamorised:

> In this cave I wrote my first story, on pieces of wallpaper. I slaved and sweat[ed] over this story, and smarted too, for the smoke always got into my eyes. It was hard to write, because the boys whispered with heads together – some bloody story – some dark deed they contemplated against those we hated – some wild plan.
>
> But at last I finished it. . . . I read it with voice not always steady nor clear. It had to do with a gang of misunderstood boys, a girl with light hair and blue eyes: dark nights, secrets, fight, blood, and sudden death.   (203: 12)

This description is not the recollection of a memory, but a mental re-enactment with the youthful Grey acting as a character within the imagination of the writer. Whatever the factual content of the related incident, it is endowed with cultural resonance rather than autobiographical significance. Though the notional relevance of the event consists in its being a first literary effort, the sense of grandiose importance derives from the American myth of the 'Good Bad Boy', its unconscious source. Leslie Fiedler describes the content of this myth:

> The Good Bad Boy is, of course, America's vision of itself, crude and unruly in his beginnings, but endowed by his creator with an instinctive sense of what is right. Sexually as pure as any milky maiden, he is a roughneck all the same, at once

potent and submissive, made to be reformed by the right woman. (42: 270)

Grey remakes himself into the all-American boy.

He endows two other boyhood memories, the Jacktown baseball game and the potato-throwing incident, with the same kind of emphasis. Autobiographically, the Jacktown game is important because it was at this game that Grey was spotted by a scout from the University of Pennsylvania who noticed his ability to pitch balls which were difficult to hit because the spin he added kept them from following a predictable course. Grey was later offered a baseball scholarship, which he accepted. The potato-throwing stunt earned him a place on the varsity ball team. Grey, in his description of these events, casts himself as a kind of Frank Merriwell.

Grey involves himself in the Jacktown game as a lark, joining the Baltimore team just for the day. He is well on his way to winning the game for his adopted team with his curveball, his advice and his forceful batting when the game is stopped by a biased umpire who complains that the 'Baltimore pitcher uses a crooked ball!'. Baffled and enraged by the curveballs they cannot hit, the Jacktown players prepare their revenge. Grey recalls, 'In great perturbation I peered out of the barn door. What should I see but the giant pitcher, carrying a rail over his shoulder, striding toward the barn, followed by the other Jacktown players and a yelling mob' (203: 76). Surmising that he is about to be run out of town on a rail, he grabs his trousers and heads for the cornfield in shirt and shoes, pursued by pitcher, players and mob. Naturally, he escapes.

The potato-throwing incident took place at the University of Pennsylvania when Grey was a freshman. He managed to enrage the upper classmen by sitting in a reserved section of a lecture theatre and by blundering into a restricted hallway. Pursued by an irate group of sophomores, Grey grabbed a basket of potatoes from a delivery boy. Then, positioned on a stairway, he managed to hold off the whole group by throwing skilfully aimed potatoes at those who led the charge up the stairs. 'I hit the first student over the eye, and he went down like a sack', Grey says. 'The next I hit in the stomach with the sound of a bass drum. I blocked the stairway with a pile of sophomores. Then I escaped' (203: 76). Once again the incidents become larger than life, and Grey is transformed into the image of the all-American good bad boy. His treatment of these events camouflages the ordinariness of his upbringing, ignores the cultural poverty of his immediate environment, and masks his sensitivity, bewilderment and loneliness. Grey reinterprets his role as writer according to the romantic vision of the artist hero. In 'Breaking Through: The Story of My Own Life', Grey becomes the hero of a creative struggle toward self-expression and self-fulfilment: 'When, with little more equipment than a tremendous determination, I gave up a fairly flourishing profession to become a writer, I crossed my Rubicon' (203: 11). He has decided to write at great cost to his comfort and well-being. The struggle has just begun. He retreats to his 'garret': 'I wrote in a little bare room with a stove, a table, and a chair. The time came when I had to put my hand into the open stove every quarter of an hour to keep it from freezing. But I kept on writing' (203: 12).

Like the romantic artist hero, he struggles on, unappreciated by 'hard-hearted publishers' and critics (203: 11). His reward is the poetic fervour, the burning inspiration he speaks of in his journal: 'It is midnight. I have just ended my novel, *Wanderer of the Wasteland*. Twelve hours today – twenty eight pages – and I sweat blood. Yet at this moment, I feel strong, keen, passionate, still unspent. The spell is in me yet' (226: 153).

It is this reinterpretation of his experiences, more than any other factor, which endangers his effectiveness as a writer, for he tries to write appropriately 'literary' passages. The result is his purpler prose and the anomalies which spring from his combination of stiltedly formal narration and attempted colloquial dialogue.

When Grey recasts his personal experiences in the West, he draws on the myth of the glorious frontier as reshaped by Owen Wister, whose work he knew (226: 65). In the Foreword to *To the Last Man* (1922) Grey echoes the sentiments of Wister's Foreword to *The Virginian:* 'I have loved the West for its vastness, its contrast, its beauty and color and life, for its wildness and violence, and for the fact that I have seen how it developed great men and women who died unknown and unsung.' Such a perspective tends to paint people and events larger than life, more intense or extreme. Wister keeps this tendency in check, but Grey does not. In 'The Man Who Influenced Me Most', Grey pays tribute to Jim Emett, a Mormon he had met on his first trip west with 'Buffalo' Jones. 'I learned of innumerable feats beyond comprehension',

Grey remarks with admiration. 'The desert had developed him. Like an Indian, if he was to survive there, he must endure.' At this point Grey's vivid imagination takes over and Emett's superhuman feats are envisaged and catalogued:

> Loneliness, hunger, thirst, cold, heat, the fierce sandstorm, the desert blizzard, poverty, labor without help, illness without medicine, tasks without remuneration, no comfort, but little sleep, so few of the joys commonly yearned for by men, and pain, pain, always some kind of pain – these were the things that taught Emett endurance. (213: 136)

The tribute to an individual becomes a glorification of endurance itself, an emphasis borrowed from the myth of the glorious frontier, of the West as the testing-ground of character. The balance between vulnerability and endurance which gives each its emotional power is lost.

The transformation of a man into a superhero leaves little room for the recognition of the ironies and conflicts of that man's position or for the acknowledgement of the subtleties and contradictions of human emotions. Grey's tendency to inflate and exaggerate is therefore an important handicap to him as a writer. One can see the extent to which this tendency shapes Grey's fiction by comparing his autobiographical account 'Death Valley' (1920) with the experiences of Adam Larey in the novel *Wanderer of the Wasteland* (1923). When Grey visited Death Valley in 1919, he met a man residing in a shack on the edge of the desert whose livelihood consisted in growing alfalfa for the mules in the borax mines. He was hospitable and informative about local conditions. In *Wanderer of the Wasteland*, Adam finds a shack perilously located at the foot of a potential landslide. It is inhabited by a man who keeps his wife prisoner in the dangerous shack to punish her for previous infidelities. Grey crossed Death Valley in the spring:

> Facing the sun, we found the return trip more formidable. Hot indeed it was – hot enough for me to imagine how terrible Death Valley would be in July or August. On all sides the mountains stood up dim and obscure and distant in haze. The heat veils lifted in ripples, and any object not near at hand seemed illusive. (205: 769)

Adam crosses this desert in July:

> Often he was thrown to his knees. And when the midnight
> storm reached its height the light of the stars failed, the outline
> of mountains faded in a white, whirling chaos, dim and
> moaning and terrible. Adam felt as if blood and flesh were
> burning up, drying out, shrivelling and cracking. He lost his
> direction and clung to the burros. . . .   (222: 166)

Grey's reworking of his own experiences in this intense and exag-
gerated form has led critics to dispute the realism of his work.
While Burton Rascoe issues the scathing denunciation, 'I have
been among ranchmen and cowboys of the Southwest and I have
never seen such purple cows' (233: 19), Frank Gruber protests,
'He saw the places he wrote about, he did the things his characters
did. . . . He knew the taciturn Mormons, the Indian traders, the
cowboys, and the ranchers. He knew Texas Rangers, gunfighters,
gamblers, dance-hall girls' (226: 166–7).

Grey's credibility is indeed questionable; he was quite capable
of remembering inaccurately. His memory of his dental trade as a
'fairly flourishing profession' when this was not the case is an
example. He even listed the year of his birth incorrectly in several
books. The question of whether to treat a specific account as fact
or fantasy becomes irrelevant, however. Whatever the degree of
truth, the literary treatment given to specific incidents removes
them from the level of individual experience, and places them on
the more generalised level of cultural mythology.

Grey not only mythologised his life experiences, but also
attempted to provide himself with experiences proper to his
culturally informed image of the idealised male role. He went on
numerous expeditions to remote parts of the West, explored an
unknown jungle river in Mexico, and travelled half way round the
world looking for big game fish and netting a number of record
catches. Such escapades provided Grey with a basis for revolt as
well as a handy refuge.

Grey's exploits, anecdotes and much of his fiction display his
rebellion. He revolted against social authority, against social
conventions, and later against what he viewed as the loose social
mores of the day. The autobiographical episodes examined earlier,
which Grey retold with evident relish and embellishment, indicate
his desire to rebel against his father's authority and the social

expectations at university. The Jacktown game seems to indicate a more generalised aggressiveness: Grey must have known that his intervention would upset players, spectators and any betting involved.

By heading for the woods in fact or in imagination, Grey retreated from life's complexities and demands. The cultural mythology allowed him to justify his consequent avoidance of practical, routine matters, from school work to business arrangements, while asserting his masculinity. He masked his embarrassment or bewilderment by portraying himself as a man of strenuous practicality with little time for mundane details; since his wife could cope admirably, they need not demand the attention of a tough masculine mind.

As a boy, he escaped to the woods. When pressures became too great at university, he retreated to the library. Later in life he would go off fishing or head for the remoter areas of the West. Or, he would write. Grey's writing seems to have helped relieve his 'black moods'. 'This morning bad news in letters and telegrams threw me off', Grey confessed in his journal entry for 26 April 1919: 'I fumed and fretted. It is so difficult to make these business decisions. I do not know what is good, or what is wrong. I have got to make a great effort to drive away the spell of blackness or sink into it. So I will go to writing!' (226: 150).

Grey's writing provided only a partial and temporary relief. As Steele and Swinney explain, merely projecting his unresolved conflicts provided no basis for understanding or acceptance, and his unresolved problems returned to haunt him (239: 86). Frank Gruber's observation that Grey grew progressively more depressed despite his successful career as a writer would seem to support this interpretation (226: 154–5).

Part of Grey's problem was that he wanted to claim all the contradictory virtues of his culture at once. He wanted to be both the tough, practical adventure hero and the idealistic romantic; both the writer who stimulated his readers' imaginations and the writer who helped to educate his audience by giving them information on geography, history, nature lore, folklore and legend (229: 111). He also wanted to be both the artist struck by inspiration and a practical working writer. Finally, Grey wanted to be known as both a popular writer and as an author of literature; he wanted 'to write literature and yet have a large audience' (203: 80).

Grey's pre-eminence as a popular writer has never been

disputed; Donald R. Arbuckle has summarised Grey's achievement well: after *Riders of the Purple Sage*, any book he wrote could be guaranteed to sell 500,000 copies, and from 1917 to 1924 each annual best-seller list contained a Zane Grey novel. This, Arbuckle points out, is 'a record unequalled to this day' (97: 96).

Grey's desire to be taken seriously as an artist has met with much scornful laughter, however. At first he was treated with indulgence by critics, but as time went on he was seen, at best, as a primitive. At worst, he was savaged. By the time of his death, the *New York Times*, which had hailed the publication of *The Heritage of the Desert* by announcing Grey's 'right to be claimed among the best of those American novelists who have chosen the frontier as their field' (234: 558), was dismissive: 'Judged by any accepted literary standard, the more than 50 novels he wrote were bad' (245: 23).

Grey himself seems to have been inordinately sensitive to bad reviews. 'It was so bitter, so hateful, so amazingly unjust that it made me ill', he said of one harsh review. In the mid twenties, he even wrote a twenty-page article in defence of his books and style, but was advised not to publish it as it was likely to give his critics additional ammunition. Still, it is hard to discount the cruelty behind such comments as Heywood Brown's observation that 'the substance of any two Zane Grey books could be written upon the back of a postage stamp' (226: 164).

Grey did make an important contribution to the Western subgenre, but one which is different in kind from Wister's innovatory work. Grey's writing is much closer to recorded daydream than to a self-conscious attempt at synthesis. His work does not mature, either in terms of a developing literary skill or in terms of an evolving world view. This has led critics to perceive a sameness in Grey's output and to denounce him as a 'one-book author', but this assessment is unfair. Although the daydream he explored, probably unselfconsciously, in his Westerns remained the same throughout his career, Grey explored all the corners of this dream, and in doing so he uncovered many of the hidden assumptions of the Western formula. In Grey's work, more than in that of any other Western-writer of the period, one begins to glimpse the assumptions and implications of the genre. Quite apart from the issue of popularity, this makes him an important writer of the Western. This is why Grey should be studied carefully.

In the settings he chooses, Grey explores several different kinds of lawlessness: the lawlessness that springs from the openness of the West, that which exists in the dominions of the outlaws, and that which results from the corruption of the law by self-serving officials. Grey's anarchic, open West is very close to Wister's idea of lawlessness as a state of pre-civilisation, but Grey tends to treat this concept literally. What is envisaged by Wister as an open society troubled by violent, unsocial behaviour becomes a vast uninhabited desert or forest in Grey's imagination. Consequently, Grey gives the reader a fuller impression of the vast emptiness of the landscape.

Like Wister, Grey applauds the openness because it ensures the ascendancy of the fittest, but as we have seen, Grey sees the resulting contest in Darwinian terms. None the less, his standard of survival is virtually identical to Wister's measure of success: Grey's heroes achieve wealth, social recognition and personal happiness. This is true of Dale and Las Vegas Carmichael in *Man of the Forest* (1920), of Hare in *The Heritage of the Desert*, and of Adam Larey, though two books, *Wanderer of the Wasteland* and *Stairs of Sand* (1943), are required in his case.

In some respects Grey goes beyond Wister's formulation. Because physical strength and spiritual worth are carefully separated, his treatment of the 'best man' allows for new possibilities. A person of poor moral fibre never prevails in the long run, but both the good man who declines to use his strength and the strong man who is morally reprehensible are explored as possibilites. An example of the former has already been provided in an earlier discussion of *The Heritage of the Desert*. The latter is dealt with in works which focus on an outlaw community.

Although outlaw society is merely a more extreme case, treating it as a special instance allows Grey to explore the more disturbing implications of social Darwinism with a freer conscience, to criticise the amorality of the philosophy, and to vent his disapproval of materialism. Glimpses of outlaw society are provided in *The Lone Star Ranger* (1936), but it is most thoroughly canvassed in *The Border Legion* (1916).

Passions run high in outlaw society, and arguments are likely to end with violence. There is no basis for mutual trust. As Kells, the outlaw-leader in *The Border Legion*, points out, 'No man can have friends on this border. We flock together like buzzards. There's safety in numbers, but we fight together, like buzzards over carrion' (202: 102). Such acute self-assertiveness brings the whole concept of 'society' and 'social responsibility' into direct conflict with the underlying social Darwinism.

As though this were not disturbing enough, in *The Border Legion* we learn that it is Gulden, a cannibal whose strength comes directly from his lack of self-restraint, who is best equipped to thrive in a lawless environment: 'He's beneath morals. He has no conception of manhood, such as I've seen in the lowest of outcasts. . . . And here on the border, if he wants, he can have all the more power because of what he is' (202: 116). Fortunately, Gulden cannot realise his full potential because he is stupid. He is eventually brought down by a conscience-stricken outlaw chief who willingly sacrifices himself, but this sleight-of-hand manoeuvring toward a happy ending does not submerge the alarming implications of Gulden's threatened triumph.

The third variant, the corruption of the law, greatly expands the domain of the Western formula by allowing for a fairly populous, apparently law-abiding community. Grey approaches this type of lawlessness from different points of view. In *The Border Legion*, we are privy to the machinations of those in power. *Riders of the Purple Sage* is told from the point of view of an intended victim. Both *Twin Sombreros* (1941) and *The Lone Star Ranger* follow detective-like figures as they search for the true villains.

The corrupt leader is apparently the best man, but his status and power belie his true worth. His relationship to the law as seeming servant but actual beneficiary is also troubling. The corrupt leader is often difficult to unmask, as is the case in *Twin Sombreros*, but this in itself raises no disturbing social issues. The ambiguity does become disquieting in *The Lone Star Ranger*, where the outlaw's conduct is alternately excused and condemned.

Two conflicting appraisals of Chesaldine are given. When talking with the outlaw's daughter, Duane pleads for the man he has brought to justice: 'I once heard a well-known rancher say that all rich cattlemen had done a little stealing. Your father drifted out here, and, like a good many others, he succeeded. It's perhaps just as well not to split hairs, to judge him by the law and morality of a civilized country' (210: 285–6). The worrying implications of this assessment are magnified when one recalls an earlier description of the outlaw: 'And herewith was unfolded a history so dark in its bloody regime, so incredible in its brazen daring, so appalling in its proof of the outlaw's sweep and grasp of the country . . . , that Duane was stunned' (210: 256).

Duane must admire Chesaldine's ambition, competence and impressive success, praiseworthy traits applauded in the American ideology. Consequently, like the gangster films of the thirties, the outlaw raises the embarrassing possibility of a non-essential, perhaps even inverse, connection between morality and the success ethic. To understand the equivocal nature of the outlaw figure, one must look at the actions and characteristics which define the typical criminal: he attempts to achieve the power and status of the 'best man' without engaging in direct individual competition; he steals property in the dead of night or with the aid of corrupt legal institutions; he shoots people *in the back* and he relies on the collective strength of a group of followers. In other words, he attempts to subvert the code of the West, of individualistic competition.

In so far as outlaws such as Chesaldine demonstrate an ability to operate within the code of the West, their villainy is mitigated. The resulting moral ambiguity seems particularly striking because it appears against a background of simplistic moral polarity. Indeed, these ambiguous characters take on a rather spurious depth, produced by the tensions between different sets of values within the book rather than by any deep ambivalence within the characters themselves.

This brings us back to the double-edged nature of law in the Western. The corrupt leader uses legal institutions to increase his power, to gain unfair advantages over those he can not dominate in equal competition. In *Twin Sombreros*, Surface is accused in these terms by Brazos: 'Yu're not even Western, Surface. Yu don't belong oot heah. An' if yu're gonna stay I advise yu to get law an' order – a hell of a lot'. In reply 'Surface controlled a malignant rage. He had sense enough to see that he was impotent in the Western creed of man to man' (220: 170). Chesaldine is also accused of using the law, but the weakness this implies is contra-indicated by his willingness to confront Duane man to man. While much of the action and violence of the Western are ostensibly directed toward the restoration of law, the legal institutions are themselves scorned as the refuge of the weak. In fact, the law which is restored is not legalistic; it is the law of the survival of the fittest as determined by the rituals of individual competition.

In *Twin Sombreros*, the actions of Brazos strip a thief of his ill-gotten gains, execute two murderers while letting a friend of the court go, restore property to its rightful owner, and remove a crooked sheriff from office by arranging his death. Brazos has acted as judge and executioner. He is the law. He is the strongest. But in actual legalistic terms he has neither restored the law nor acted with the consent of any legal body. In fact, he has deliberately circumvented the proper legal channels: 'Wal, I reckon yu won't get oot of heah alive. I'm not trustin' the justic of Las Animas . . .' (220: 176).

Instead, Grey's heroes restore the *status quo* in a series of encounters between the individualistic hero and individual members of the villainous group. Brazos first deals with Orcutt, then with Syvertsen, then Bess, then Surface, then finally Bodkin. Likewise, in his confrontations with the powerful officials of the Mormon Church, Lassiter (*Riders of the Purple Sage*) demonstrates how weak they are as individuals. The *status quo* the hero restores is just as inherently lawless as the crisis situation.

The surprising tolerance of criminal activity provides further evidence of the special character of 'law': 'Every rancher has stolen cattle, knowingly or not, and he's testy about it', Renn Frayne admits in a letter to Brazos (220: 41). In *The Lone Star Ranger* Duane comments 'That Blandy. His faro game's crooked. . . . Not that we don't have lots of crooked faro-dealers. A fellow can stand for them. But Blandy's mean, back-handed, never looks you in the eyes' (210: 215). It is not criminal behaviour but criminal conspiracy which is threatening. As Duane remarks, 'Western Texas had gone on prospering, growing in spite of the hordes of rustlers ranging its vast stretches; but a cold, secret, murderous hold on a little struggling community was something too strange, too terrible for men to stand long' (210: 219–20). This sensitivity to conspiracy is interesting in that it foreshadows the more central role this element plays in the hard-boiled detective novel.

Zane Grey also gives fuller development to Wister's concept of the West as a land of exploitable wealth, and, characteristically, he handles the concept more pictorially. The exploitable resources include a vast array of mineral deposits, the abundance of wildlife and the potential of the land for grazing and farming. However, the harshness of the natural environment, the uncertainty of survival in a hostile world and the lawlessness hinder accumulation and shadow continued possession with uncertainty. One recalls the lush portrayal of Naab's oasis in *The Heritage of the Desert* and the description of the prospectors who are found dead near an arsenic spring with gold in their pockets in *Wanderer of the*

Wasteland. Such descriptions bring the abundance into shocking juxtaposition with the tenuousness of possession.

Lawlessness implies a close relationship between property and power which is explicitly acknowledged in *The Border Legion*: 'Don't you hold your claim – your gold – by the right of your strength? It's the law of the border' (202: 253). Property changes hands as the balance of power shifts; extensive wealth requires more determined and capable protection. Rich ranchers provide the most tempting target for rustlers. The rich gold strike attracts outlaws. And, in the desert, it is the terrible Death Valley, with its furnace winds, arsenic springs and poisonous air, that holds the greatest mineral treasure. Thus the property-holder is tested according to the level of his ambitions.

While desirable, it is impossible to secure a lasting reward. Grey tries to circumvent this problem by bestowing wealth at the end of a book, neatly discouraging the reader from contemplating a problematic future. In some cases, he moves the hero and heroine east, another form of evasion. The latter is an interesting attempt to maintain a synthesis of East and West while keeping useful distinctions, and, predictably, it produces more problems than it solves.

Wanderer of the Wasteland shows that the characteristics essential for survival in the West may make a man unfit to enjoy his rewards in the East; indeed, they may even render him unfit to live in a civilised state. Dismukes spends forty years of hardship slaving to accumulate half a million dollars' worth of gold. 'I'm rich', he says to Adam when his goal is reached; 'The years of lonely hell an' never-endin' toil are over. No more sour dough! No more thirst an' heat an' dust! No more hoardin' of gold! The time has come for me to spend. I'll bank my gold an' draw my checks' (222: 181). He talks of seeing the world, of buying a farm that is green, where he can hear the sound of running water. He dreams of marrying and having a family. But his travels teach him that he is no longer capable of living anywhere but in the desert, alone: 'On one hand was the dream of my life – the hope of a home an' happiness – what I had slaved for . . .', admits Dismukes. 'On the other hand the call of the desert! . . . Ah! The desert was my only home. I belonged to the silence an' desolation' (222: 210). Dismukes's admission is a dangerous one for the Western formula: it shatters the synthesis which makes the West the proving-ground for Eastern values. Some of the sting is drawn from this admission –

it is a religious, mystical force which compels Dismukes to return – but the larger implications cast a shadow none the less.

When Grey does not indulge in such evasions, he is forced to tackle the troubling vulnerability of the aged. In *Man of the Forest*, an employee dismissed for stealing tries to confiscate his former employer's property. The reader's attention is drawn away from the dying rancher, however, for the threat is depicted as a test of the worthiness of his niece, the intended heiress. This neatly sidesteps the real issue. Such handling serves another end as well: the young lady and her male protector appear to be 'earning' the wealth they inherit, thereby defending the fairness of such expectations.

As an emblem of power, the defence of property carries heightened significance. Thus, in *Riders of the Purple Sage*, Tull systematically strips Jane Withersteen of her property to demonstrate that she is helpless. Holly Ripple (*Knights of the Range*, 1939), Helen Rayner (*Man of the Forest*) and Jane Withersteen all find themselves faced with forced, undesirable marriages if they prove unable to defend themselves, for weakness effectively negates all one's rights.

This places Grey's women in a position which heavily reinforces traditional concepts of sex roles: Grey carefully demonstrates that women depend on men for their property and personal rights, even their lives, not to mention their 'honour'. All his embattled heroines are ultimately at the mercy of the men who fight over them and their property; they are essential adjuncts of the material reward handed out at the end of a book to the victorious combatant. To be sure, this is given a romantic overlay in which the heroine pines for the man who is protecting her, but her essential weakness makes her an object in a power play. Joan articulates this dilemma in *The Border Legion*: 'Men were the embodiment of passion – ferocity. They breathed only possession, and the thing in the balance was death. Women were creatures to hunger and fight for, but womanhood was nothing' (202: 254).

The men who fight for these embattled heroines are oversized characters, big enough to dominate their womenfolk physically and to fill the vast landscape. 'When señor becomes a man he will be a giant', a Mexican says of Adam in *Wanderer of the Wasteland* (222: 19). Adam does grow up to become a man capable of crushing an enemy with his bare hands (222: 122). Deeds are correspondingly oversized. Pan Handle Smith and Texas Joe (*The*

Trail Driver, 1936) can achieve deadly accuracy with their six-shooters in the middle of the night with only the split-second lightning-flashes to aim by. Gulden's death struggle (*The Border Legion*) is that of a giant: four men, uncounted rounds of ammunition and a knife are needed to kill him. And then he lingers. Lassiter rescues a child from a band of rustlers. Bleeding copiously from the five bullet wounds he has received, he carries the child and guides an exhausted woman up the side of a canyon wall. Upon reaching a ledge, he pushes a huge balancing rock down the cliff to foil pursuers. Such deeds would seem preposterous if set in the usual everyday world, but, as Cawelti has commented, the West lends people and deeds an epic stature (102: 39ff). Grey takes full, sometimes too full, advantage of this tendency in the formula.

But in character, as in setting, Grey tends to push the standard conceits of the formula to the point where they yield up their assumptions and implications. He examines such extreme cases as the gun-fighter syndrome and gold fever, both aberrations encouraged by the social environment of the Western and by the value structure of the American dream. The Gun-fighter syndrome is the need to compete gone haywire; gold fever occurs when the desire for gain no longer recognises any restraint or sense of proportion.

The Lone Star Ranger is Grey's most detailed study of the gunman; here the formative social pressures are carefully delineated and the distorting influence of the skill is thoroughly explored. In part, Duane is compelled to fight by 'an inherited fighting instinct, a driving intensity to kill', a product of his frontier heritage (210: 3,12). Social forces reinforce this tendency, for his quick draw and his father's notoriety result in a reputation which he must defend with his life. He is forced to develop his skill until the gun becomes 'a living part of him' (210: 41). His whole being and personality become distorted in the process.

The extent to which the gun dominates the man can be seen with other gunmen as well: both Black (*The Lone Star Ranger*) and Lassiter (*Riders of the Purple Sage*) become shrunken, transformed when deprived of it. Duane himself realises the dangerous warping power of his profession: 'Sometimes he had a feeling of how little stood between his sane and better self and a self utterly wild and terrible. He reasoned that only intelligence could save him – only a thoughtful understanding of his danger and a hold upon some ideal' (210: 104). In the end, despite his ideals and his heroism, Duane must accept the full horror of what it means to be a gunman:

> He realized it now, bitterly, hopelessly. The thing he had intelligence enough to hate he had become. At last he shuddered under the driving, ruthless, inhuman blood-lust of the gunman. . . . And those passions were so violent, so raw, so base, so much lower than what ought to have existed in a thinking man. Actual pride of his record! Actual vanity in his speed with a gun! Actual jealousy of any rival!   (210: 294–5)

Duane is tormented by his victims and is driven by 'the need, in order to forget the haunting, sleepless presence of his last victim, to go out and kill another' (210: 294). This portrait is a far cry from Wister's heroic gun-fighter, the Virginian. Indeed, Grey pioneered in portraying the gunman as the obsessed, ultimately doomed figure who would later become a cliché of the Western formula. By pushing tendencies to their relentlessly logical conclusion, Grey demonstrates how such a figure is a natural outgrowth of the overdeveloped competitive drive unrestrained by law. And again, he indicates his own ambivalence toward the aggressive qualities encouraged by social Darwinism.

The effects of gold fever are most thoroughly explored in *The Border Legion*. The lust for gold destroys all sense of value, proportion and priorities; it eclipses all needs, instincts and standards beyond the impulse for personal enrichment. Grey describes the effect of a big gold strike on the men involved:

> It was a time in which the worst of men's natures stalked forth, hydra-headed and deaf, roaring for gold, spitting fire, and shedding blood. It was a time when gold and fire and blood were one. It was a time when a horde of men from every class and nation, of all ages and characters, met on a field where motives and ambitions and faiths and traits merged into one mad instinct for gain. It was worse than the time of the medieval crimes of religion; it made war seem a brave and honorable thing; it robbed manhood of that splendid and noble trait, always seen in shipwrecked men or those hopelessly lost in the barren north, the divine will not to retrograde to the savage. It was a time, for all it enriched the world with yellow treasure, when might

was right, when men were hopeless, when death stalked
rampant. The sun rose gold and it set red. It was the hour of
Gold! (202: 242)

Here we have in their most extreme form the social implications
of the economic aspirations associated with the American dream.
Grey presents an unusual portrayal of America as 'melting-pot';
here the people of the world come together not to savour the
benefits of freedom, but to lust after gold: the economic drawing-
power of the new world takes on a sinister edge. Men are brought
together in such a way that social instincts are destroyed: 'Daily
the population of Alder Creek grew in the new gold-seekers and
its dark records kept pace. With distrust came suspicion and with
suspicion came fear, and with fear came hate – and these, in
already distorted minds, inflamed a hell' (202: 241).

In explaining gold fever, Grey once again speaks of the
regression of man to the savage state. It would seem that the West
brings out the savage in man, but not the Indian savage, the
white-man savage; the two are not the same. 'You can always
trust Indians to go to the freightin' posts for you. But never let
any white man in this desert know you got money. That's a hard
comparison, an' its justified', Dismukes tells Adam (222: 61–2).
The uncivilised Indians do not suffer from gold fever. 'I did meet
desert men who could have helped me', Dismukes continues. 'But
they passed me by. The desert locks men's lips. Let every man
save his own life – find his own soul. That's the unwritten law of
the wastelands of the world' (222: 63). He suggests that Adam
find a community of Indians, however, for they will help him to
learn the ways of the desert. The Indians do take Adam in and
care for him. But the Indian community cannot be seen as a viable
alternative to the white man's civilisation, for it is doomed to
extinction. This is a grave handicap within the framework of social
Darwinism, and one which exposes Grey's ambivalence toward
both this philosophy and the assumed beneficence of the social
'progress' it demands.

What kind of savage, then, is it that the West brings out in
men? It is the magnification of those values enshrined in the
American dream and basic to a capitalistic economy which makes
a man savage. When these civilised instincts are given free reign
in the lawlessness of the West, they clearly demonstrate the need
for the restraints of civilisation.

This is where the role of women becomes crucial; for it is they, and not the violence-prone males, who exert a restraining influence on the aggregate society of the West. Women are seen as the true harbingers of civilisation: they are religious, deplore violence and are concerned with the welfare of others. Jane Withersteen (*Riders of the Purple Sage*) is a good example of the Grey heroine: she shows concern for the welfare of her employees and neighbours, she begs Lassiter not to use his guns on her enemies, and she maintains her religious convictions despite the perfidy of the Mormon elders.

Good women such as Jane Withersteen, advocates of the values of Christian humanism, distract attention from the brutality of the American-dream values. The issue of ideology becomes redefined as a matter of sex-role differences. None the less, it is both interesting and telling that the sterling qualities of such heroines create problems for their hero protectors. Their influence is at once progressive, toward a more humane set of values, and potentially crippling. Lassiter endangers himself, Jane and the security of her property-holdings as long as he restrains himself in accordance with her wishes. Dale faces a similar dilemma in *Man of the Forest*.

None the less, Grey follows Wister's lead, marrying hero and heroine after the double process of initiation. While the heroine is undergoing the resulting process of self-abnegation, the hero prepares to become a responsible member of society, a husband and family man. Sometimes, as with Lassiter in *Riders of the Purple Sage* and Buck Duane in *The Lone Star Ranger*, he hangs up his guns, a considerable sacrifice of significant import for a Western hero.

Grey's heroes do not make the transition to capitalists, however; the continuity of values between East and West is not as consciously emphasised in this respect. The synthesis attempted in Grey's Westerns is articulated in terms of civilisation and nature rather than East and West. Indeed, Dismukes's dilemma, once he has achieved success in *Wanderer of the Wasteland*, implicitly questions the notion of continuity, as does Grey's use of the East as a place for happy endings.

But Grey's exposure of discontinuities must be kept in perspective. Grey's heroes are all self-reliant, independent, competent and strong. They all have an internalised code which acts as their 'moral compass'. The plots of Grey's Westerns allow these heroes to achieve personal happiness as well as social and financial success. These are stock American values, stock American dreams, and they would be recognised by Grey's readers as such. By placing such heroes and plot patterns in the wild and woolly West, Grey emphasises the continuity of key American values.

The range and seriousness of the ideological issues Grey explores in his Westerns have not been recognised. In large measure this is because Grey's failings as a literary stylist give his work an apparently shallow finish. This in turn can be traced to his misunderstanding of the stylistic requirements of the colloquial style, to his misdirected literary pretensions and to his poor ear for the vernacular. Indeed, these factors are related: his desire to appear 'literary' undoubtedly clouded his understanding of the potential of the colloquial style, while his poor ear prevented him from using it skilfully.

When Grey is bad, he is awful. He has a poor ear for conversation, and his dialogue reflects this:

> 'No time – for a woman!' exclaimed Jane, brokenly. 'Oh, Lassiter, I feel helpless – lost – and don't know where to turn. If I *am* blind – then – I need some one – a friend – you, Lassiter – more than ever!'
>
> 'Well, I didn't say nothin' about goin' back on you, did I?'
>
> (216: 157)

He has no awareness of levels of language; he seems unaware of the important differences between the colloquial style and a more literary approach. As a result, one finds him moving quickly from a stilted literary level to an awkward attempt at colloquial speech. In *Riders of the Purple Sage*, a child's speech is set against Grey's attempt at a literary style. The effect is undoubtedly meant to be ironic, but is instead merely embarrassing for its awkwardness and lack of subtlety:

> 'Does oo love me?' she asked.
>
> Lassiter, who was as serious with Fay as he was gentle and loving, assured her in earnest and elaborate speech that he was her devoted subject. Fay looked thoughtful and appeared to be debating the duplicity of men or searching for a supreme test to prove this cavalier.
>
> 'Does oo love my new muvver?' she asked, with bewildering suddenness. (216: 269)

It would be decidedly out of character for Lassiter to speak to anyone in 'earnest and elaborate speech'. His reply to Jane's impassioned plea for help, quoted previously, is more appropriate in use of dialect, though it does not ring true in its choice of words.

Such inconsistencies can even be found within a single speech. In *Man of the Forest* Dale says 'Warm! Neck broken. See the lion's teeth an' claw marks. . . . It's a doe. Look here. Don't be squeamish, girls. This is only an hourly incident of every-day life in the forest' (212: 149). With 'This is only an hourly incident . . .', the pace and level of language changes strikingly. The change serves no purpose; it jars the reader's inner ear.

Grey is capable of better writing. His pictorial imagination lends an intensity and immediacy to his descriptions, making them effective and memorable. In a perceptive analysis of Grey's work T. K. Whipple comments 'Mr. Grey does not dodge big scenes and crises, . . . he has distinct liking for intense situations, and he has the power which Stevenson so admired of projecting these high moments in memorable pictures' (243: 506). One thinks of the precariously located cottage overlooking Death Valley (*Wanderer of the Wasteland*), Lassiter's rolling of the rock in *Riders of the Purple Sage* or Augustus Naab's anguish at the end of *The Heritage of the Desert*. Grey's rhetoric also reflects this pictorial intensity. The passage quoted earlier on gold fever provides a particularly effective example, as does the following passage from *The Heritage of the Desert*:

> The creatures of the desert endured the sun and lived without water, and were at endless war. The hawk had a keener eye than his fellow of more fruitful lands, sharper beak, greater spread of wings, and claws of deeper curve. For him there was little to eat, a rabbit now, a rock-rat then; nature made his swoop like lightning, and it never missed its aim. . . . The lizard flicked an invisible tongue into the heart of a flower; and the bee he caught stung with a poisoned sting. The battle of life went to the strong. (207: 253–4)

Grey effectively depicts the impact of an unforgiving environment on its inhabitants.

On occasion, Grey's descriptive passages come close to the sparse style usually associated with hard-boiled fiction. The tense anticipation before a trap is sprung on a gang of bank-robbers is conveyed through selected details noted in passing by the narrative eye:

> There was no excitement in the street. He crossed to the bank corner. A clock inside pointed the hour of two. He went through the door into the vestibule, looked around, passed up the steps into the bank. The clerks were at their desks, apparently busy. But they showed nervousness. The cashier paled at sight of Duane. There were men – the rangers – crouching behind the low partition. All the windows had been removed from the iron grating before the desks. The safe was closed. There was no money in sight. A customer came in, spoke to the cashier, and was told to come to-morrow.
>
> Duane returned to the door. He could see far down the street, out into the country. There he waited, and minutes were eternities. He saw no person near him; he heard no sound. He was insulated in his unnatural strain. (210: 299)

Such passages show that Grey is capable of better writing than the purple prose he is associated with. The restrained description above avoids the excessive use of adjectives and adverbs. By noting the absence of glass, the expectation of violence is made chillingly plain; this is the essence of dramatic understatement.

5

Frederick Faust

'Max Brand', 'Evan Evans' and 'George Owen Baxter' are among the better known pen names of Frederick Shiller Faust, born in Seattle, Washington on 29 May, 1892, the son of Gilbert Leander Faust and Elizabeth Uriel Faust, Gilbert's third wife. Faust grew up in the San Joaquin Valley, living in extreme poverty. His father had drifted through the West failing at a variety of occupations in many different towns. The family moved frequently, often more than once a year (276: 13). Necessity forced a younger brother and an older sister to be continually farmed out to relatives while Faust was kept at home because of poor health; he was even sent to the mountains one summer to recuperate. He read his first book, Malory's *Morte dè' Arthur*, at the age of seven and quickly became a voracious reader; by ten he had 'written enough to know that [he] wanted to write more', and it was at this time, he says, that 'a sense of high destiny overcame [him] once and for all' (276: 19). His mother died when he was eight, and he was orphaned at thirteen.

Thereafter he lived with relatives or friends of relatives, staying on ranches, farms or in the small towns of central California and moving frequently: 'making my way', he later wrote, 'by my own efforts and the charity of others' (276: 15). At sixteen, he arrived in Modesto to attend a highly regarded secondary school. He stayed at first with Thomas Downey, the principal and a distant relative, but later left 'in order to avoid the appearance of being dependent on a relative' (271: 11).

Faust demonstrated considerable academic ability: he finished a year's course in classical history and literature, which Downey had provided for his spare time, in three months, and asked for more. His writing also showed promise. Faust graduated from Modesto High School as a student 'pre-eminent in liberal arts courses and quite competent in science, algebra, and calculus' (271: 14).

94

With a $50 loan from Downey, he prepared to enter the University of California at Berkeley. His freshman year was not a particularly successful one: he was rejected by a number of fraternities, and the translation of *König Ottokar* which he worked on with Leonard Bacon was not accepted by the English Club. His standing improved considerably in his sophomore year: he was elected to the editorial board of the *Occident*, the undergraduate literary magazine, and became a member of the English Club, 'a highwater mark of campus culture' (271: 19). Heinie Faust, as he was then known, became a notable campus figure.

He had more than seventy-five pieces published in the *Occident*, some after he had left university. He also contributed to the *University Chronicle*, a quarterly which recorded university activities; he became editor of the yearbook; associate editor, then editor of the campus humour magazine, the *Pelican*; and wrote a column for the *Daily Californian*, the campus newspaper. His poem 'One of Cleopatra's Nights' won the university's Cook Prize. He also wrote a blank-verse play, *Fools All*, and worked with George A. Smithson, instructor in English philology, on a translation of *Beowulf* which was later submitted for publication.

Faust gained a more unsavoury reputation for exploits of a different kind. He was recognised, he recalls, as 'the most famous drunk on campus', and was known as a braggart and a roughneck (271: 20). He angered the administration by enrolling in courses, then dropping them without official sanction if they did not interest him. He infuriated campus officials by offering to take anyone's final examination in any subject for $5; he guaranteed a passing grade. He satirised faculty and administrative dignitaries and their values in his campus newspaper column. His behaviour and the ideas and values he expressed in his writing eventually became a campus issue. He was denied his degree because of unexcused absences from classes, but it is likely, as Robert Easton points out in *Max Brand: The Big Westerner*, that the true grounds for his dismissal were moral and personal. Berkeley would later offer him an honorary degree, and Faust would refuse to accept it.

After being thrown out of university in 1915, his senior year, Faust began a rather bizarre set of adventures. He headed for India, but stopped in Honolulu to take a job as reporter, then as sports editor, of the *Star-Bulletin*. When he learned that members of the nationalist group he had intended to join in India had been hanged, he changed his plans and decided to head for Canada to enlist as a soldier in the First World War: 'The more I think about it', he wrote in a letter dated 15 September, 1915, 'the more plainly I see that the only part of the world where there is anything doing today is dear old Europe and everyone who hopes to enter heaven ought to be over on the Western front collecting chilblains and 42 centimeter shells' (276: 21).

Faust met up with a classmate, 'Dixie' Fish, and together they worked their way to Canada aboard a freighter carrying contraband ore. The ship almost sank in a storm, but was eventually towed into Vancouver, where both Faust and his friend joined the army. They suffered the inevitable delays with impatience, longing to be at the front. Fish bought himself an honourable discharge for $15 and headed for New York. There he joined the Ambulance Corps and sent Faust money to enable him to follow, but Faust was either unwilling or unable to buy his discharge, and attempted to desert. However, he 'Spent a little too much time saying goodbye to some of the boys . . . and one of the police who knew me on the boat and the battalion telegraphed ahead to Victoria where I found an escort of large sided detectives in formidable overcoats awaiting me' (276: 22).

He was arrested and given the choice of buying his discharge or serving a two-year jail sentence. He paid his money, found himself broke and attempted to re-enlist. This time a doctor rejected him on medical grounds, because of a varicocele, so he made a deal with the authorities whereby he would have an operation, then enlist. By mid March 1916, he was out of hospital and firmly established in the 'American' Battalion of the Canadian Army, stationed in Toronto. By April he could happily report in a letter, 'I think we beat it Wednesday. We have had to sign our overseas papers and that listens like business' (276: 23). The battalion became ensnarled in red tape, however, and Faust deserted again, knowing that he could be sentenced to death for a second offence.

He headed for New York, arriving in August, having walked across Nova Scotia, down through Maine, and shipped as a stoker on a ship from Bangor to New York. The Ambulance Corps would not take him and the British consul would not allow him to enlist in the British Army, so Faust reconciled himself to remaining in the city and took a job at Wanamaker's Department Store until he could find a post on one of the daily newspapers. 'I am pretty well decided now', he wrote in a letter dated 28 September, 1916, 'that I shall not try to get over to the front unless someone actually approaches me on the street and sticks a ticket in my hand . . .' (276: 25).

During this time Faust was submitting poems for publication and collecting rejection slips. He took another position working in the subway at William and Beekman Streets, and wrote a disgusted letter to the *New York Times* asking whether 'this' was the best he could expect from American society after receiving a good university education. The letter attracted the attention of Mrs Moffet, Mark Twain's sister and the mother of a college friend, and she provided Faust with a letter of introduction to Robert H. Davis, chief executive of the Frank A. Munsey publishing-firm. When he went to see Davis, Faust was given a plot and told to write a story. The result was 'Convalescence', published in *All Story*, 31 March, 1917 for which he was paid $78.

At about the same time, William Rose Benet of the *Century*, who had been encouraging Faust to continue writing poetry, accepted 'The Secret' for publication in the magazine's February 1917 edition. He paid Faust $50. Faust announced the sale of these two works in a letter of 5 February 1917 to his fiancée, Dorothy Schillig, a girl he had met at the University of California: 'I wouldn't go through the eternal agony of writing careful prose for all the blood of Jesus and a dozen new Holy Grails. Not for me' (276: 26). None the less, writing prose offered him a dependable, comfortable income; writing poetry did not, and Faust wanted to marry. So he began churning out his seemingly endless stream of salable prose, married Dorothy Schillig in May, and renewed his attempts to get to the front.

He was rejected by the draft board because of a recurrence of the varicocele. Following an operation to correct it at his own expense, he enlisted with the understanding that he would go straight to the front. Instead he was shipped to Camp Humphreys in Virginia. He finally secured a transfer and arrived in New York in time to see the end of the false armistice celebration: 'The bloody war is over. . . . I went to New York Thursday night and just missed a great celebration' (276: 34). Despite his persistent attempts to reach the front, Faust felt that he had failed: 'oh, for one little chance to play the man – just for a minute. But all I can do is wait for a discharge to go back to New York with a training camp and no war behind me. A fine tradition to hand down to our children' (276: 36).

To appreciate Faust's sense of failure here, one must recognise the lasting impact of his early experiences. The poverty and hardship of his childhood have often been seen as formative influences, as spurs to his ambitiousness; indeed, Robert Easton sees Faust's preoccupation with giants and giantism in this light, but the imprint of Faust's childhood is deeper and more complex.

Faust's recollections indicate that his childhood instilled a strong element of self-doubt. In a short autobiographical sketch, he portrays his mother with great admiration and affection, but also recalls, 'I think she had a haunting fear that I would be either a dullard or prove weak minded. She used to go over my lessons with me at night, but I could not learn. And I think it nearly broke her heart. It actually took me three months to learn how to write down figures . . .' (276: 13).

His perception of his father as a glorious failure and his perceived likeness to his father must have caused him even more profound uncertainty and uneasiness. In another fragment of the sketch quoted earlier, he justifies his father and his own admiration for him:

Dear old Daddy. Everyone loved him who knew him well. He had been a very brilliant lawyer when he was young and for a time everything he touched turned to gold. Then luck changed. He invested everything in the first Southern California land boom – and lost everything when the boom went bust. Then he went to Seattle. In a few years he was president of a bank and a director of several big concerns and owned a big lumber mill. Then came bad investments and the lumber mill burned down.

He was a heavily built man, but he had been an athlete in his youth and even when he was old he walked with a quick step and a snappy military swing of his arms. I could pick him from a crowd a block away by his walk alone. . . .

His homecoming at night was always a big event of the day to me. And after supper he used to tell me all sorts of stories. I liked them better than books. He was a bit of a mystic and there was a queer atmosphere about his stories that I never found in a book.

We used to understand each other without speaking a word.

Sometimes we would say the same thing together, our minds were so alike. And I was just a bit of a kid then. . . . God bless the man who invented Heaven and that beautiful fancy of meeting after death. How I long to believe in it! (276: 14)

But Faust was capable of viewing his father in a much harsher light as well:

My father was a passionate man with a good deal of brain but also with an unhappy talent for acting parts and giving them a certain German false sentimentality. I loved him a great deal but I kept seeing through the sham until I almost wished that I could be blind and accept him as he wanted me to accept him. In this way something hard, cold, critical was born in me – or perhaps it existed from the first, in a child of parents whose added ages reached ninety years. (275: 15)

Faust's ambivalence towards his father and his perceived likeness to him made him wish to prove himself a practical success. It also led him to view his own success as a writer with contempt and suspicion. This ambivalence helps to explain why Faust was ashamed of his family's poverty and why he reacted with pugnacity to a world he viewed as essentially hostile. He grew up fighting for his place, and seeking emotional fulfilment not from human contact, but from books and his daydreams;

I went for years with a swollen and scarred face because the fights at one school had hardly healed before I had to begin them again in another. All of this, you see, was forcing me thousands of miles away from normalcy in human relations. . . . I grew up tall, gangling, crushed with shame because of dodged bills at local stores, learning to withdraw from children of my age, thrown utterly into a world of books and daydreaming, daydreaming, daydreaming. (276: 15; 275: 18)

Faust's need to prove himself in competition of a direct, immediate kind can be seen in his schoolyard fights and in his boxing, upon his arrival at university, in the Freshman – Sophomore 'smoker', a competition which pitted first-year students against second years in a smoke and drink-laden atmosphere. His need to test himself can also be seen in his keen interest in horse-riding, tennis and squash, and in his pride at having proved himself at a variety of jobs involving physical labour. His answer to Downey's warm welcome at Modesto, 'I can pay my own way' (271: 9), and his ruffian antics at Modesto and Berkeley provide further evidence, as does his keen sense of failure at having missed the really big test of the First World War.

Faust is said to have remarked on many occasions that man's chief business is fighting of one kind or another and that to die in battle is the best kind of death (271: 64). *Time* quotes him as explaining his enormous productivity in terms that echo this sentiment: 'No one is more than forty to fifty per cent efficient, but when a man is backed into a corner by a man who intends to kill him, he can be as high as ninety per cent efficient' (273: 44).

His doubts about his ability to deal with the world on what he saw as its own terms must have been further exacerbated by his poor health as a child, his two medical rejections from the army, and a weak heart which became apparent when he suffered a heart attack at the age of twenty-nine.

With these concerns driving Faust, it is easy to see why the Western story with its crucial theme of the 'best man' provided an ideal framework for his fantasies. Some of the resulting fictions are transparent in their attempts to rework childhood experiences and to exorcise the resulting shame and self-doubts. In *Destry Rides Again (1930)*, a young lad makes up for his father's cowardice by risking his life to save the hero, Destry. His reward is to be taken on as Destry's protégé, thus earning a new and more deserving father. In *Marbleface (1934)*, the hero learns to compensate for a weak heart by developing steely nerves; his practical success, honesty and humility vindicate a rascally father figure in the eyes of the town.

Larramee's Ranch, Speedy and *The Tenderfoot* all deal with the seemingly inconsequential man with hidden potential which, when discovered, endows heroic stature. The hidden strength can be physical, as in *The Tenderfoot*, or a matter of character, as in *Larramee's Ranch*, where the best man is a cripple who cannot even shoot a gun; sometimes it is a blend, as in *Speedy*. It is also noteworthy that the uncovering of hidden potential is sometimes paired with the disclosure of the true weakness of a generally acknowledged hero, as in *Brothers of the Trail* and *South of Rio Grande (1930)*.

This theme of hidden potential should not be confused with the more conventional handling of the Western theme of environment as crucible. In both *The Tenderfoot* and *Larramee's Ranch* the inner strength is uncovered quite suddenly rather than developed over time. The hero is astounded by his discovery, and, although grateful, treats his newfound capabilities with suspicion. Although different from developed strength, the two notions are linked; in both the West brings out the best in man. Faust's preference for the former, a magical solution, is understandable; it avoids the unpleasant implications of failure within the Protestant ethic.

Faust needed to separate his own ambitions as a writer and his own literary endeavours from his father's story-telling. Consequently, he turned toward poetry, where his failure to achieve artistic goals was keenly felt, and firmly separated poetry from prose. He is said to have used two desks: one with a quill pen for writing poetry, the other with a typewriter for doing prose. Mornings he worked on poetry; afternoons, when exhausted by his efforts, he produced prose.

For Faust, poetry was the result of long painful hours of self-conscious effort; on 17 April, 1927, he recorded in his journal 'Three lines verse, 28 pages prose. A perfectly beautiful day' (276: 49). Poetry was 'artistic', formal; Faust though it 'a sacred art', requiring antique themes, noted Leonard Bacon (249: 44; 271: 72). Faust's poetry never attained his high standards, but he continued to hope for a breakthrough. One senses great longing in his 1933 statement, 'If I could write one powerful poem, no matter how short, it seems to me that dying would be an easy matter' (271: 173). Only two poetry books and a few poems bear his own name. The rest, a vast output said to total some 25 million words, was published under an estimated nineteen different pen names.

While writing poetry was an inherently worthwhile activity, churning out prose was not. Faust referred to his books as 'bread and butter', never discussing them with his children; he even forbade them to read the prose which brought him fame and considerable wealth (275: 34). These badges of success were a source of some satisfaction, as was his lavish lifestyle, but the money provided an unwelcome reminder that he had sold out:

Money and prose and prose and money make a bad combination for a goal. Verse has already been the God of my worship and verse has been shabbily served by me. . . . I wonder if I shall have the courage, ever, to give up a fat income for the sake of verse. I doubt it. And I despise myself for my cowardice.

(276: 45–6)

He derived amusement from the awe his gift of 'improvisation' inspired, but felt contempt for his fiction and for his role as story-teller to the masses. In 1937 he wrote to Carl Brandt, his agent, airing his dissatisfaction: 'Listen, Carl, the only guy that ever had a right to write *Of Mice and Men* without a let-down ending, is Heinie Faust. Why the hell can't I do something? Why can't I see you and talk about something except cheese to fit the *Collier's* market?' (271: 199).

Faust was intelligent enough to recognise the need his fictions filled within himself, and this further underscored his self-contempt and his disdain for his fiction. From Hollywood, Faust wrote to Grace Flandrau in New York,

> To revert to the Cosmopolitan story, the source of this and of all my fiction which has sold (or nearly all) has been an escape from reality. There was perhaps too much reading and too much actual pain in my childhood. It made me build daydreams, bubbles into which I could escape and find a bright and blue and golden world all for me. I denied pain. So in my stories men may start bad but they must wind up good. Women are angels and men are heroes. And a certain number of child-minded people, even millions of them, read this brainless drip and like it. (271: 222)

One must, I think, pair this statement with Sergeant Jack Delany's recollection of a conversation with Faust the night before he was killed. Faust was a war correspondent in Italy at the time, preparing to accompany Delany's division into battle when the sergeant tried to persuade him to stay behind until the objective was taken. Faust protested,

> All my life I've written fiction. . . . I've put the heroes in tight spots and then by an extra stretch of the imagination, I've got them out of those spots. It always was pretty easy to do – easy because it was fiction.
>
> But this is fact. And these man [*sic*]; though they really are youngsters, are potential or actual heroes. They're in a tight

spot – I didn't put them there, and no extra stretch of my imagination can get them out of it. (275: 124)

The next day, 11 May, 1944, Faust went with the advancing troops and was killed by mortar fire during the assault.

Faust's fiction has been condemned and praised as adult fairytales, and there is much in his works which is appropriate to such a categorisation, but Robert Easton hits closer to the mark when he comments that Faust saw the West in terms of 'the myth of the timeless man, reliving the age-old, cyclical stories of the son in search of an illustrious father or the warrior who had an Achilles heel' (271: 218–19). Unfortunately, he does not recognise the true significance these myths had for Faust, nor does he develop a full argument for the mythic timbre of Faust's writings.

'Myth' is a slippery term, and a distinction must be drawn between the sense in which Faust is a mythic writer and the way Zane Grey uses myth. Grey assimilated the myths of his culture and used them to endow even the mundane aspects of his past with heroic import. In his fiction too, Grey explored the ideological myths which provided a ready-made value structure and sense of identity, and used them to supply the 'answers' he sought. This act of faith eliminated any need to generate personal myths.

Faust was influenced by the Greek myths he had absorbed in his extensive reading. He used the patterns furnished by these myths in a detached and selfconscious manner. He even claimed a Western modelled on the *Iliad*. But Faust could never use myth to give his experiences a heroic cast or view fiction as a substitute for life. His use of the classics does not explain the mythic resonance of his work.

Faust's most interesting work is mythic because it comes from the same wellspring as myth. Myth derives from the need to resolve a problem of overwhelming significance while disguising its presentation. Acknowledgement of the problem would precipitate overwhelming anxiety, so the distancing-process is important. There is a need to repeat this process over and over because the problem is at base unresolvable. The problems which generated Faust's intensely personal myths were the unresolved conflicts of his youth, centring on his acceptance or rejection of his father, with the implications this decision held for his own identity. Thus Grace Flandrau says of Faust's work,

'It had to pour out like automatic writing, like the material of a dream.' She said it had to be fiction, written out of some disassociated fragment of youthful personality, or else it had to be highly conscious verse, during the writing of which 'he probably thought too much, or rather, too exclusively. So that, distinguished as it was, it suffered from the absence of his daemon.' (271: 270–1)

Unlike Wister and Grey, Faust was not enamoured of the Western landscape and had little interest in proclaiming or exploring the essential Americanness of the West. Landscape plays only a minor role in his Westerns: 'His setting was a never-never land', Robert Easton has commented. 'He used a minimum of actual circumstance . . . chiefly because he was a natural tale teller and wanted to free his work from everyday reality' (271: 67). It is a tribute to the strength and versatility of the Western formula that in Faust's work, where 'setting' does not matter, the key elements can be found in abundance.

The artificial distinction between East and West is maintained, with the West depicted as more open, physically and socially, and more lawless than the East. In *Trailin'*, Anthony Woodbury, seated in the library of a Long Island mansion, explains his feelings to the man he assumes is his father: 'I'd rather be out in the country where men still wear guns, where the sky isn't stained with filthy coal smoke, where there's an horizon wide enough to breathe in, where there's man-talk instead of this damned chatter over teacups – ' (266: 26–7). Needless to say, the young man soon heads west.

In *South of Rio Grande* we see the contrast of East and West from the Western point of view when, on seeing a greenhorn in trouble, the deputy comments, 'If I had my own way, I would have a special State fund for such cases as this; to put them on the train and ship them back East, where a man can be as small and as soft as you please so long as he knows how to walk and talk' (263: 15). The contrast becomes much more ambivalent when the deputy describes the town's seamy lawlessness, however: 'It was a ragged, mean, low-down, crooked, dirty border town . . . and [I] wondered that the thin sides to its wooden shacks could hold in the murders, the stranglings, the knife fights, the gun plays, the robberies, treacheries, and thousand kinds of crime which they had known' (263: 16). The sheriff even comes to see law as a positive good. None the less, contempt for the law as the refuge of the weak is the more common attitude. Chris Verner, a reformed bank-robber and successful farmer in *Larramee's Ranch*, strikes a keynote of the traditional attitude: 'Me and the law have got on tolerable well without leanin' none on each other for support' (259: 176).

Such characters as Jerry Ash in *Marbleface* and Vincent Allen in *The Tenderfoot* head west to avoid real or imagined criminal prosecution in the East. Their flight supports the illusion of the West's openness. Jerry Ash is relieved when he arrives in Piegan, a small town four days hard riding from the railroad, and assumes his freedom is secure. Although a detective does come to arrest him, the lawman is ridiculed and sent packing. The town's attitude is summed up in the following exchange:

'You – behind me!' he snapped. 'I'm Detective Charles Richardson, of New York City. I have a warrant for this man's arrest.'

Said Harry: 'I'm Harry Blossom, of Piegan, and you'll have to go to hell and back before you serve that warrant on Pokerface.' (260: 144)

Even the sheriff refuses to assist the New York policeman, committing a penitentiary offence in 'losing' the warrant. He justifies his action on the grounds of friendship. The contrast between the sheriff's loyalty and the detective's greed makes the sheriff's behaviour appear noble, but the value-set implicit in his behaviour remains problematic.

To place loyalty above law as Faust does quite explicitly in *Marbleface*, *Singing Guns*, *Brothers of the Trail* and *The Tenderfoot* exalts lawlessness of a very different kind from that which Wister and Grey portray with such enthusiasm. For Wister and Grey, the non-institutional law their heroes uphold is a necessary alternative to the non-existent, ineffective or corrupt legal institutions. The premium Faust places on loyalty strains the atavistic values at the base of the Western formula and introduces a conflicting ethical standard.

In *Singing Guns* (1928), the resultant conflict between individualism and self-denial can be seen very clearly. The two main characters are Owen Caradac, a sheriff, and Annan Rhiannon, a criminal. Caradac and the society he represents all profess social

Darwinist values. Caradac defines himself as a hunter of men (262: 7). When the sheriff tracks him down, however, it is Rhiannon who wins the shoot-out. Caradac's life is therefore forfeit 'by the law of the West, by the law of the wilderness, by the law of all beasts and the men who hunt for one another', but he does not die (262: 14). Rhiannon, who has shot him in self-defence, nurses him back to health. Caradac's gratitude takes the form of self-denial. He mixes his blood with that of his victor and pledges 'night or day, mountain or desert, *in the law or outside of it*, your blood is my blood, and my blood is your blood, so help me God!' (262: 14, emphasis added).

From this point on, Caradac leads a double life. On the one hand he maintains his position as sheriff and continues to pursue criminals; on the other he harbours a known criminal. When his duplicity is discovered, the populace is outraged. According to the code, he should either have defeated Rhiannon or have perished in the attempt; the code can not accommodate mercy and gratitude. Caradac responds by defending Rhiannon as the best man, thus placing the issue back within its familiar framework: 'How many men has Rhiannon killed?' enquires a representative of the Governor. 'From behind – from the side – sneaking by night, or ever taking an advantage – not one!' responds Caradac. The governor's representative goes on to observe that he has killed a good many, but Caradac has a ready retort: 'George Washington killed a lot more' (262: 137).

Caradac is aided in his argument by the fact that Rhiannon has taken a rundown farm and transformed it into a thriving operation, a model of what hard work and ingenuity can accomplish. His case is also bolstered by the essential amorality of social Darwinism, which tempers the townsfolk's resentment and forces a local banker to admit, 'What harm did he ever do? Scratched the surface once in a while! Just scratched the surface. Good for our systems. He stirred us up when we got too settled!' (262: 133).

Rhiannon himself, the 'best man', operates within a different value system: he has a strong sense of social responsibility. Although he realises that the killing which drove him from society was justifiable as self-defence, he cannot excuse himself for what he sees as the misuse of his strength: 'But I seen that I wasn't fit to live around with people. Take when a man hits you; you got no right to get mad. Not when you're like me!' (262: 17). He has voluntarily removed himself from society to protect it from his anger. Admittedly, it is a rather warped sense of social responsibility which necessitates robbing society to supply his needs and killing pursuers on occasion. Still, Rhiannon sees his exile as self-denial. He wants to be a social being, and longs for a wife and family.

He challenges Caradac's 'hunter ethic', especially his practice of hunting men with a price on their heads. Rhiannon recognises that Caradac's 'reward' is 'blood money'. Here the two value systems clash unresolvably, and Caradac, caught between the two, feels confusion and guilt: 'Nobody else minds. The papers are full of what I done to him. Nobody grudges me what I get out of that sort of work', he protests. 'But *you* grudge me!' (262: 48).

In the overall scheme of the book, however, it is not Caradac who needs to defend his actions. It is Rhiannon's compassionate values which are inexplicable within the formula's framework, while his criminality and subsequent social rise are defensible. Rhiannon is pardoned by the governor, Caradac keeps his job, and Rhiannon earns the rewards appropriate to his new status as 'best man': a good woman and a comfortable fortune. Ironically, this happy ending is less forced than the traditional resolution of a Grey or Wister Western. By introducing the value of loyalty and the notion of social responsibility, Faust allows for characters who are capable of long-term interpersonal involvement.

In *Destry Rides Again*, Faust gives extended, sympathetic treatment to the forbidden notion that the morally superior hero need not be the strongest or most skilful. The young Harry Destry boasts that he is the best fighter in Wham, and treats his victims with a sort of 'affectionate contempt' (253: 6). One of his victims, Chester Bent, does not take his defeat gracefully; in revenge he framos Destry for the robbery of the express. While Destry spends six years in jail, Chet builds his fortune with the money from the robbery and develops his strength and shooting-skill for a second encounter. When they face each other for a second duel, Chet says,

> D'you think that I didn't start preparing for the day you'd get out of prison the day you went into it? Little things are fairly sure to float up to the surface, in time, and there was never a minute when I didn't half expect that I'd have to face you with a gun. The six years you've missed I've been working.
>
> (253: 198)

In their second encounter, Chet beats Destry to the draw, but the sheriff intervenes on Destry's behalf. Destry gives chase and is again beaten, this time in hand-to-hand combat. He must admit that he has met his master, an admission made more bitter because Chet has duped him. Chet is the best man in terms of the individualistic ethic: he is clever, strong, skilful and financially self-made. But he is also dishonest, vicious, cruel and a betrayer of his avowed friends. The good-hearted Destry is a failure, without occupation, duped and defeated, who wins in the end by luck alone, killing Chet and securing the traditional rewards: wealth and a good woman.

Only the letter of the formula is upheld, and, alarmingly, Destry discovers that every victor is a potential victim. As a result, he learns compassion and the importance of loyalty. Compare Wister's statement from *The Virginian*, 'All America is divided into two classes, – the quality and the equality' (197: 147), with Destry's mature outlook:

> Equal. For all men are equal. Not as he blindly had taken the word in the courtroom, with wrath and with contempt. Not equal in strength of hand, in talent, in craft, in speed of foot or in leap of mind, but equal in mystery, in the identity of the race which breathes, through all men out of the soil, and out of the heavens.   (253: 187–8)

Faust has come a long way from the formula as articulated by Wister in *The Virginian*. The distance is not suprising. Faust did not view the world from the centres of power as Wister did; Faust's friends did not shape the events of their time as Wister's did; Faust did not come from a long distinguished lineage as did Wister. Faust's attempts to soften the brutality of social Darwinism can be seen as an attempt, perhaps an unconscious one, to defend his father. It can also be seen as a defence of the 'equality' from which he came against the 'quality' who held the centres of power. Or it can be seen as an attempt to compensate for the social poverty of his youth and the constant battles he endured by emphasising non-competitive virtues. Whatever the preferred explanations, the fact remains that in Faust's Westerns there are relics of an ideology incompatible with the basic framework of the Western formula. Indeed, many of his works reveal the interweaving of two antagonistic ideologies. This conflict is evident in the treatment given to wealth as well.

For Faust as for Grey and Wister, the West is a land where the individual has great opportunity for personal enrichment. *Gunman's Gold* begins with these lines:

> The strategy of Lee Swain was simple. It consisted in being in the right place at the right time. He had managed to get there, through skilful planning, so often that he had stacked up what he considered a nest egg. He had done that in the Eastern States. When he wanted to make the nest egg grow into a whole brood of thriving birds, he decided to go West. (256: 5)

The potential of the land is shown by the rich mines in *Gunman's Gold, Marbleface, South of Rio Grande* and *Destry Rides Again,* and by the richness of the farmland in *Singing Guns* and *Larramee's Ranch.* In book after book, wealth and a girl are parcelled out at the end as a reward for the hero, but there are exceptions.

The tenuousness with which wealth is held is also manifest. In *Gunman's Gold* (1933), two prospectors are shot dead as they work. Bank-robberies or train heists occur in many books. More interesting are those books in which trickster figures use their wits to cheat others out of wealth. In *Montana Rides!* (1933), Montana successfully poses as the kidnapped heir of a wealthy rancher in order to siphon off some of the rancher's riches. He does not carry the plan through, however. In *Marbleface,* Colonel Riggs creates a short-lived speculative boom in Piegan by dishonestly besting a rival town both for the status of county seat and for the advantage of a railway connection.

The relationship between tenuousness, acquisitiveness and cleverness is given more positive and more explicit treatment in *Speedy.* Unlike the essential dishonesty of the ploys just discussed, Speedy's endeavours are seen as fair contests. The con-man hero even warns his intended victim 'We're all men, we all have a share of brains, we all want money, we all want an easy time. Well, your dollars are your treasure; your wits are the soldiers that guard it. If I can put your soldiers to sleep, I take your money. That's my game, and it's a good game. It beats chess all hollow' (264: 17).

Whether it is gained by fair means or foul, Faust's attitude to wealth is ambivalent. Often one glimpses a distrust of riches and a dislike of those who possess them. One aspect of this already noted is Rhiannon's critique of 'blood money' in *Singing Guns*. In *Brothers of the Trail*, Rickie Willard defends his outlaw brother: 'There's a thousand gents up there in the mountains ready to die for him still, because he never did no harm. All he ever nicked was the big gents, the big operators that had so many millions they could afford to lose a few thousands here and there!' (252: 32). Rickie is careful to explain that the gang does not prey on poor folk even when resources are needed. This contempt for the wealthy is an inversion of the contempt for the underdog victim expressed by Wister in *The Virginian*.

Money is feared for its dangers as much as it is desired for its possibilities. It is recognised as a weapon as much as a status symbol. By paying Ralph Carr's debts in *Brothers of the Trail*, for example, Harry Loomis feels that his entitlement to Ralph's daughter is strengthened. In *Destry Rides Again*, Chet Bent uses money to frame Destry and later, when he pays his expenses, to purchase his gratitude and to blind and weaken him. Frances Jones, in *The Tenderfoot*, succinctly articulates the insidious power of money over the poor: 'Mother died before I could remember her. The rest of the time dad was fightin' wild hosses and a mortgage. He could beat the hosses, but he couldn't beat the mortgage. He used to say that a mortgage was like bad rheumatism: you couldn't get it out of your system' (265: 33).

It is not surprising that wealthy men are often portrayed unsympathetically in Faust's Westerns. In *Speedy*, both well-to-do lawyers are made to look ridiculous when they fall victim to Speedy's schemes. There is a touch of villainy as well when Chalmers is described as 'dramatically pulling out his wallet, like a revolver, from his breast pocket' (264: 30). Mr Julius Maybeck (*Larramee's Ranch*) stands as the archetypal capitalist who expects gratitude for minor philanthropy from those he exploits. He has built a bank 'in the guise of a Greek temple among the little bungalows of the village' (259: 136) and longs for a commemorative statue with the inscription, 'To Julius Overman Maybeck, philanthropist and financier, whose genius, whose generosity, and whose foresight created this city and all that is in it . . .' (259: 138). In his hunger for public recognition, he has forgotten to acknowledge his primary motivation.

Not all wealthy men are villainous, of course, and it is not insignificant that wealthy transplanted Easterners tend to fare worse than their Western counterparts. Certainly this helps to fit the distrust of wealth into the value framework of the Western formula, as do such comments as Tom Holden's exclamation on learning of Larramee's fortune: 'Inherited money, eh? That's hardly fair!' (259: 49).

Faust's critique of wealth goes deeper than the social bias indicated so far, as can be seen in such books as *Speedy* and *Gunman's Gold*, two works which reject the traditional happy ending of the Western. In both the hero refuses to accept the reward held out to him at the end. Shannigan, in *Gunman's Gold*, accepts the girl, but refuses the money, twice. He will not touch a gold mine that has been the scene and motive of a murder (256: 151). Later he declines his fee for the saving of Jack Reynolds: 'If Jack had been worth his salt, I would have taken your money – and a pile of it too. I would have sent in a bill that would have made your eyes pop. But as for this job with Reynolds – I charge that all on the wrong side of the ledger. I won't talk money with you' (256: 154). The end which, in his own mind, justified his extra-legal efforts, has turned out to be unworthy. To accept money would be to disparage his work still further. Besides, money has become so corrupted by the greed, the dishonesty and the selfishness which surround it that Shannigan can not accept it as an honourable reward. The distrust of wealth on this level, together with the professional code, pinpoint an important transitional element in outlook from Western hero to private eye.

Speedy's objection to wealth is of a different tenor: he refuses both the girl and the fortune because they threaten to make him less free. With an echo of Dismuke's lament that his lifestyle has made him incapable of any other, Speedy says, 'I always thought that I was only killing time until a grand opportunity should come my way, but now that the opportunity has come, I see that the devil has been too careful a schoolteacher, for me, and I can't forget his lessons' (264: 191).

Rejections in these terms go beyond Grey's uneasiness over the efficacy of a lasting reward or the ability of a man to enjoy his reward. Faust is questioning whether the 'best man', as he defines him, can feel morally justified in accepting a reward tainted by the lawlessness of the West. And he is asking whether the possibilities which wealth brings are worth their cost: the loss of freedom and the burden of defence.

In developing his heroes, Faust subverts key formulaic attributes, redefining such ideologically charged concepts as the protean nature of identity within American society, and the importance of strength and reputation in achieving high status. Once reworked, these key concepts offer Faust extensive possibilities for exploring his personal worries and preoccupations. The issue of identity allows Faust to explore his anxiety over the relationship between parentage and identity. In *Montana Rides!*, the Montana Kid poses as the returning kidnapped son of a wealthy rancher. Although an imposter, he proves himself a worthy heir to Lavery, the owner, earning the respect and friendship of all who work with him and the love of his assumed family. The true son, whom Montana locates in an attempt to compensate for his deception, is a Mexican bandit; kidnapped and brought up by a Mexican outlaw, he has been taught to hate his real family.

What constitutes the essential characteristics of the father-son relationship, then? After Tonio Rubriz/Dick Lavery is told the true story of his parentage, he turns to the bandit and says, 'Padre, all these years have been a lie. . . . That man is my father!' (272: 122). The outlaw replies, 'You talk like a fool. You *are* a fool. Are you not my son? What is blood? The dogs and the cattle have blood. But my soul is breathed into you' (272: 123). Tonio accepts the truth of this assertion. Although he changes sides when he learns that his adopted father plans to kill his blood relatives, the book suggests that no amount of time or love or change of culture will blot out his Mexican past. He crosses the border with his family, but at the end of the book he wears the ring the outlaw has left for him.

It is easier to make Montana, the pretender, into a true co-heir with Tonio, for he is without parentage, past or obligations: when asked his true name, he replies, blushing, 'Nicknames – that's all I've had, or synthetic names that people gave me when they took me in when I was a brat' (272: 223). Although he is shamed by his namelessness, it leaves him free to become what he will. Both the sense of loss and the freedom of the orphan are thus recalled.

The freedom of anonymity is explored further in *Speedy*. The hero discusses his protean identity with a lawyer who thinks him a rogue: 'Sometimes . . . I'm a son who's been disinherited by a cruel father. . . . Sometimes . . . I'm about to go to work to earn enough money to finish my school course. Sometimes I'm recovering from an attack of the great white plague' (264: 10). When asked his name he replies, 'I've been called a good many names . . . some of them long, and some of them short. I've been called more one-syllable names than almost anyone in the world, I suppose. But the one I prefer is Speedy' (264: 11).

Speedy's identity as a con-man is a rather troubling offshoot of the self-made man, and the fact that he is a lovable rogue with a fairly strict professional code is only slightly reassuring. Such qualms are in the reader's mind, however. For Faust, the heart of the issue is a highly personal one: the fraudulence of an identity that results from the rejection or ignorance of one's parentage; from the denial of past.

Destry Rides Again explores the same ground from another viewpoint. Willie Thornton's parentage is never in question; the issue is whether the father is worthy of the son. One hears definite echoes of Faust's past when Willie confronts the truth of his father's character:

> It was for him the crashing of a world about his ears. He had not been able to avoid seeing the truth about many phases of his father's idleness and shiftlessness, but, no matter what else he might be, for these years he had loomed in the mind of Willie as a great man, because he was the companion of Destry, the famous. A hundred stories he had told Willie of adventures with that celebrated man, and now these stories had to be relegated to the sphere of the fairy-tale! (253: 89)

Willie's courage and devotion earn him a new and worthier father, Destry, who in turn feels the weight of responsibility as a chosen father: 'he felt a sudden scorn for the baser parts that were in him, the idler, the scoffer at others, the disdainful mocker at the labours of life. He wished to be simple, real, quiet, able to command the affection of his peers' (253: 187). The notion that the father should be worthy of the son must have tugged heavily at Faust, only to be countered by guilt and an argument for the importance of loyalty.

Faust's treatment of strength, while less idiosyncratic, is also unusual in that his viewpoint is that of the underdog. In his work, strength is regarded with awe and envy; it is to be attained if possible, and countered by the wily tricks of the potential victim if not. Typically, he peoples his books with physical giants, and occasionally there are even good giants such as Rhiannon. More often, his giants are minor characters such as 'Gorilla' Jones in *Gunman's Gold*, employed to demonstrate the mettle of his heroes.

Jones is a very effective jailer whose daily demonstrations of prowess keep the prisoners quiescent: 'his final exhibition was with the sandbag, which he smashed with either hand, dealing out terrible blows that seemed capable of driving straight through the body of an ordinary man' (256: 95). As he does this, he wears an expression of 'animal intensity of delight' (256: 95). The performance holds the prisoners spellbound.

When the modest and unimposing Shannigan agrees to spar with 'Gorilla' in order to win the right to see a prisoner, the giant is filled with sadistic delight. For Shannigan the encounter is not a test of his courage so much as a test of his character, for Shannigan is confident that he can win; he possesses hidden resources of tremendous strength. Pictorially, the encounter appears as David against Goliath, with the expected victim magically transformed.

Speedy's confrontation with Big Alf has a similar flavour. When Mary asks how a small man such as Speedy could have beaten him Alf is exasperated: 'How do I know? When I reached for him, I just seemed to hit myself. That's all that I know about it. When I rushed him, I just tripped on the place where he'd been standing, and sailed right on and lit on my face' (264: 50). Alf finally concludes by deciding 'Magician, that's what he is' (264: 52). The bag of tricks Speedy brings to combat are considerable, and they form a veritable handbook for the survival of the weak: he knows how to use his opponent's strength to his own advantage, when to play dead, and when it is best to use every fibre of his being to fight for his life. He can judge whether he should run, or submit to temporary defeat. His tricks are hardly the usual array for a Western hero. As we have seen, they hark back to the clever folk hero, to the trickster.

The issue of reputation also engaged Faust's interest, most notably the problem of undeserved reputation, another taboo area for American ideology, but one of great interest to Faust, who was half ashamed of his own success. In *The Tenderfoot*, Allan's false notoriety as a bloodthirsty desperado destroys him, partly because the hero comes to believe what is said about him and is overcome with unwanted guilt. Even when those closest to Allan offer reassurance, he takes their assertions as misguided kindness.

More often, the undeserved reputation proves embarrassing because the man who possesses it feels unworthy. This is the case with Jerry Ash in *Marbleface*. When he downs a robber with a lucky snap shot, he knows how fortunate he has been, but everyone else thinks him extremely skilful. When Colonel Riggs tells him that there is something calm about his presence, Ash comments, 'I could have laughed in his face, when I remember[ed] that it was my practice in schooling my nerves for the sake of my rotten, crumbling, shattered heart that had given me this calm exterior' (260: 48). Every time he tries to set the record straight, his attempt is seen as modesty, and his renown grows.

Ash's reputation is both liability and asset. While tempting to the ambitious who wish to enhance their own standing, it is also a powerful defence: 'I knew that there were fifty men in that one county who could shoot the eyes out of my head, who were far faster and surer in every way with a weapon of any kind. But the nerves of a good many of them would be upset by merely the reputation which was behind me . . .' (260: 121). Ash is eventually bettered, but his honesty and fairness bolster him in defeat, and he remains high in the regard of the townspeople.

The way Faust subverts key terms does not negate the central thematic argument of the Western formula. After all, such champions of American-dream optimism as Grey are not immune to discontinuities. However, Faust does not use gender to apportion conflicting value-sets. This makes the incompatibility more obvious and more difficult to bridge. It also lessens the importance of his female characters, for it makes them seem superfluous to the central conflict, though more involved in the ways of the West. During their infrequent appearances, Faust's women are treated more as partners than as civilisers, but they still tend to be the minor partner, the little woman in the background

The discontinuities revealed in Faust's work are also different in kind from those exposed in Grey's Grey explores a rift which is characteristic of American society as a whole and reflects the standard remedy for channelling competing values. The discontinuities in Faust's work, on the other hand, are the product of different levels of ideology. Such values as self-reliance, independence and competence belong to the ideology built into the Western formula itself. Those of the underdog – loyalty, mercy, wily cleverness and endurance – are fragments of a working-class ideology which is never crystallised within the works. While the conflict of values with which Grey deals has wide relevance within American society, the conflict in Faust's work is only relevent to those on the bottom of the socio-economic heap: those who want to justify their own lack of success or the failure of someone close to them.

None the less, Faust's work asserts the fundamental primacy of the individual as social unit. In *Singing Guns*, the sheriff may develop a close bond with Rhiannon, but in the end Rhiannon must stand or fall on his own merits. That it is not admissible for a person to be a substitute in someone else's battles is the lesson of *Brothers of the Trail*: Rickie cannot fight in his brother's stead; the Chief must fulfil his own obligations and maintain his own position. Faust's heroes do succeed, and their rewards are often the familiar ones of material comfort and personal happiness.

Group action is given an unpleasant, often a villainous, representation. The angry mob that captures the sheriff in *Gunman's Gold* is fairly typical: 'Hands were laid on the sheriff. Leering, savage, rejoicing faces appeared before him, men who never had liked him, men who long had writhed under the heavy hand with which he occasionally bore down upon the rougher spirits in town. He could guess what mercy he would receive from them' (256: 62). They are cowards emboldened by numbers; gullible enough to be easily manipulated by the villain or by the acting of a young girl, and sufficiently greedy to be quickly diverted by the prospect of personal gain. Mobs in *Marbleface* and in *South of Rio Grande* are given equally derisory treatment.

The continuity of values between East and West is also underscored. Anthony Woodbury (*Trailin'*, 1919) and Jerry Ash (*Marbleface*) are representative of the Easterners who successfully make the transition to the West. Similarly, there are many Westerners, Sheriff Caradac (*Singing Guns*) and Chris Verner (*Larramee's Ranch*), for example, who become successful ranchers or capitalists.

The complexity of the issues Faust explores in his Westerns brings into question his dismissal by critics. In Faust's case, as with Grey's, it is the crudities of his workmanship which account for the apparent superficiality of his work. His approach to his material is a strange amalgam of attitudes, and his style reflects this. A terse, hard-boiled style blends with elements of fantasy, sentimentality, folktale, and myth. He has little respect for his material, and treats it in an offhand, superficial manner. Too often the mechanical manoeuvrings of the writer are visible behind the prose.

In *Gunman's Gold*, for example, one can almost sense the line at which Faust decides he must shift the portrayal of a character to accommodate the developing story line. At the beginning of the story, Reynolds is generous and self-effacing. On p. 59, he has a small temper tantrum that throws slight doubts on his character, but by p. 65 these are put to rest when Shannigan offers what appears to be the final verdict on Reynolds: 'he's brave and pretty straight. He's not a saint, and he may not be a hero.' When questioned on p. 76, Reynolds exhibits intelligence. But on p. 111 his character takes a sudden turn for the worse, and from that point on he is foolish, selfish and greedy.

In *Singing Guns*, Faust seems to toy for about fifteen pages with the idea of turning Sheriff Caradac into a villain (262: 115–31). If this is not the case, then these pages are a rather crude attempt to give the plot another twist. In either case, they jar, an obvious contrivance. Such sudden shifts indicate the shallowness of Faust's characterisation and the careless, hurried treatment he gives to his material generally.

Although Faust's style can be broadly labelled colloquial, it suffers from the same inconsistencies as his structure. He seems content to utilise whatever style or technique serves his purpose of the moment without worrying about unity of effect. *South of Rio Grande* is a good example. The book begins as a first person narration. The language is terse and understated, exhibiting a restraint that approaches the hard-boiled style: 'The chief had hit me hard. So hard that I had to look out the window, and looking out there into the street, I saw the kid in the middle of trouble' (263: 7). But Faust does too much explaining to sustain this: 'The kid was all right; he meant no harm; but he was simply loaded with excess energy that couldn't take care of itself, and, of course, that meant trouble of the worst kind that far west of the Mississippi' (263: 15). Worse still, the narrator turns frankly sentimental: 'I'm jealous of The MacMore for the first time. . . . I wouldn't mind having a kid like you in the family myself.' His young protégé replies by gripping his hand, saying, 'You are one of the family, Joe' (263: 54).

By chapter 23, Faust has clumsily switched to third-person narration, explaining,

For what immediately follows, I have not the narrative of Dennis MacMore, though it is about him and his strange adventures that I have to speak. I have not his version, for a reason that will soon appear; but all that I describe is substantiated by my knowledge . . . , by certain eyewitnesses, and by a mere use of sheer logic. . . . (263: 166)

By chapter 31, Faust is exploiting the romantic interest of the scene unabashedly: 'How far did she see the truth about him, and how clearly did he show that he was losing his mind about her? How much was she upset . . . ?' (263: 222). On p. 250 the first-person narration resumes, and it is the laconic style which has the last word. Such a hodgepodge of techniques comes close to self-parody at times. Faust's rather backhanded reassurance that the third-person narration is 'no more a fiction than what has gone before' exhibits this self-mockery. Faust uses the term 'fairy-tale' as he uses it in *Destry Rides Again*, as a kind of epithet. It is used often, and, in books populated by giants, sorcerers, and heroes with magical ability, this too amounts to self-ridicule.

Faust's writing succeeds when it is stripped down to dialogue and a terse recounting of the ensuing action; when it uses a consistent colloquial style. In dialogue Faust seems to lose his bitterness, and demonstrates a good ear for conversation as this passage from *Singing Guns* demonstrates:

'G'wan away,' said the father to his son. 'I don't need you and I ain't asked for you. Gwynn, I'm glad to see you. I admire how you done up the old place, over there. I been by and admired to see it. I wanta buy that place. What you sell for?'

'It ain't mine,' replied Rhiannon. 'The sheriff, he owns it, Mr. Dee.'

'Ha?' exclaimed Oliver Dee. 'How old am I?'

'Fifty,' guessed Rhiannon, surrendering himself to the oddities of this conversation.

'Is that old enough to be mistered?' asked Mr. Dee.

'Maybe not,' said Rhiannon, and smiled. He rarely smiled!
(262: 60)

The passage flows naturally, and builds a picture of Oliver Dee with a few easy strokes.

Faust is at his best when he puts the giants and sorcerers to one side and writes about humans on a human level. He does this in *Destry Rides Again*, where the only hidden potential is the ability to learn and to develop. Here his energy is funnelled into deepening his characters rather than enlarging them; the bitterness is contained and directed. *Destry Rides Again* is his best book, and a good one.

6

Dashiell Hammett

Samuel Dashiell Hammett, the son of Richard Thomas Hammett and Annie Bond Hammett, was born in Saint Mary's County, Maryland on 27 May, 1894. He was of Scottish and French ancestry; Dashiell was an Americanised version of De Chiel, his maternal grandmother's family name. Both Hammett's father and grandfather were known as business failures, heavy drinkers, gamblers and ladies' men; proud, pugnacious, stubborn, independent and ambitious, though inherently lazy. Hammett's mother, nicknamed 'Lady' by her inlaws, treated her husband and his family with disdain. She was equally proud and independent, and outspoken in her disapproval. Her influence over Hammett may be judged by his avowed intention never to behave as his father had toward his mother.

As a youth, Hammett flared up when his sense of honour was attacked, but was otherwise introverted; he spent much of his free time reading mysteries and adventure novels from the local library. His formal education ended when he was thirteen and was told to help his father with his latest business disaster. He was forced to leave the highly regarded Baltimore Polytechnic Institute after only one semester. His father's business failed, and Hammett began working at a series of jobs which he described in a brief autobiographical account in *Black Mask:* 'I became the unsatisfactory and unsatisfied employee of various railroads, stockbrokers, machine manufacturers, canners, and the like. Usually I was fired' (370: 128). By the age of twenty he had contracted gonorrhoea and was drinking heavily.

Some time during 1915 Hammett answered 'an enigmatic want-ad' (370: 128) and became an employee of Pinkerton's National Detective Agency. Although he says that he 'stuck at that until early in 1922, when I chucked it to see what I could do with fiction writing', his employment with Pinkerton's was not continuous (370: 128). The first interruption came when he enlisted in the

Motor Ambulance Company of the United States Army on 24 June, 1918. He was stationed near Baltimore. During his year of service he rose to the rank of sergeant. Like Faust and many others in the training-camps, Hammett came down with influenza, but in his case the disease activated tuberculosis, the first of a series of lung ailments that would eventually cause his death. After his honourable discharge from the Army on 29 May, 1919, Hammett rejoined Pinkerton's, but by November of the following year his health had deteriorated to the point where he required hospitalisation. Again he left the agency, this time to enter the Cushman Hospital for disabled veterans in Tacoma, Washington. There he met Josephine A. Dolan, the nurse he would marry on 7 July, 1921. By this time Hammett had been transferred to a San Diego hospital, then discharged. It was not long before he was again working for Pinkerton's, this time in San Francisco. He ended his career with Pinkerton's late in 1921 or early in 1922.

Hammett gives a number of reasons for leaving Pinkerton's: that he wanted to write, that he had been deprived of a much anticipated trip to Australia, and that 'I would have been fired anyway, except for a literary quality about my reports' (356). His continuing battle against tuberculosis was certainly another factor, and he may well have begun to feel distaste for the kind of work he was doing. By the time Hammett joined Pinkerton's in 1915, the agency had acquired an unsavoury reputation for its brutal strike-breaking and industrial espionage. William W. Delany had written a dirge-like ballad, 'Father Was Killed by the Pinkerton Men', and the agency had been investigated by Congressional committees in the wake of the violence in Homestead, Pennsylvania, in 1892. At the resulting hearings, a member of the United States Secret Service had testified, 'There is not one out of ten [Pinkerton's men] that would not commit murder; that you could not hire him to commit murder or any other crime' (56: 21).

The Pinkerton years decisively shaped Hammett's sense of himself and his society. Richard Layman argues that the detectives' code, taught to Hammett as part of his training, became the basis for his value system: 'The code was pragmatic and unwritten; it provided an operative with an approach to his job that would allow him to do it well with as little physical and emotional risk as possible. Essentially, the code was built around three elements: anonymity, morality, and objectivity' (358: 11–12). Morality was conceived in personal rather than civil or religious terms; his job was 'to protect good people from exploitation by bad people, and the means to that end require[d] no justification' (358: 12). Success often necessitated breaking the rules.

It is likely that this code appealed to Hammett because it helped him to reconcile his conflicting impulses. He was close to his mother and wanted to live up to her expectations of him as a man of honour, but his temperament made this difficult. Lillian Hellman summed up this tension years later when she called him a 'sinner saint' (337: 10). The Pinkerton code allowed him to justify any action so long as it played some part in the defence of 'good people'.

Lillian Hellman believed that these years were crucial in the development of his political beliefs as well. She recalls an anecdote he frequently recounted of an offer of $5000 from an officer of the Anaconda Copper Company to kill Frank Little, the labour-union organiser. Hammett claimed to have been strike-breaking for Pinkerton's when the offer was made. 'He seldom talked about the past unless I asked questions,' recalled Hellman, 'but through the years he was to repeat that bribe offer so many times that I came to believe, knowing him now, that it was a kind of key to his life' (355: 35–6). She goes on to explain,

> He had given a man the right to think he would murder, and the fact that Frank Little was lynched with three other men in what was known as the Everett Massacre must have been, for Hammett, an abiding horror. I think I can date Hammett's belief that he was living in a corrupt society from Little's murder. In time, he came to the conclusion that nothing less than a revolution could wipe out the corruption.   (355: 36)

Both Layman and Hellman are probably correct in their assessments, for these concerns are reflected in Hammett's writing and his actions. The code surfaces in his passion for privacy, in his preoccupation with the nature of objectivity in his writings, and in his seemingly calm acceptance of radical shifts in tactical policy by the Communist Party. Whether the Little incident is apocryphal, as Layman claims, or appallingly real, it is significant in that it articulates Hammett's awareness of the truth of Pinkerton's role as participant in the vicious power struggle barely hidden by American economic and social institutions. This insight was the lesson of Hammett's Pinkerton years, and it permeates his writing, providing him with the social milieu for his stories.

After Hammett left Pinkerton's, he enrolled in stenography and writing-courses at Munson's Business College in San Francisco, training himself for journalism. He studied over the next year and a half, too ill to do more than read and write; indeed by 1925 his health was so bad that he was forced to send his wife and baby daughter to stay with relatives for six months because he feared infecting his small child. During these years he traded his first freelance ad, written on speculation, for a pair of shoes. His publishing-debut was made in October 1922 with a 100 word anecdote, 'The Parthian Shot', which appeared in the *Smart Set*. Writing and advertising had displaced his initial interest in journalism, and he confined his efforts to these fields. He entered the pulp-story market with 'Immortality', printed in the November 1922 *10 Story Book*. His first appearance in *Black Mask* came a month later with 'The Road Home', and the Continental Op was introduced in 'Arson Plus' the following October, also in *Black Mask*. As early as 1924, George W. Sutton, Jr, then editor of the magazine, could comment that 'Mr. Hammett has suddenly become one of the most popular of our *Black Mask* writers' (362: 28).

Writing fiction based on the awareness he had gained during his Pinkerton years permitted him to reassert the validity of his Pinkerton code: as a writer he was expected to explore the seamy life in order to expose social corruption. This allowed him to put his years with the agency into a new perspective, as preparation for a literary career. His growing awareness of Pinkerton's true role no longer allowed him to view with equanimity his participation in such cases as the Fatty Arbuckle rape case or the Anaconda Strike.

Though he was having considerable success placing his stories, he was not making much money. In anticipation of the birth of his second child, Hammett abandoned fiction-writing in March 1926 for a salaried position as advertising-manager to Albert S. Samuels, a jeweller on Market Street. Advertising gave him a measure of financial security, but lacked the element of moral certainty he sought. His code, calling for anonymity, objectivity and morality, no longer applied. Perhaps this explains his wife's recollection of the job as a confusing experience for Hammett.

Hammett's personal life became more and more unsettled; he gambled, drank heavily and had a series of affairs. His work required him to produce sentimental advertisements such as the one picturing two lovers standing atop the globe with the caption, 'A Samuels diamond puts you on top of the world!' (362: 19). It is unlikely that the bitter irony of such sentimental fictions escaped him, or that people's need for them eluded him. His awareness of the manipulative character of the advertisers' trade is displayed in a series of articles he wrote for trade journals between October 1926 and March 1928. Despite the impact the job had on Hammett, it was short-lived, lasting only six months before his health forced him to give up full-time employment. Once again he turned to writing. To protect his two young daughters, he was forced to leave his home once more, and this time the move effectively ended his marriage.

During 1927 Hammett published book reviews, poems, and articles in addition to his fiction. Layman counts seventeen appearances in seven different magazines that year. Among them were the initial two instalments of Hammett's first novel, *Red Harvest*, in the November and December issues of *Black Mask* (358: 77). He managed to earn more that year than he had ever earned before and his career was clearly on the rise. His family would soon be abandoned.

Hammett's productive writing-career was very short, but between December 1922 and March 1934 he published over sixty short stories, many in *Black Mask*, but a number were printed in such slick magazines as *Collier's*, *Liberty*, and *American Magazine*. His five novels also appeared during these years: *Red Harvest* (1929), *The Dain Curse* (1929), *The Maltese Falcon* (1930), *The Glass Key* (1931) and *The Thin Man* (1934).

In 1930, with a backlog of fiction still to be published, Hammett stopped work on *The Thin Man*, and went to Hollywood 'for a year', leaving the sixty-five page manuscript unfinished. In November of that year, he met Lillian Hellman, entering into an intense, tempestuous relationship which lasted the rest of his life. The impact of this on Hammett can be seen in the marked shift in tone between his previous novels, together with the unfinished manuscript, and the final version of *The Thin Man*. The companionship he found with Hellman changed his mind about the possibility of relationships being both positive and close, and this change is mirrored in *The Thin Man*. This shift is also hinted at in Hammett's explanatory note on the fate of the earlier manuscript: 'One thing and/or another intervening after that [his move to Hollywood], I didn't return to work on the story until a couple of

more years had passed – and then I found it easier, or at least
generally more satisfactory, to keep only the basic idea of the plot
and otherwise to start anew' (328: 161). This offers the first hint
that Hammett had begun to outgrow his formula.

Hammett's connection with Hollywood lasted until mid 1950,
but his involvement was not continuous and he was contracted to
various studios during this time, providing original material for
six films in all. During the late thirties, while he was commuting
back and forth between New York and Hollywood, Hammett
became increasingly involved in the politics of the left. It is thought
that he probably joined the Communist Party in 1937 or 1938.
When he enlisted in the Army in September 1942 as a private, he
was initially sent to a containment centre for personnel considered
potentially subversive. His transfer to Adak, one of the Aluetian
Islands, after the protests of Eleanor Roosevelt forced the closure
of Camp Shenango, seems to have been intended as further
imprisonment (358: 187ff).

Hammett's political activities, the assistance he gave to
developing young writers, particularly to Lillian Hellman, and his
teaching at the Jefferson School in New York absorbed the energy
and enthusiasm he had once put into writing. Clearly he had
changed his political views and personal priorities: the man who
interested the FBI from 1941 until his death on 10 January 1961
had evolved from a loyal Pinkerton operative. Hammett's writings
were an important stage in that evolution. The point of view
expressed in his fiction has been characterised as 'pre rather than
proto-Marxist' by Steven Marcus, who calls the world view largely
Hobbesian (360: 373). Lillian Hellman reinforces this assessment
when she prefaces the anecdote about Frank Little's murder with
the comment, 'It was true that Hammett became a committed
radical and I didn't, but strangely enough when we first met I
think it was I, and not he, who had come to certain unshakable
conclusions' (355: 35). Lillian Hellman did not meet Hammett until
1930, after he had written the great bulk of his fiction.

The articulation of his vision of power and corruption helped to
forge the political convictions which turned him away from
writing, toward political involvement. The hard-boiled detective
formula provided Hammett with an appropriate vehicle for
exploring and articulating his insights on corruption, but it would
not have been compatible with a more Marxist approach because
the formula itself is so bound up with ideology. Perhaps this is

another factor in his subsequent silence; his vision began to outgrow the old forms, but he could find no new ones with which he felt comfortable as a writer. This would explain his lack of concern over the fate of his detective heroes, and his willingness to abandon them to other writers. Clearly they no longer mattered so much as they had when he felt compelled to explain their significance to the readers of *Black Mask*. As early as 1932 he indicated to an interviewer that he did not want to continue writing detective stories, but instead wanted to write a play, and later some straight novels (367: 516).

Hammett's keen observations on the corrupting influences within society started him searching for alternatives. This search was given a personal urgency; in order to submerge the guilt evoked by his ignoble behaviour, he sought to ally himself on the side of the angels. His writing, which had managed to hold the guilt in check for a time, became inadequate as it crystallised his perception of societal ills. His voracious reading provided him with the basis for his new political convictions (337: 13).

His prolonged mental growth and the ironic twists his own life took made Hammett acutely aware of his own limitations of perspective and so of judgement. Consistency of viewpoint is therefore not to be found, for what mattered to Hammett was his allegiance to his code; his defence of 'the good' as defined by his level of awareness at the time. He admitted to Lillian Hellman that 'a great deal about communism worried him and always had and that when he found something better he intended to change his opinions' (337: 13). His presidency of the Civil Rights Congress, his sponsorship of numerous organisations and his high profile in the left-wing press brought him to the attention of the FBI, and virtually assured his later clash with the forces of McCarthyism. These activities shed little light backward on his fiction, however, for, by the time he went to jail for contempt of court in 1951 and faced McCarthy himself in 1953, he had grown beyond the insights of his fiction.

To understand the man who wrote that fiction and the vision behind it, one must go back much further. Like Faust, Hammett had to battle with debilitating illness, and, even more than Faust, Hammett came to value toughness, the ability to survive physically and psychologically in the teeth of a brutal universe. The importance of toughness is graphically demonstrated in his fiction.

Hammett never coveted the strength that Faust idealised, nor the conspicuous symbols of success which Faust sought. Hammett's experiences, like Faust's, imbued him with a keen sense of the ironies of the fiction-making process, but, unlike Faust, he did not retreat into demon-ridden fantasy. Faust had felt the gulf between fact and fiction as a personal shame associated with his father's shortcomings. Hammett's awareness of the gulf between subjective awareness and objective reality accumulated as he witnessed the strange turns of his own life. The lives of those he intruded on in his detecting, advertising and later in his writing showed him the manipulative nature of the fiction-making process. For Hammett the gulf did not reflect a personal failing, for he saw it as all-pervasive: he treated it as a cosmic joke in which he was both victim and perpetrator. The Flitcraft anecdote in *The Maltese Falcon* perfectly encapsulates the bitter irony of what Hammett sees as the human condition: Flitcraft assumes not only a universe structured on human notions of rationality and justice, but also a correspondence between his perception of the structural rules and the actuality. A chance falling beam shows him the fallacy of both assumptions.

Hammett's strong sense of irony, together with his acute awareness of social hypocrisy imparts a biting humour to the sardonic comments he collected in 'From the Memoirs of a Private Detective':

7

Of all the men embezzling from their employers with whom I have had contact, I can't remember a dozen who smoked, drank, or had any of the vices in which bonding companies are so interested.

8

I was once falsely accused of perjury and had to perjure myself to escape arrest.

19

In 1917, in Washington, D. C., I met a young woman who did not remark that my work must be very interesting.

22

I know a forger who left his wife because she had learned to smoke cigarettes while he was serving a term in prison.

28
I know a man who once stole a Ferris-wheel.   (346: 417–22)

Hammett's *Black Mask* correspondence also shows his keen awareness of the reconstructive process through which live material is transformed into fiction. In a letter of June 1924 regarding 'The Girl with the Silver Eyes', Hammett says,

> Taken in a lump, the story is pure fiction, but most of its details are based on things that I've either run into myself or got second hand from other detectives. For instance, 'Tin-Star' Joplin's roadhouse is in California, though not near Halfmoon Bay, and he is exactly as I have set him down. 'Porky' Grout's original died of tuberculosis in Butte, Montana, two or three years ago.
> (347: 127)

Hammett's letter may even be a further fiction; he was known to take advantage of the gullibility of both readers and editors on occasion. 'I found I could sell the stories easily when it became known I had been a Pinkerton man', he told an interviewer years later. 'People thought my stuff was authentic' (356). In his novels, Hammett sought to explode his fictions from within. This self-exposure is particularly visible in *The Dain Curse*, as already discussed in Chapter 2.

The gulf between appearance and reality, social pretence and social fact, formulation and experience, haunted his life and haunts his fiction. It accounts for his sense of the endemic corruption of American society, for his interest in the role of writer as fiction-maker, and for his empathetic appreciation of expectations held in defiance of a cosmos ruled by chance.

Hammett's rather cynical view of the manipulative nature of writing should not be construed as a disregard for craftsmanship; if anything it increased his awareness of the importance of good workmanship. Lillian Hellman watched him as he worked on *The Thin Man* and recalls, 'I had never seen anybody work that way: the care for every word, the pride in the neatness of the typed page itself, the refusal for ten days or two weeks to go out even for a walk for fear something would be lost' (337: 16–17). He could be highly critical of his work. He called *The Dain Curse* 'a silly story', *The Maltese Falcon* 'too manufactured', *The Thin Man* 'boring', but found *The Glass Key* 'not so bad . . . the clews were nicely placed there, although nobody seemed to see them' (367: 518; 356).

Unfortunately, Hammett's respect for the craft of writing, his insight into the ironies of the fiction-making process, his need to feel himself engaged on behalf of a noble cause, and his changing perception of the legitimacy of his past stances all made it inevitable that he would outgrow the formula he had helped to pioneer. 'I stopped writing', he said in 1957, 'because I found I was repeating myself. It is the beginning of the end when you discover you have style' (356). It must have pained Hammett to have outgrown his formula; to have gained sufficient distance to appreciate the appropriateness of the style. He had advanced to a point where using it approached self-indulgence or, worse, self-parody. No longer generated by the need to come to terms with a certain view of life, his style became an object for self-conscious imitation. This Hammett would not countenance.

In his five novels, Hammett does not repeat himself. All his novels explore two key ideas: an existential vision of human order against cosmic chaos, and a recognition of the corrupting influences of the exchange mentality. The locus of concern changes from book to book: *Red Harvest* focuses on the corruption of the individual; *The Glass Key* shows how interpersonal relationships are jeopardised by current mores; *The Thin Man* reconsiders the possibility of close personal ties. *The Dain Curse* turns the working assumptions of the detective story inside out, while *The Maltese Falcon* explores the limitations inherent in the fiction-making process. Each work is a unique product within a logical progression of developing insights.

Hammett uses the city as an evocative metaphor for 'things as they are', not as a uniquely depraved environment; the problems of the city are not left behind when the Op journeys into the countryside. Attention is fixed firmly on the present. There is no historical perspective to offer hope or nostalgia, making the city's profound lawlessness claustrophobic. Crimes are committed frequently and with relative ease; murder, blackmail, fraud, extortion, bribery, theft, and assault follow in rapid succession while the bootleg whisky flows freely.

The police are unable to deal effectively with the lawlessness. In *The Thin Man*, the policeman involved in the Wynant case stands gaping in astonishment when the murderer is identified: 'What do you want me to do?' Nick Charles growls, 'Put him in

cellophane for you?' (353: 181). The Chief of Police in *Red Harvest*
finds himself unable to face the violence of Personville. When
called upon to visit the scene of yet another murder, he says, 'I
don't want to. I don't know as I could stand it just now' (352: 128).
The opposition of police to criminal is often more apparent than
real. In *The Dain Curse*, Sheriff Cotton frames his wife's lover,
while in *Red Harvest* Dinah Brand sees the police as a corrupting
influence: 'He had been a pretty good guy, straight as ace-deuce-
trey-four-five, till he got on the force', she complains. 'Then he
went the way of the rest of them' (352: 80). The Western features
corrupt lawmen, of course, but the officials in Hammett's novels
are less artificially damned. The sulphurous aura of betrayal that
hangs about Grey's corrupt officials is replaced by motives drawn
to a human scale. Noonan protects the interests of corrupt friends
in *Red Harvest*, while the District Attorney in *The Maltese Falcon* is
anxious to amass an impressive career record. The contrast
between honest townsfolk and criminals is also denied, as in the
case of Personville, discussed in Chapter 1. Justice becomes a sad
pretence when the separation of the guilty from the innocent is
so equivocal; the circle of suspicion widens rather than narrows.

Hammett may treat corruption on a human scale, but lawlessness assumes cosmic dimensions. The discovery of truth is made
impossibly difficult by the gulf between appearance and reality.
Meaning becomes hopelessly tied to the framework of interpretation which context supplies, blocking every attempt to discern
truth objectively. These problems are graphically demonstrated
when the Op struggles to understand the events of *The Dain Curse*,
as the discussion in Chapter 2 demonstrates.

The detective can never obtain an account untainted by the
observer's preconceptions or self-interest. Mrs Leggett's explanation in *The Dain Curse* is designed to hurt Gabrielle, while Fitzstephan's is intended to prove his insanity. The detective is effectively
trapped in a world of mirrors, while Hammett compels the reader
to acknowledge a similar predicament. Both are lost in the fun
house, as Steven Marcus explains:

> [the Op's] major effort is to make the fictions of others visible
> as fictions, inventions, concealments, falsehoods, and mystific-
> ations. When a fiction becomes visible as such it begins to
> dissolve and disappear, and presumably should reveal behind
> it the 'real' reality that was there all the time and that it was

masking. Yet what happens in Hammett is that what is revealed as 'reality' is a still further fiction-making activity – in the first place the Op's, and behind that yet another, . . . the writer . . .

(360: 371–2)

The fabric of formulations which hides a vacuous, disordered reality is readily apparent in *The Maltese Falcon*. Indeed, it is explicitly stated in the Flitcraft parable. Flitcraft had assumed that by being a good 'citizen – husband – father', he was 'in step with his surroundings'. Spade explains that 'The life he knew was a clean, orderly, sane, responsible affair' (351: 59). Then, 'a falling beam' misses Flitcraft by a hair as he walks between office and restaurant, tearing the mask away. Flitcraft is made aware that men die 'at haphazard like that' and live 'only while blind chance' spares them (351: 59). He readjusts to this realisation by acting haphazardly, leaving his wife, children and business and missing a golf appointment. After lunch he simply steps on a bus and wanders randomly. But no more beams fall, and he settles down again, marrying a woman not unlike his first wife and playing golf most afternoons after four. Spade explains, 'He adjusted himself to beams falling, and then no more of them fell, and he adjusted himself to them not falling' (351: 60).

The Flitcraft parable neatly displays cosmic randomness set against man's need for order and consequent faith in a congruence between his perception of order and some absolute reality. Spade understands that the Flitcrafts of the world must preserve their faith in appearances, for to strike through the mask is to encounter the terror of chaos. In 'The Poetics of the Private Eye: The Novels of Dashiell Hammett', Robert I. Edenbaum notes the consequent importance of appearances in defining reality. He points out that a character such as Spade, who recognises the arbitrary nature of this assumed congruence, can manipulate what passes for reality by altering appearances.

Spade does just this, and, because he is the only character who accepts this vision fully, he has great power. He alone preserves his awareness of the vulnerability of his formulations and remains poised to sidestep the inevitable 'falling beam'. When Spade tells Brigid the Flitcraft parable, he means it as a warning; he is telling her not to place too much faith in the sentimental fiction she has built around them both. The ending shows that she has not heeded his advice, for she is stunned when Spade steps out of the relationship as she has portrayed it, redefining his role from lover to detective.

The impenetrability of the third-person narration in *The Maltese Falcon* confounds interpretation, and so underscores the point of the Flitcraft parable. The narrative eye always stays with Spade, but we never see the scene from his point of view. We are never told his thoughts, only given his words and actions. Spade may have involved himself with Brigid, Gutman and Cairo in order to solve the murders, recover the falcon and prosecute the thieves; or he may be an opportunist who finds he must turn everything over to the police in order to save himself. Some understanding of Spade is possible because the vision underlying the book is his vision, but this does not help us to interpret his actions or to place a moral value on them.

Hammett creates a tension between the value-free, opaque narrative surface and the reader's expectations as engendered by the formula. Although the reader's expectations are fulfilled in the end – the criminals are brought to justice – only appearances have been satisfied, and appearances have proved deceptive throughout the book. There are Brigid's pseudonyms – perhaps 'Brigid' is one of them – and her stance as a flustered schoolgirl. Gutman's purring compliments are as meaningless as Wilmer's pose as a tough gunman. Finally, there is the central irony of the book: the enormously valuable falcon is a fake. The reader is left wondering whether his satisfaction at the triumph of justice is yet another betrayal by appearances.

The suspicion that the fulfilment of the reader's expectations is yet another fiction is reinforced by the profundity of the lawlessness, both social and cosmic. In such a world no order can be restored, even temporarily, by Spade's actions; the final formulation is forever poised on the brink of disintegration. Lawlessness on this level could not be contained in a classical detective story, but it can work in this formula, from the tradition of the Western, because lawlessness is one of the central threads of that tradition. Even so, Hammett is pushing dangerously, but exhilaratingly close to the limits of the formula.

The Dain Curse and *The Maltese Falcon* contain Hammett's most extended treatment of cosmic lawlessness, but the same vision can be glimpsed in his other books as well. It stands behind the Op's technique of 'stirring things up' in *Red Harvest*, in marked contrast to the expected practice of piecing together evidence (352: 77). One glimpses it in the frantic, boozy lifestyle of Nick and Nora Charles in *The Thin Man*. And one senses it in *The Glass Key* as the narrative moves from control to disintegration, from the well-ordered machinery that runs Madvig's city to the fragmentation of loyalties at the end of the book. Such a progression is contrary to expectation, for a mystery plot necessarily works from incongruity to resolution. In *The Glass Key*, this process is devalued by the overwhelming degeneration.

Hammett's setting allows the individual maximum freedom to achieve prosperity, but emphasises the cost of such freedom. He underscores the seamy side of individualism, especially the damage done to interpersonal relationships by the 'exchange mentality'.

Because the world he creates is often associated with a general squalidness, the degree of affluence is often overlooked. The tsar of Personville has made a fortune from the town; he unblinkingly writes the Op a cheque for $10,000, while his son leaves a $5000 cheque stub as a clue to his last day's activities. Wealth is even more in evidence in *The Dain Curse*, where the Op describes the Leggetts' living-room: 'the dull orange rug under my feet was probably both genuinely oriental and genuinely ancient, . . . the walnut furniture hadn't been ground out by machinery' (339: 11). The temple is a monument of luxury to the gullible wealthy, and even the Leggetts' cleaning woman has a boyfriend who keeps a $1000 bankroll in his pocket. Thousands are spent in search of the fabulously bejewelled Maltese falcon. In *The Glass Key*, vast sums change hands in an evening's gambling, while large pay-offs are made and larger kickbacks expected.

Wealth is not glamorous, but shabby and meretricious. Dinah Brand provides the most memorable example, with her run stockings, slovenly appearance and insatiable greed. Often the shabbiness is less pictorial, more a quality of life. Personal happiness, worth and prosperity become disassociated, and affluence brings victimisation rather than fulfilment. Even Edgar Leggett and Clyde Wynant, both of whom have achieved prosperity through honest hard work and cleverness, are not exempted by their virtues: both are murdered. All are caught in a perpetual struggle, and the crassness of the struggle reinforces the impression of baseness.

Spade states the interrelationship between wealth and power quite succinctly when he says, 'Most things in San Francisco can be bought, or taken' (351: 51). Every individual is a potential victim, and must concentrate his energies on forestalling this inevitable fate. Interpersonal relationships become power struggles, and people become objects to be manipulated; self-sacrifice, mercy and compassion are too dangerous to contemplate. 'I'm not going to play the sap for you', Spade tells Brigid (351: 197). The result is the 'exchange mentality': individuals circle one another with extreme suspicion, taking calculated risks, bargaining carefully with whatever assets they possess and hoping desperately to obtain some advantage that can be pressed further. Sex is exchanged for security, money buys sex or a strong arm, and strength exacts temporary loyalty.

'Forget the bank roll and go in for charity', the Op tells Dinah Brand in *Red Harvest.* 'Pretend I'm Bill Quint' (352: 33). She merely laughs and tells him that she has used Bill's inside information on labour relations to make money on the stock-market. Much of the discussion in *The Maltese Falcon* centres on who has bought what from whom, and for how much. When Spade discusses Cairo's offer of $5000 for the falcon with Brigid, the bargaining begins again:

'It is far more than I could ever offer you, if I must bid for your loyalty.'

Spade laughed. His laughter was brief and somewhat bitter. 'That is good,' he said, 'coming from you. What have you given me besides money? Have you given me any of your confidence, any of the truth, any help in helping you? Haven't you tried to buy my loyalty with money and nothing else? Well, if I'm peddling it, why shouldn't I let it go to the highest bidder?'

'I've given you all the money I have.' Tears glistened in her white-ringed eyes. Her voice was hoarse, vibrant. 'I've thrown myself on your mercy, told you that without your help I'm utterly lost. What else is there?' She suddenly moved close to him on the settee and cried angrily: 'Can I buy you with my body?'

Their faces were a few inches apart. Spade took her face roughly between his hands and he kissed her mouth roughly and contemptuously. Then he sat back and said: 'I'll think it over.' His face was hard and furious.   (351: 54)

Besides her offer of money and sex, Brigid is attempting to use sentiment as currency. She is asking for self-sacrifice in payment for love, appealing to a need that Spade feels keenly despite his awareness of the implacability of the exchange mentality and the impossibility of love in a world ruled by such precepts.

In the end her offer is refused and Spade turns her over to the police for the murder of his partner, but he acknowledges the force of her appeal before he does so. He points out her cold-blooded arrangements for the deaths of his predecessors and gives her seven reasons for turning her in, finding only her claim to love as a counterbalance. In exasperation he tells her, 'If that doesn't mean anything to you forget it and we'll make it this: I won't because all of me wants to – wants to say to hell with the consequences and do it – and because – God damn you – you've counted on that with me the same as you counted on that with the others' (351: 199).

If the bargaining breaks down, it is not unusual for characters to take what they want without further ceremony. When, in *The Glass Key*, Shad O'Rory finds his attempts to buy incriminating information from Ned Beaumont are failing, he tries to extract it by beating him. *The Dain Curse* shows murder to be the ultimate ego-centred act of the individualistic ethic. Alice Dain murders her sister to obtain her brother-in-law for herself. Joseph Haldorn tries to murder his wife because she objects to his attempts to acquire Gabrielle as mistress. And, when Owen Fitzstephan's advances are rebuffed by Gabrielle, he murders her protectors.

From *Red Harvest* to *The Thin Man*, Hammett explores the same question: is it possible for any two people to form a close tie that is immune to the corrupting influence of the exchange mentality? In *Red Harvest*, one is given a panoramic view of this mind-set; the scope is wide, but none of the relationships is given close scrutiny. Indeed, they are too shallow to merit a penetrating eye. Alliances are forged and broken with relative ease on the basis of convenience or expediency. One watches Dinah Brand's shifting allegiance as she determines who is best able to offer protection or the opportunity for financial aggrandisement; her commitments are summarily broken when her assessment changes. Her escapades are acted out against a power struggle among rival gang-leaders for the control of Personville. These men negotiate allegiances as tenuous as those of Dinah Brand; power is their medium of exchange.

The focus is narrowed to a family unit in *The Dain Curse*, where, in addition to their murderous outbursts, Alice Dain and Owen

Fitzstephan exert the powerful destructive influence of totally egocentric individuals. They warp family ties and blight Gabrielle's development, causing her to shun close personal ties because she fears her own potential to hurt others.

The Maltese Falcon pits love against the exchange mentality, and demonstrates the mockery made of the finer sentiments in a world dominated by such bartering. Honour is meaningless when 'I give you my word . . .' tends to preface a lie (351: 50). Trust and affection are debased when Gutman can say, 'Well, Wilmer, I'm sorry indeed to lose you, and I want you to know that I couldn't be any fonder of you if you were my own son; but – well, by Gad! – if you lose a son it's possible to get another – and there's only one Maltese falcon' (351: 179). Love takes on a bitter irony when Spade tells Brigid, 'You're an angel. I'll wait for you. . . . If they hang you I'll always remember you' (351: 195).

The Glass Key follows the corruption and consequent breakdown of Ned Beaumont's friendship with Paul Madvig. Ned makes it plain that his loyalty has not been bought, and that Paul is not entitled to treat him as a subordinate. Ned accepts Paul's money as a token, but not as payment:

> Ned Beaumont, looking down at the cheque, shook his head and said: 'I don't need money and you don't owe me anything.'
> 'I do. I owe you more than that, Ned. I wish you'd take it.'
> Ned Beaumont said, 'All right, thanks,' and put the cheque in his pocket.
> Madvig drank beer, ate a pretzel, started to drink again, set his seidel down on the table, and asked: 'Was there anything on your mind – any kick – besides that back in the Club this afternoon?'
> Ned Beaumont shook his head. 'You don't talk to me like that. Nobody does.'   (348: 79)

Paul's treatment of Ned's loyalty as subordination due to him, as a commodity purchased, angers Ned. That his loyalty is not purchased on these terms becomes clear when Ned tricks Madvig's rival, Shad O'Rory, into giving him useful information while refusing to give incriminating information to Shad, even under duress. When Ned is taken to hospital after his brutal ordeal, he refuses treatment until he has given Paul the details he has learned.

Paul's misinterpretation is inevitable, for as a politician he is forced to think within the framework of the exchange mentality: he buys votes, temporary loyalty, and even tries to purchase a wife. He comes to distrust Ned despite all that Ned has done, for he can no longer comprehend altruism. When Ned warns him of Janet Henry's treachery Paul says, 'That's enough. . . . What is it, Ned? Do you want her yourself or is it – . . . . It doesn't make any difference. . . . Get out, you heel, this is the kiss off' (348: 172).

Ned proves his loyalty once again by saving Paul and revealing the true murderer of Taylor Henry, but his saving of Paul exhausts his friendship, and he leaves knowing that Paul has never understood and never will. When Ned agrees to take Janet with him to New York saying, 'Do you really want to go or are you just being hysterical?. . . . It doesn't make any difference. I'll take you if you want to go', his response is not that of one who has transferred his loyalty; it is a shrug of profound weariness (348: 217). And when Paul, misunderstanding, has wished them luck and left, the extent of the fragmentation and despair is underscored by the last two sentences of the novel: 'Janet Henry looked at Ned Beaumont. He stared fixedly at the door' (348: 220). The gaps between people are unbridgeable.

The relationship between Nick and Nora Charles in *The Thin Man* is the only one to survive its social environment. Their marriage is able to withstand the machinations and temptations of the Wynant–Jorgensen family, but this relationship is not a final answer to the social menace of the exchange mentality. The careful nurturing they give to the marriage is itself an acknowledgement of vulnerability. Theirs is an uneasy truce of long standing between two aggressively independent individuals. The repartee which characterises it refuses to acknowledge sentiment despite mutual affection: 'You damned fool,' Nora says when she regains consciousness after Nick's fight with the gunman Shep Morelli, 'You didn't have to knock me cold. I knew you'd take him, but I wanted to see it' (353: 30). Sentiment has become too debased by its social utility to remain simply expressive, and must be avoided.

The vulnerability of their relationship to the social pressures is also reflected in their determination to separate themselves from society. They shun involvement, preferring to be determinedly amused. The Charleses are tourists in New York, having left San Francisco to avoid overbearing relations whose demands threaten involvement. Initially, the Wynant family provide them with entertainment. When Nick and Nora find themselves at the centre of a murder investigation, they remain detached, speculative. After Nick reveals the killer, they resume their drinking. The cost of such a successful marriage is isolation. In *The Thin Man* the dangers of the exchange mentality have been evaded rather than overcome.

Hammett's hero is the anonymous organisation man of unimposing stature and low status, the not too tall, 'middle-aged fat man' of *Red Harvest* and *The Dain Curse* (339: 100). Even in *The Glass Key* and *The Maltese Falcon*, where the hero is younger and taller, he is weary; worn down by his struggles and the awareness of his impending defeat by some chance falling beam. Such heroes stand in marked contrast to the tall, sun-tanned giant of the Western. The Op's success has narrower limits, his evaluation of his society has turned caustic and his morality more equivocal. But, in a world where survival is accounted success, the Op survives and, for a time, prevails.

The Op is constantly faced with his own vulnerability and, like Faust's underdog heroes, must use his hidden potential to avoid victimisation. The magical powers which strengthened Faust's heroes are replaced by toughness. Physically, the Op must be tough enough to withstand a cruel beating or the wearing toll of constant vigilance. Philosophically, he must look into the cosmic void and accept the randomness that passes for order. Mentally, he must dispassionately acknowledge the inevitability of his own victimisation, and use this indifference as a weapon. Spade does this when he answers Gutman's threat of torture with a shrug: 'If you try anything I don't like I won't stand for it. I'll make it a matter of your having to call it off or kill me, knowing you can't afford to kill me' (351: 169).

Self-reliance becomes an essential defence mechanism, an adjunct to toughness. The irony of this retreat into self is that a perverted form of self-reliance has led to the exchange mentality. It becomes necessary to distinguish between the egocentric form and the more acceptable protective variety by developing a hero's code which demands disinterested involvement, self-restraint, the rejection of strong interpersonal commitments, and a sense of fair play.

The presence of a client emphasises the hero's professionalism, underscoring the purity of his motives in contrast to the self-aggrandisement of the exchange mentality; this is enshrined in the rules of the Continental Detective Agency, which forbid taking

rewards or bonuses (352: 58). The contrast between the considerable violence directed at the hero and the hero's actions emphasises the latter's self-restraint. The rejection of strong interpersonal
ties declares the disinterested nature of the Op's involvement and
frees him from the muddling influence of sentiment: 'I'm only a
hired man with only a hired man's interest in your troubles. . . .',
he tells Gabrielle (339: 148). The code demands that the detective
assign guilt fairly despite the temptation to manipulate evidence
in a universe where justice is ultimately a meaningless concept.
Beyond this, the respected adversary is sometimes accorded the
courtesy of being warned of an impending confrontation: in *Red
Harvest*, for example, the Op cautions Max Thaler to leave town
to avoid the approaching bloodbath. The 'ifs and buts' of *The Dain
Curse* and the Flitcraft parable in *The Maltese Falcon* also act as
oblique admonitions.

The code is not only a group of behavioural guidelines, but a
set of reader expectations as well. Hammett acknowledges these
by building the code into his books, but his hero's actions often
wander into the area of unacceptable behaviour. One can ask
whether Spade's concern with the falcon is really disinterested, or
whether the Op had shed his self-restraint when he sets off the
purging of Personville. The equivocal morality projected by such
actions is the result of the hero's involvement with a corrupt
world, and as such it further underscores the detective's vulnerability. The hero's moral status is often discussed by critics, but
the judgements reached are less significant than the ambiguity
which supports the debate.

It is Hammett's style which achieves the fine balance needed to
prevent the reader from judging the hero's behaviour with any
certainty. This style uses a particular variation of the colloquial
stance, the objective technique as defined by Philip C. Durham
in his excellent unpublished doctoral dissertation, 'The Objective
Treatment of the "Hardboiled" Hero in American Fiction' (1949).
Taking his definition from Mario Praz's 'Hemingway in Italy',
Durham refers to a distinctive quality produced by

a peculiar artistic technique – an exclusive concentration upon
what Ernest Hemingway called the 'sequence of motion and
fact', which produces an emotion, rather than upon the direct
portrayal of emotion or thought [or] upon any rhetorical effort

– such as calling attention to a tear-jerking scream – to arouse or direct the response of the reader.

Durham goes on to point out that 'By using this technique these authors appear to create an attitude of casualness and detachment which makes the emotional reaction all the more effective . . .' (291: 3–4). This deadpan stance allows the narrator to look at violence dispassionately; to report without comment. The results can be, and are meant to be, shocking; the brutality is underscored by the starkness of its presentation. Violence is made to seem more than a mere contest; it is barbarous: the bloodless shoot-out of the Western gives way to explicit death.

Durham identifies a number of stratagems associated with the objective technique: the use of simple, stripped-down sentences, the portrayal of actions as a series of component movements, the use of understatement, and the practice of giving descriptively equal treatment to human beings and to inanimate objects. These devices emphasise brutality by objectifying those involved; people are treated as mechanisms, equated with things. Philip Durham has demonstrated Hammett's use of the objective technique, but the true achievement of Hammett's style only becomes apparent when one realises the extent to which it maintains the balanced tensions and ambiguities of his world view.

By viewing people and things with indiscriminate interest or indifference, Hammett strips human beings of their special status and reinforces the value-set of the exchange mentality. Compare, for example, the following passages from *The Maltese Falcon*. The first describes preparations for an evening snack; the second portrays Brigid's attempts, later that evening, to seduce Spade in order to evade his questions:

> He had put the coffee-pot on the stove when she came to the door, and was slicing a slender loaf of French bread. She stood in the doorway and watched him with preoccupied eyes. The fingers of her left hand idly caressed the body and barrel of the pistol her right hand still held.   (351: 79)

> She put her hands up to Spade's cheeks, put her open mouth hard against his mouth, her body flat against his body.
> Spade's arms went around her, holding her to him, muscles bulging his blue sleeves, a hand cradling her head, its fingers

half lost among red hair, a hand moving groping fingers over
her slim back. His eyes burned yellowly.   (351: 82–3)

Spade's mechanical preparations for supper match her deliberate
provocation: the fondling of the pistol and the caress of the body
are equivalent actions; both are objectified. If anything, the gun is
given gentler, more affectionate treatment.
        The objectification of persons is further emphasised by the
mechanisation of their actions. This is achieved by breaking actions
down into component movements, as when Spade disarms Cairo
in *The Maltese Falcon*:

> Spade, by means of his grip on the Levantine's lapels, turned
> him slowly and pushed him back until he was standing close in
> front of the chair he had lately occupied. A puzzled look
> replaced the look of pain in the lead-coloured face. Then Spade
> smiled. His smile was gentle, even dreamy. His right shoulder
> raised a few inches. His bent right arm was driven up by the
> shoulder's lift. Fist, wrist, forearm, crooked elbow, and upper
> arm seemed all one rigid piece, with only the limber shoulder
> giving them motion. The fist st[r]uck Cairo's face, covering for
> a moment one side of his chin, a corner of his mouth, and most
> of his cheek between cheek-bone and jaw-bone.   (351: 44)

By breaking Spade's punch into a series of component movements,
Hammett slows the action and heightens the tension. He also
provides only 'the sequence of motion and fact'; there are no
interpretative cues as to the motivation for the action. We are
provided with a record of movements which might as easily be
the movements of an automaton as those of a man; reasons and
emotions which would humanise the participants are omitted.
Because Spade's movements are presented as unmotivated, the
reader's sense of the brutality of the event is heightened. The
brutality is further underscored by the slow-motion concentration
and by the efficient deliberateness implied by the catalogue of
movements.
        The objectification of character is even more striking when this
technique is used at a point where some display of emotion is
expected, as when Spade is informed of his partner's death. He
smokes a cigarette, then gets dressed; the process is minutely
described:

Spade's thick fingers made a cigarette with deliberate care, sifting a measured quantity of tan flakes down into curved paper, spreading the flakes so that they lay equal at the ends with a slight depression in the middle, thumbs rolling the paper's inner edge down and up under the outer edges as forefingers pressed it over, thumbs and fingers sliding to the paper cylinder's ends to hold it even while tongue licked the flap, left forefinger and thumb pinching their end while right forefinger and thumb smoothed the damp seam, right forefinger and thumb twisting their end and lifting the other to Spade's mouth. (351: 12)

Where we expect emotion, we are presented with movement, efficient and deliberate. The reader is forced to recognise his distance from the hero, to acknowledge his ignorance of Spade as a person while admiring Spade's efficiency as a mechanism. The movement is vividly clear, but its meaning is equivocal: Spade might be totally unaffected by the news or he might have been numbed by it. The ambiguity of the text is maintained. Such impenetrability has led John Whitley to argue that Hammett's hero has no personality, no 'recognizable interior self', merely a 'deliberately created void' (372: 454). Less convincingly, it sustains Peter Wolfe's contention that Spade's toughness 'is leavened by both tenderness and subtlety' (374: 111ff). Such debate is a measure of Hammett's achievement, for it reflects the delicate balance he achieves, the provocative uncertainty.

The ambiguity of the text is also maintained by the short, stripped-down sentences, which make limited use of adjectives and adverbs. When the Op awakes from his nightmares in *Red Harvest*, he finds himself clutching the handle of an ice pick which protrudes from the body of his companion, Dinah Brand. The narrative at this point discloses nothing in its sequence of subject–verb, simple declarative sentences: 'My eyes burned. My throat and mouth were hot, wooly. I went into the kitchen, found a bottle of gin, tilted it to my mouth, and kept it there until I had to breathe. The kitchen clock said seven-forty-one' (352: 145). The absence of modifiers leaves the reader stranded, without interpretative clues to help evaluate the meaning of the death, the degree of responsibility the Op must accept for it, or the Op's own reaction to finding himself in such a position.

In dialogue, the short, stripped-down sentences emphasise the efficiency and restraint of the hero, especially when they are set against the more verbose responses of other characters. When Noonan asks the Op to run a dangerous errand for him in *Red Harvest*, the contrast of styles is marked:

> 'I hate to start this without giving Whisper a chance,' Noonan said. 'He's not a bad kid. But there's no use me trying to talk to him. He never did like me much.'
> He looked at me. I said nothing.
> 'You wouldn't want to make a stab at it' he asked.
> 'Yeah, I'll try it.'
> 'That's fine of you. I'll certainly appreciate it if you will. You just see if you can talk him into coming along without any fuss. You know what to say – for his own good and all that, like it is.'
> 'Yeah,' I said and walked across to the cigar store, taking pains to let my hands be seen swinging empty at my sides.   (352: 47)

While Noonan is emotive, the Op is dispassionate. The style underscores the hero's potency; it emphasises his efficiency and restraint. Noonan's verbosity provides an effective foil. This same technique is used very effectively in *The Maltese Falcon* to help flesh out the character of Gutman.

Hammett's prose leaves one with the impression of a descriptively restrained, opaque narrative surface, but, as we have seen, the narrative treatment of different characters is by no means uniform. The treatment he affords a single character also varies subtly over the course of a book. Spade's usual self-restraint is understandably broken when the falcon is delivered to his office. The lavish description of unwrapping the bird stands out against the norm of descriptive austerity:

> His face was hard and dull. His eyes were shining. When he had put the grey paper out of the way he had an egg-shaped mass of pale excelsior, wadded tight. His fingers tore the wad apart and then he had the foot-high figure of a bird, black as coal and shiny where its polish was not dulled by wood-dust and fragments of excelsior.
> Spade laughed. He put a hand down on the bird. His widespread fingers had ownership in their curving. He put his other

arm around Effie Perine and crushed her body against his.
'We've got the damned thing, angel,' he said.   (351: 145–6)

The unusually lavish description gives a vivid pictorial image of
the scene. It also emphasises Spade's savage triumph; gloating is
apparent in both his expression and his actions. He tears the
package, 'crushes' his secretary; his eyes shine and he laughs. The
dearth of modifiers in the work as a whole ensures that such
interpretative cues have great impact. Spade's words belie the
excited descriptive thrust of the passage, as do his later claims of
disinterested involvement: 'Don't be too sure I'm as crooked as
I'm supposed to be' (351: 199). The discrepancies maintain the
aura of ambiguity and underscore the rift between action and
speech, appearance and reality.

Descriptive understatement portrays people as objects; it underscores the brutality of an event by dispassionately portraying violence as movement. Conversational understatement, on the other
hand, tends to humanise the speaker. When Spade says simply,
'We've got the damned thing, angel', he is understating his reaction. Similarly, the Op's simple admission 'I was afraid' in *The
Dain Curse* seems mild when one considers that he is facing a
crazed killer (339: 87). Such comments demonstrate that there is a
self restraining the hero, for they display an awareness that goes
beyond mere reflex reaction, beyond the merely mechanical.
Conversational understatement can be seen most clearly when it
is overdone, as it is in this passage from *The Dain Curse:*

> I was in a swell mood when I got up from my knee. Playing
> nurse-maid to a crazy girl wasn't enough: I had to be chucked
> around by her boy friend. I put all the hypocrisy I had into my
> voice when I said casually, 'You oughtn't to do that,' to him
> and went over to where the girl was standing by the door.
>   (339: 77)

'I put all the hypocrisy. . . .' lacks subtlety, but it clearly pinpoints
the deliberateness of the understatement. The disparity between
action and reaction underscores the implied threat and creates a
tough humour.

Sometimes the understatement shades off into wisecrack,
adding a wry humour to the irony which permeates Hammett's
writing. The Op's comment, 'I've got a mean disposition.

Attempted assassinations make me mad' (352: 62), and Spade's observation to his secretary, 'You're a damned good man, sister' (351: 147), are two examples. However, the wisecrack is by no means as pervasive in Hammett's writing as it is in Chandler's.

By balancing the human with the mechanical, by setting the thrust of one device against the counterpoint of another, Hammett keeps the philosophical tensions of his work intact. The limitations of the circumscribed context or present perspective add to the reader's dilemma. Attention is continually engaged by the immediate foreground. The focus is so precise that one sees everything in sharp detail, but lacks the distance necessary to permit judgement of the phenomenon. The frustrations involved in this narrowed viewpoint reflect Hammett's vision. He sets the reader's need to order and interpret against a narrative designed to confound interpretation. The reader becomes the butt of a Flitcraft-type joke, and his discomfort mirrors Hammett's view of the human condition.

7

Raymond Chandler

On 23 July, 1888, Raymond Thornton Chandler was born in
Chicago, the first and only child of Florence Thornton Chandler
and Maurice Benjamin Chandler. His mother was Irish; she had
met and married Maurice while staying with relatives in Nebraska.
When Chandler was seven, his parents divorced. That same year
he came down with scarlet fever. Florence soon returned to Britain
with her son, and Chandler did not see his father again; but he
would remember him as 'an utter swine', and would later worry
about what portion of his father's deficiencies he had inherited.

The move to his grandmother's home in south London did not
provide the young boy with a happier home life. To the upheaval
of divorce and illness was added the culture shock of encountering
Victorian formality after the casual lifestyle and relative disregard
for class divisions found in the Midwestern United States. To make
matters worse, he and his mother were constantly humiliated as
the refugees of an unsuccessful marriage living on the charity of
others. Chandler would long remember such petty acts of abase-
ment as his grandmother's refusal to serve his mother wine at
dinner when it was offered to everyone else (406: 4). Chandler's
helplessness must have added to his discomfort. As the only child,
and only resident male – the household was supported by an
uncle living in Waterford, Ireland – his loneliness and confusion
were exacerbated.

It seems to have been this Irish uncle who dictated the household's move to Dulwich, where Chandler entered the first form
of Dulwich College, a public school of reputable academic standing
but little social prestige, in the autumn of 1900. Chandler did well
despite his frequent absences due to illness and several shifts
between classical studies, intended as a preparation for university,
and the modern curriculum, designed for those headed for business. During these moves, his inclinations battled with a sense of
economic realism: his uncle was unwilling to finance a university

education. Chandler never settled into a comfortable place within the college community: his absences and shifts between classical and modern studies, his status as a day boy and his mediocrity in sports separated him from his peers. The knowledge that he would not be allowed to go to university despite his interests and proven academic ability increased his sense of humiliation and injustice. Dulwich had a positive impact none the less: it provided him with a code of behaviour, that of the Victorian gentleman, induced a certain self-confidence in the manipulation of language, and inculcated a sense of social and academic superiority and privilege.

By 1905, his uncle had decided that Chandler should prepare to enter the Civil Service. Accordingly, Chandler left Dulwich for a sojourn in Europe designed to improve his languages. He spent most of the ensuing two years in Paris and Munich, returning to England in the spring of 1907 to prepare for a special examination to fill vacancies in the Admiralty. Out of 600 applicants, Chandler placed third and was offered a post as Assistant Store Officer, Naval Stores Branch. His uncle was well pleased, for this was what he had envisaged for his nephew; a secure future now seemed within the lad's grasp. Chandler soon shattered this complacency: he grew disenchanted with his clerical duties and quit after six months to pursue a precarious career as a freelance journalist. The result was 'a bombshell; perhaps no one had ever done it before. My Irish uncle was livid with rage' (399: 22).

Over the next four years Chandler published some twenty-seven truly awful poems together with a number of anonymous paragraphs in the *Westminster Gazette* and a series of his reviews and essays in the *Academy*. None of this work is particularly noteworthy, but it does reveal preoccupations which would later surface in his detective fiction. Chandler became discouraged when he did not break into the more lucrative literary markets. He 'managed to get a loan of £500 from [his] irate uncle (every penny of it was repaid with six percent interest)', and prepared to emigrate (399: 25). He viewed this departure for the United States dispassionately; it was neither the abandonment of a much-loved homeland, nor a homecoming.

Inevitably, as he wandered across America with his 'beautiful wardrobe [and] public school accent', he was treated as an alien (399: 25). He stopped for short spells, first in St Louis, then in Nebraska, where he had relatives, before making his way to the

California home of the Lloyd family, friends he had made on the transatlantic voyage. Arriving in California, he began working at a series of odd jobs. He went to night school to learn book-keeping – he claims to have finished a three-year course in six weeks – and landed a job as book-keeper and accountant for the Los Angeles Creamery, a position obtained through the intercession of the Lloyds. Chandler's friendship with this family would prove to be an enduring one of great influence over the course of his life.

By 1916, Chandler was firmly settled in an old residential section of Los Angeles and had been joined by his mother. The United States entered the First World War the following year. Although Chandler decided to enlist in August 1917, it was not the US Army he joined but the Canadian forces. By 26 November he and his outfit were on their way to England, and on 18 March, 1918 Chandler was sent to France. His battalion was in a reserve position, but saw heavy action none the less. Three months after arriving in France, Chandler was found unconscious, the sole survivor of an artillery barrage. Guilt and isolation were once again his lot.

He was sent back to England suffering from a concussion, but recovered quickly. Chandler decided to join the Royal Air Force, was accepted as a cadet in July and began training. However, the war was soon over, and by the end of December he found himself stationed in London awaiting his return to Canada. He was not commissioned in the RAF, but had risen to the rank of sergeant in the infantry and been awarded the British War and Victory medals. He was demobilised at Vancouver on 20 February 1919, and began to make his way slowly south to California.

It was on his return to Los Angeles after the war that he fell in love with the wife of a friend, and she with him. Cissy Pascal was quickly granted a divorce, but the subsequent marriage was delayed because Chandler's mother disapproved of a marriage partner eighteen years his senior. The marriage took place on 26 February 1924, within two weeks of his mother's death.

Chandler's determination to marry Cissy distanced him from his peers once again. The marriage is also symptomatic of his rather ambivalent attitude to women. His reverence for his 'sainted' mother and his Victorian upbringing encouraged a chival-rous regard for 'the lady'. His fear of impulses which linked him to his hated father encouraged him to project his own mixture of titillation and disgust onto the women he met: 'There was a time in my life as a young man when I could have picked up any pretty girl on the street and slept with her that night. (Bragging again, but it is true.) I didn't do it because there has to be something else and a man like me has to be sure he is not hurting anyone. . . .' (408: 421). In fact, Chandler did not approach the subject of sex without squeamishness. In marrying Cissy, he chose a partner of whom he could be fondly solicitous, one who guaranteed a quiet domesticity, and one whose age and dignity allowed him to combine deference with surrender.

While waiting to marry, Chandler took two apartments, one for Cissy, another for his mother and himself. During this time he also changed jobs, becoming an accountant to the Dabney Oil Syndicate, a post offered him through the influence of the Lloyds. By the time of his marriage, he had been working for the Dabney firm at least two years and had risen rapidly in the company, eventually becoming a company vice-president at the substantial salary of $1000 a month.

Chandler did not handle his success well. Although he later remembered himself as a tough business man and a fine administrator, at least one employee characterised him as the office 'martinet' (406: 36). He was aggressive and abrasive enough to involve his company in numerous lawsuits. Chandler's difficulties are not surprising: he had been an outsider all his life, so it is unlikely that he was well equipped to deal with colleagues or employees on any but the most formal terms. To relieve the pressures and overcome his difficulties in dealing with people, he began to drink. He alienated friends by his morose behaviour, his frequent suicide threats and his bizarre outbursts. His drunkenness and absenteeism undercut his position in the company, as did a series of affairs with his female employees.

Despite his influential friends, Chandler was given a warning, then fired in 1932. His own account of his dismissal fails to acknowledge his irresponsible behaviour: 'My services cost them too much', he explained, 'Always a good reason for letting a man go' (406: 40). Losing a well-paid position during the Depression must have been a shattering experience. This was a crisis intensified by the marital troubles his drinking and suspected infidelities had caused.

Chandler retreated to Seattle, where he had army friends, but quickly returned when his wife was hospitalised with pneumonia.

Soon he was helping the Lloyds with their side of a legal battle which involved the Dabney Oil Company. By supplying information about the financial manoeuvrings of the firm, he aided their case and must, to a degree, have felt himself revenged. Out of gratitude and pity, these friends once again came to his aid, providing him with an allowance of $100 a month. Chandler, now forty-four, tried once again to support himself by writing. To locate a market, he started reading through a variety of slick magazines and pulps.

His ideas had changed little since his early attempts at prose. Compare, for example, the introduction to *Pearls are a Nuisance* with 'The Tropical Romance', published in the *Academy* some forty years earlier. In 'The Tropical Romance' Chandler wrote,

> Certainly the violent romance of the tropics had its faults. It did not paint life as season-ticket-holders see it. It was apt to display the raw edge of things, and to provide murderous-minded authors with a great many opportunities to enlarge on the surgical aspects of sudden death. . . . Its alarmingly swift justice did not cause one to admire the vacillating movements of political reform. . . . Nevertheless, to it belonged, in its day, the magic of the places where life is a mighty colourist, and it made that magic live as no other literature has ever done. And they were men, those somewhat shop-soiled heroes with tarnished morals and unflinching courage. (377: 69)

Now, years later, Chandler discovered in the *Black Mask* detective story another genre with much the same appeal:

> I don't think this power was entirely a matter of violence, although far too many people got killed in these stories and their passing was celebrated with a rather too loving attention to detail. . . . Possibly it was the smell of fear which the stories managed to generate. Their characters lived in a world gone wrong, a world in which, long before the atom bomb, civilization had created the machinery for its own destruction and was learning to use it with all the moronic delight of a gangster trying out his first machine-gun. . . . As to the emotional basis of the hard-boiled story, obviously it does not believe that murder will out and justice will be done – unless some very determined individual makes it his business to see that justice

is done. The stories were about the men who made that happen. They were apt to be hard men and what they did, whether they were called police officers, private detectives, or newspapermen, was hard, dangerous work. It was work they could always get. There was plenty of it lying around.   (387: 7–8)

James Whitfield Thomson points out the continuing enthusiasm for rough vitality (420: 16f). The passages also suggest that the British adventure story influenced Chandler's work. The extent to which the much-heralded realism of Chandler's hard-boiled fiction is really romanticism brought down to earth by local colour is also apparent. The nostalgia of his youthful vision is carried over in his laments for 'a world gone wrong'. The misanthropy has become more directly apparent, and is augmented by the rather peculiar view of women discussed in Chapter 1.

Though his social attitudes show little growth, his fascination with the American voice and his admiration for specific American writers did lead to a striking change in the style of his work. Chandler began an apprenticeship, imitating the writers he admired: Ernest Hemingway, Dashiell Hammett and Erle Stanley Gardner.

Chandler publicly acknowledged his debt to Hemingway and Hammett in his much-quoted essay 'The Simple Art of Murder'. In 1932 he paid Hemingway the compliment of writing a short parody, 'Beer in the Sergeant Major's Hat (Or the Sun also Sneezes)', which he dedicated 'with no good reason to the greatest living American novelist – Ernest Hemingway' (407: 23–5). Hammett's influence can be seen most markedly in 'Nevada Gas', 'Spanish Blood', 'Guns at Cyranos' and 'Noon Street Nemesis', all published in 1935–6. In these, as James Whitfield Thomson has convincingly argued, Chandler masters the mechanics of the objective technique as practised by Hammett (420: 63ff). Chandler then moved on, trying to circumvent what he saw as the limitations of this stance:

It has too great a fondness for the *faux näif*, by which I mean the use of a style such as might be spoken by a very limited sort of mind. In the hands of a genius like Hemingway this may be effective, but only by subtly evading the terms of the contract, that is, by an artistic use of the telling detail which the speaker never would have noted. When not used by a genius it is as flat as a Rotarian speech.   (407: 21)

In Hammett's writing Chandler saw the possibilities of the colloquial style fettered by the objective voice:

> Hammett's style at its worst was almost as formalized as a page of Marius the Epicurean; at its best it could say almost anything. I believe this style, which does not belong to Hammett or to anybody, but is the American language (and not exclusively that any more), can say things he did not know how to say or feel the need of saying. In his hands it had no overtones, left no echo, evoked no image beyond a distant hill.   (389: 234)

Chandler never grasped Hammett's awesome achievement. His criticism reveals his own expectations, his need for projected heroism and sentimental idealism. Chandler wanted to inject these into the hard-boiled subgenre and to explore the possibilities of the colloquial style which stood behind the objective technique: 'All I wanted to do when I began writing', he later recalled, 'was to play with a fascinating new language, to see what it would do as a means of expression which might remain on the level of unintellectual thinking and yet acquire the power to say things which are usually only said with a literary air' (399: 214).

Back in 1935, Chandler had lesser immediate ambitions. He was learning to write by synopsising, then expanding, a novelette by Erle Stanley Gardner. Chandler later confessed to his model, 'In the end I was a bit sore because I couldn't try to sell it' (399: 73). The lessons Chandler hoped to learn were probably ones of plotting, which he never did master, and pace. He told Gardner that he admired his 'perfection of control over the movement of a story' such that 'Every page throws the hook for the next' (399: 51).

Chandler learned most of his craft well and quickly. After working on his first original story, 'Blackmailers Don't Shoot', for five months, he sent it to *Black Mask*. It was published in December 1933, and he was paid $180, a penny a word. 'After that', Chandler says, 'I never looked back, although I had a good many uneasy periods looking forward' (399: 26). Indeed he must have, for he was a slow, careful writer, and at pulp word rates that made for a meagre income. None the less, Chandler spent five years working on carefully crafted stories before trying his hand at a novel, *The Big Sleep* (1939). His financial situation did not improve, though two more books followed, *Farewell, My Lovely* (1940) and *The High Window* (1942).

It was not until 1943, when Chandler began to tap the big money in Hollywood, that he knew anything like financial security. Initially, he was engaged by Paramount to work with Billy Wilder on the film script of James M. Cain's *Double Indemnity*. His thirteen-week contract earned him $750 a week, a considerable sum. His connections with various Hollywood studios, while not continuous, would last till 1950.

Critical acclaim came before financial security. Even *The Big Sleep* attracted considerable attention, though the reviews were mixed. *Farewell, My Lovely* was highly praised, and one reviewer, Morton Thompson of the *Hollywood Citizen-News*, wrote, 'I am perfectly willing to stake whatever critical reputation I possess today or may possess tomorrow on the literary future of this author. Chandler writes throughout with amazing absorption in the tasks of craftmanship' (406: 89).

Such praise must have pleased Chandler greatly and reinforced his high regard for craftsmanlike writing. In a letter to Mrs Robert Hogan, dated 7 March 1947, he wrote, 'A good story cannot be devised; it has to be distilled. In the long run, however little you talk or even think about it, the most durable thing in writing is style and style is the most valuable investment a writer can make with his time' (399: 75).

Chandler was convinced that the effectiveness of the hard-boiled detective novel was due to the emotional impact of its style rather than to the breakneck action of its plot: 'My theory was that the readers just *thought* they cared about nothing but action; that really, although they didn't know it, the thing they cared about, and that I cared about, was the creation of emotion through dialogue and description' (399: 219). He goes on to provide a much-quoted example of a man who is murdered while trying to pick up a bothersome paperclip: 'The things [sic] they remembered, that haunted them, was not, for example, that a man got killed, but that in the moment of his death he was trying to pick a paper clip up off the polished surface of a desk and it kept slipping away . . .' (399: 219). While Chandler's assessment of the importance of emotional impact is sound, the sentimentality evoked by such details contrasts markedly with the stark horror and shock produced by an effective use of a fully objective style.

It is this evocation of sentiment through a notionally objective style which is Chandler's achievement; it enabled him to give the objective technique the overtones, the echoes, he found lacking in the work of his predecessors.

Although Chandler could savour his vindication on the critical front as well as the wealth, Academy Awards and lionisation his involvement with Hollywood brought, success would again prove his undoing. He began to drink and his previous debacle repeated itself: drinking produced moodiness, another spate of philandering with the office secretaries, and further marital unhappiness.

Billy Wilder has noted that Chandler's contact with Hollywood thoroughly unsettled him. It appears that the social atmosphere of Hollywood both drew and repelled Chandler. It removed him from the cloistered environment in which he had done his best writing and made it impossible for him to return to those conditions undisturbed (402: 44–51). Natasha Spender provides the most informed explanation: she saw within Chandler a deep anxiety whenever he was called upon to take a role other than that of the alienated outsider, an anxiety she attributed to his 'deep distrust and disbelief in the generosity of human nature' (418: 137).

Stephen Knight has recognised this as the basic message of Chandler's fiction, and it has led him to certain conclusions regarding the audience and appeal of Chandler's novels:

> The pressure of the form and content suggests that an isolated, intelligent person, implicitly hostile to others and basically uninterested in them, can verify his own superiority by intellectual means and create a defensive withdrawal. . . . A richly satisfying message is fabricated for the alienated person of some education, and the natural audience has not failed to find Chandler comforting. (404: 138)

It is always dangerous to deduce audience from appeal, but the noticeable critical approval Chandler has gained from just such an audience, and a highly influential one at that, should be considered.

To write well, Chandler needed a detached, lonely existence where he could develop his writing without feeling self-conscious about either his reputation or the latent content of his work. These conditions were only present at the beginning of his career as a mystery-writer, when he developed a style of wit and power and created a hero onto whom he could project an unrealistic, idealised self-image.

While making Marlowe consistent with formulaic expectations, he created a hero tough enough physically to cope with a world he himself felt unequal to as a sickly child. He created a hero tough enough emotionally to cross the social minefield of inter-personal relationships with self-assurance, without the sense of panic Chandler himself experienced. He created a hero who did not need his mother or any other woman and who did not revere any. He created a hero who would never be spoiled by success; indeed, one who would never have any success beyond the satis-faction of a job well done. And he created a hero who was capable of balancing sentimental romanticism with tough cynicism. Chandler's hero is an alienated outsider who vindicates that stance by his demonstrable superiority in a society unworthy of his services.

Chandler's marked attachment to his hero is unusual. His anxiety over Marlowe's fate in the media and his frequent compari-sons in correspondence between Marlowe and himself show the depth of this attachment. This bond can also be seen in the changes Marlowe undergoes through time. Chandler becomes increasingly indulgent toward his hero and more expansive in his treatment, through Marlowe, of his own preoccupations. One watches him explore his feelings about women, exorcise his bitter-ness over his Hollywood experiences, and sink into morbid exam-ination of his own self-pity and self-disgust.

By the end of Chandler's writing-career, Marlowe began to look anachronistic and absurd, especially in *Playback* and 'The Poodle Springs Mystery'. This is due partly to subtle changes in the social setting in which Marlowe operated, partly to the increasingly self-conscious treatment of hero and style. These changes destroy the formula's capacity to balance Chandler's conflicting emotional needs – and it was this balance which had given his work its vibrancy. As a result, Chandler began to push his writing toward self-parody.

To see Chandler at his best, one must look at his first two novels, *The Big Sleep* (1939) and *Farewell, My Lovely* (1940). In these, one can appreciate his enduring contribution to the hard-boiled formula: a colloquial style which combines stark witticism and irony with subtle shadings of emotion, a hero who balances tough cynicism with romantic idealism, and a city setting of beauty and brashness which sustains, extends and in a sense explains the hero who moves within it.

Chandler vividly describes the changing moods of the different neighbourhoods of Los Angeles, but his city is as much a metaphor for 'things as they are' as Hammett's. Chandler measures his city with a historical perspective, however. The decline is judged by memories of a simpler and somewhat better time, and Marlowe mourns the irredeemable past. He articulates his sense of loss directly in *The Little Sister* (1949):

> I used to like this town. . . . A long time ago. There were trees along Wilshire Boulevard. Beverly Hills was a country town. . . . Los Angeles was just a big dry sunny place with ugly homes and no style, but good hearted and peaceful. It had the climate they just yap about now. People used to sleep out on porches. Little groups who thought they were intellectual used to call it the Athens of America. It wasn't that, but it wasn't a neon lighted slum either.   (384: 180)

Simplicity and innocence have been replaced by commercial sleaziness. Chandler uses the expected lawlessness of the formula to reflect his personal disillusionment with society. Crime runs rampant: *The Big Sleep* features six murders, blackmail, robbery, a pornographic-book trade, a stolen-car workshop and racketeering. *Farewell, My Lovely* adds abduction to a similar inventory. The crimes have a sordidness which is not present in the self-serving ruthlessness of Hammett's world. Geiger's death in *The Big Sleep*, surrounded by ornate oriental trappings, gargoyles and tassels, with a flagon of laudanum on the desk and the camera focused on a doped, naked girl, has a particular nastiness. Mrs Florian's death (*Farewell, My Lovely*) in her squalid home is mean and sordid.

Lawlessness is deeply woven into the fabric of society. Captain Gregory articulates the frustration and bitterness of the police when he tells Marlowe,

> Being a copper I like to see the law win. I'd like to see the flashy well-dressed mugs like Eddie Mars spoiling their manicures in the rock quarry at Folsom. . . . You and me both lived too long to think I'm likely to see it happen. Not in this town, not in any

town half this size, in any part of this wide, green and beautiful
U.S.A.   (378: 197)

The wealthy use their power, carelessly disregarding the corruption which ripples from their intended goal. The Grayles in *Farewell, My Lovely* and the Sternwood family in *The Big Sleep* exert the
shadowy influence of vast family fortunes; their indiscretions are
not pursued by officialdom. The enormously successful mobsters
such as Eddie Mars and Laird Brunette (*Farewell, My Lovely*) bully
or buy the protection they need.
The offhand dishonesty extends down through much of society.
There are doctors, such as Dr Sonderborg (*Farewell, My Lovely*),
who pander to the addictions of their patients; gigolos such as
Marriott (*Farewell, My Lovely*); and small-time blackmailers such as
Brody (*The Big Sleep*). Not even the survivors of a better age escape
untainted: the Sternwood's butler conceals a murder, and Anne
Riordan, the good girl in *Farewell, My Lovely*, steals police evidence.
Galbraith, a crooked Bay City policeman, sums up the problem
for Marlowe:

A guy can't stay honest if he wants to. . . . That's what's the
matter with this country. He gets chiselled out of his pants if
he does. You gotta play the game dirty or you don't eat. A lot
of bastards think all we need is ninety thousand FBI men in
clean collars and brief cases. Nuts. The percentage would get
them just the way it does the rest of us. You know what I think?
I think we gotta make this little world all over again.   (379: 201)

Galbraith's solution is Moral Rearmament. Marlowe is sceptical:
'If Bay City is a sample of how it works, I'll take aspirin', he says
(379: 201).
The division of the world into victims and wealthy victors so
characteristic of social Darwinism exists without comment. There
is no social criticism, no hope held out for a better future, just the
nostalgia on which E. M. Beekman comments. Of Marlowe he
says,

In this character there is a fierce grief which has little opportunity
to be assuaged – a grief for a loss, perhaps a primeval Eden,
perhaps a community of decent men. Not a grief, however,
simply for a loss of innocence, but a bitter frustration about the

fact that things *are* as they are though they shouldn't be that way. There is a revulsion for this world yet also a distaste for his own defiant nobility, a nobility very much like a pawned code of honor.   (376: 167)

This is the 'fierce grief' of an outsider who has longed for a niche in the society that has rejected him, and that he, out of bitterness and an intense feeling of injustice, rejects. Chandler had no 'social consciousness', as he defiantly announces:

> P. Marlowe has as much social conscience as a horse. He has a personal conscience, which is an entirely different matter. . . . P. Marlowe doesn't give a damn who is President; neither do I, because I know he will be a politician. There was even a bird who informed me I could write a good proletarian novel; in my limited world there is no such animal, and if there were, I am the last mind in the world to like it, being by tradition and long study a complete snob.   (399: 214–15)

The result, as Russell Davies has noted, is a widely directed misanthropy, but one which does leave room for individual acts of loyalty or love. Harry Jones, a minor character in *The Big Sleep*, refuses to 'put my girl in the middle for anybody', lies to a hitman about her whereabouts, and drinks his cyanide 'like a little gentleman' (378: 169,173). Chandler bestows a qualified and condescending approval. More generally, there is disdain for the rich hypocrites, the corrupt cops, the little crooks and big racketeers, and underneath this there is a deep distrust and dislike of just about everyone. This attitude is brought into high relief when Marlowe meets someone, such as Anne Riordan or Red Norgaard, whom he should trust; he holds himself back, unable to overcome his wariness.

In Hammett's world of the exchange mentality, one senses the Op's hunger for human contact. One sees the risks the Op is willing to assume in order to come as close to an intimate relationship as the social dynamics of his world will allow. There is a sense of compassion in Hammett's work; an empathy with those caught in the merciless struggle for survival and a recognition of the need for love. Marlowe, on the other hand, carefully isolates himself from those who would provide such fellowship.

Chandler's treatment of wealth, like his treatment of lawless-

ness, is an interesting blend of the expected formulaic elements
and his own misanthropy. The possessors of wealth are judged
unworthy, and the means to wealth are seen as corrupting and
immoral.

Chandler's criticisms are those levelled at the newly wealthy by
a more patrician eye. He objects to the bad morals, lack of dignity,
and bad taste of the *nouveau riche*. The wealthy families in his
books do not stand above the fray; their indiscretions provide for
a common meeting-ground between them, the jostling lower
classes and the mobsters, a meeting which reflects badly on their
claim to exclusivity. Often wealth is used to erect a showy façade
which conceals intellectual and emotional poverty as well as
hypocrisy. Marlowe finds that Mrs Reagan (*The Big Sleep*) and Mrs
Grayle (*Farewell, My Lovely*) both discard their refinement very
quickly: 'To hell with this polite drinking', Mrs Grayle says to
Marlowe after her first drink; 'Let's get together on this. You're a
very good-looking man to be in your sort of racket' (379: 111). It
is not long before Marlowe is warning her not to get shrill.

From the top of society to the bottom, the possession of wealth
is linked to a desperate urgency. In Mrs Reagan we taste the
hunger to live quickly, exquisitely and immediately which drives
people to the Los Angeles night world. In Chandler's description
of the Bay City seafront we feel the urge for fast action, rewards
now, regardless of cost:

> Outside the narrow street fumed, the sidewalks swarmed with
> fat stomachs. Across the street a bingo parlour was going full
> blast and beside it a couple of sailors with girls were coming
> out of a photographer's shop where they had probably been
> having their photos taken riding on camels. The voice of the
> hot dog merchant split the dusk like an axe. A big blue bus
> blared down the street. . . .   (379: 207)

In this world of peepshows and sidewalk cars, cotton candy,
greasy french-fries and popcorn, there is a tawdriness not present
in the Western; a sense of empty people seeking bogus thrills.
The exuberance of Western spreeing is replaced by a meretricious
escapism.

The means to wealth are a further reflection on the wealthy:
they are dirty, demeaning or downright dishonest. When Marlowe
leaves the Sternwood house he notices the oilfields which have

been the source of the family fortune: 'The Sternwoods, having moved up the hill, could no longer smell the stale sump water or the oil, but they could still look out of their front windows and see what had made them rich. If they wanted to. I don't suppose they would want to' (378: 25–6). Chandler's first-hand experience of the oil business comes immediately to mind.

The more blatantly dishonest roads to wealth – blackmail, pornography, murder, extortion and various rackets – make possession characteristicly tenuous. Marriott is murdered by the woman he has profitably blackmailed (379). Brody is killed before he can cash in on the racket he has stolen (378). Disproportionate wealth is often the mark of a crooked individual. The new radio in her shabby home makes Mrs Florian suspect. When Marlowe comments that Lieutenant Randall is wearing a nice suit, Randall takes the remark as an affront to his integrity: 'The flush dyed his face again. "This suit cost twenty-seven-fifty," he snapped' (379: 169). In these circumstances Marlowe's vow of poverty is understandable.

Within Hammett's world wealth corrupts and destroys interpersonal relationships because of the strains of the exchange mentality. Chandler's consideration of wealth is quite different; it is based on his misanthropy. 'P. Marlowe and I do not despise the upper classes because they take baths and have money', Chandler wrote in the letter quoted earlier; 'we despise them because they are phoney' (399: 215). Carmen Sternwood would be 'a child who likes to pull wings off flies' regardless of her financial circumstances, and, although Geiger probably hopes for financial gain when he dopes Carmen and takes nude photographs, his actions have a stealthy nastiness that goes beyond the profit motive (378: 18). Chandler seems to argue that it is not wealth which corrupts people, but people who abuse wealth.

Within this seamy world, Chandler's hero is an especially vulnerable figure. His susceptibility to physical brutality makes this painfully apparent. When caught off guard by Art and Canino in *The Big Sleep*, for example, or by the Indian in *Farewell, My Lovely*, he is knocked senseless, then dealt with while unconscious. Marlowe is also a much more socially marginal figure than the Op, as his shabby office, empty filing-cabinets and genteel poverty reveal. His lack of status and connections add to his vulnerability. In *Farewell, My Lovely*, Lieutenant Randall acknowledges Marlowe's right to practise his profession, but warns, 'any acting-captain with a grouch can break you' (379: 186). This threat is regularly hurled at Marlowe, whose unheeding perseverance underscores his personal courage and determination.

Marlowe is continually compelled to demonstrate his personal superiority, his status as 'best man', and to confront the marginality which is society's dismissal of his worth. He does this by succeeding where others fail; by uncovering guilt and bringing wrongdoers to justice. He must also prove himself to be an honourable man. Chandler's misanthropy demands an absolute separation between Marlowe and the moral squalor of his society. The result is his code, his self-imposed set of moral imperatives which he wields as a shield against an evil society.

Marlowe's code requires poverty because money is associated with corruption. Disinterested involvement in other respects is also important: 'That's the way it is', Marlowe tells Mrs Reagan when she tries to seduce him. 'Kissing is nice, but your father didn't hire me to sleep with you' (378: 147). Because he is disinterested, Marlowe can enjoy participation while maintaining distance; obligations and expectations are defined formally and exactly.

Once professional responsibility has been assumed, total commitment is demanded. Marlowe pursues Lindsay Marriott's murderer because Marriott was killed while under his protection. He does this despite both his antipathy for Marriott and his awareness that Marriott had hired him under false pretences. Marlowe's loyalty is impersonal, often without warmth, but it is absolute. As he tells General Sternwood, 'The client comes first, unless he's crooked. Even then all I do is hand the job back to him and keep my mouth shut' (378: 204).

Marlowe's code also demands fair play, despite the hazards involved. In *The Big Sleep* he becomes involved in a rather one-sided shoot-out with Canino. Marlowe comments 'Perhaps it would have been nice to allow him another shot or two, just like a gentleman of the old school. But his gun was still up and I couldn't wait any longer. Not long enough to be a gentleman of the old school. I shot him four times . . .' (378: 194). Where the line between etiquette and foolhardiness is finely drawn, Marlowe knowingly places himself at risk. The gentlemen of the old school worked within more amenable circumstances. Marlowe's nostalgia and disappointment are again invoked.

Marlowe participates very little in the violence which surrounds him, except, occasionally, as a victim. When violence erupts, he is self-restrained, prefering threats to direct action. Even when he must react quickly, as when Mrs Grayle shoots Moose Malloy or when Agnes attacks him, his initial response is too restrained and he must use greater force to be effective. His restraint seems mechanical. He is too aloof; he has no passions which require self-control. Marlowe's self-restraint is therefore less impressive than that of the Op in Hammett's fiction.

A chivalrous regard for women is also required, despite the contrast between the behaviour of those treated as ladies and the expectations implicit in the code. Marlowe's deference is often tempered by sarcasm, and this combines with his misanthropy to produce the strange attitude to women which has often been noted in Chandler's work and which has led to much speculation over Marlowe's, and Chandler's, sexual preferences.

The usual double standard does not work for Marlowe, though he pays lip service to it when he tells Lieutenant Randall that Anne Riordan is 'a nice girl. Not my type', and goes on to explain, 'I like smooth shiny girls, hard-boiled and loaded with sin.' (379: 171). But Marlowe rejects the 'smooth shiny girls' as well, going so far as to tear his bed to pieces to remove the tainted sheets on which Carmen has tried to seduce him. Marlowe's rejection makes him sexless; there is no sense of self-sacrifice in his abstention. Even the wistfulness which hangs over his visit to Anne Riordan's house has more to do with the comforts of a well-tended home than with restrained sexuality.

In Hammett's world, women are dangerous precisely because the hero feels their attraction so compellingly that they can use their sexuality as a trap. By contrast, when Marlowe finds a naked woman in his bed, he thinks, 'It's so hard for women – even nice women – to realize that their bodies are not irresistible' (378: 153). Hammett's women are strong figures. They use or withhold their favours in accordance with their desires and their assessment of the situation, as do Dinah Brand and Brigid O'Shaughnessy. Chandler's women are weak, trapped by their lusts and by their need for protection: they are incomplete without men. Inevitably, the resulting pursuit of Marlowe by the Sternwood daughters, Mrs Grayle and even Anne Riordan seems undignified where it does not appear depraved.

Despite his elaborate courtesy, Marlowe assumes the worst of the women he meets. Anne Riordan raises the issue of Mrs

Grayle's love life with Marlowe: 'She would have one, wouldn't she?' she asks. 'Who hasn't?' Marlowe replies. Her response clearly amazes him: '*I* never had. Not really' (379: 87). His jaw drops open.

Marlowe's attitude makes his resolve to avoid strong personal ties understandable. He deliberately distances himself, as he does in the following exchange with Mrs Reagan:

> '. . . you're as cold-blooded a beast as I ever met, Marlowe. Or can I call you Phil?'
> 'Sure'.
> 'You can call me Vivian.'
> 'Thanks, Mrs Reagan.' (378: 63)

He does the same thing when Anne Riordan's domesticity threatens to come too close. Marlowe builds a wall around himself verbally; through his rudeness he cuts himself off from obligations, expectations and sympathy.

Chandler's treatment of women reflects cultural ideals, as shown in Chapter 1, but his personal foibles are also visible. His upbringing in a household of women, his great regard for his 'sainted' mother, and his determination not to be a 'swine' like his father shaped this curious blend of sentimental idealism, disappointed rejection and avoidance of sexuality. Chandler was sensitive enough about his portrayal of women to alter Marlowe's celibacy in the books written after *The Little Sister*, probably in response to allegations that Marlowe was a homosexual. In these Marlowe's love life alters rather unconvincingly. Marlowe was Chandler's *alter ego*, and his code reflects the same kind of panic indicated by the altered state of Marlowe's sex life; both reveal a wall hastily erected to keep out the night.

Despite Chandler's heated pronouncements that he is *not* a political writer, his work does reinforce the prevailing American ideology. Chandler's cynicism and misanthropy act as perfect compliments to the individualistic ethic. His concern with criminal conspiracy further reinforces the individualistic bias. In his books, criminal networks are sometimes extensive, with the key individuals remaining shadowy figures, as with Laird Brunette. Sometimes they are small-scale operations involving single rackets such as Geiger's book trade, Amthor's clinic and Sonderborg's sanatorium.

As the formula dictates, the threat of these conspiracies is neutralised. Sometimes the villains pick up and run, as Sanderborg's group does, or dissolve, as with the inheritors of Geiger's trade. Apparent conspiracies are often not what they seem: both Marriott's murder in *Farewell, My Lovely* and Rusty Reagan's disappearance in *The Big Sleep* are mistakenly connected with conspiracies until Marlowe demonstrates otherwise. Marlowe breaks up the smaller rackets and reveals the true villains.

Still, the aura of intrigue remains, for the conspiracies are infused with an emotional potency which is difficult to dispel. A mystique of evil invincibility surrounds the kingpin racketeers who are not brought to justice. The vast web of connections and influence which incorporates racketeers and police, and the shadowy potency of the large operators leave the impression of mysterious wheels within wheels, of an evil force that can be pruned back, but never killed. Chandler's misanthropy takes on a larger and more sinister dimension.

Severe constraints are placed on what can be accomplished by an individual, but the basic underlying assumption remains: the individual is society's only hope. Marlowe embodies that hope in a society whose values are out of joint: 'He is the hero, he is everything', Chandler wrote in 'The Simple Art of Murder', and concluded 'If there were enough like him, I think the world would be a very safe place to live in, and yet not too dull to be worth living in' (389: 237).

Chandler's plots are unsophisticated in the use they make of the formulaic elements. In part, this is the result of his lack of distance from his material. He seems unaware of the philosophical assumptions beneath the formula and is incapable of appreciating the ironies involved. Chandler also had trouble with the mundane aspects of plotting, as one can see from his description of his method:

> With me a plot, if you could call it that, is an organic thing. It grows and often it overgrows. I am continually finding myself with scenes that I won't discard and that don't want to fit in. So that my plot problem invariably ends up as a desperate attempt to justify a lot of material that, for me at least, has come alive and insists on staying alive.   (406: 68)

Anyone who has read Chandler's novels will not doubt this

description. His plots are complicated, difficult to remember and often haphazard.

Chandler clearly regretted that he did not have 'one of these facile plotting brains, like Erle Gardner or somebody' (399: 214). But he was concerned with the time and energy needed to compensate for this failing rather than with any deleterious effects produced. He did not consider plot an important ingredient: 'The technical basis of the *Black Mask* type of story was that the scene outranked the plot in the sense that a good plot was one which made good scenes' (387: 8).

In a sense, Chandler's poor plots do not appear to matter. The descriptive portrayal of his scenes is dramatic and effective enough to sustain his books. But, when we compare Chandler's use of plot to Hammett's, it is clear that the failure does matter. Hammett's skilful manipulation of the mystery plot gives his books added depth and density. Chandler cannot use plot as a tool, for he has enough trouble getting his characters from one scene to the next.

Unlike his treatment of other elements of the hard-boiled formula, Chandler's style was carefully and self-consciously developed. His awareness of the dynamics of style, his playful approach to language and his desire to push the formula to the limits of its capacity resulted in a style of great sophistication and flexibility, especially in his early books. By using elements of the objective technique, he enhanced the impact of the colloquial style.

The cadence and pace of his prose mimic those of speech. His use of short, stripped-down sentences maintains the clipped, rushed tempo of an exciting incident being retold:

> The man in overalls gunned his motor, shot a glance up and down the alley and ran away fast in the other direction. He turned left out of the alley. We did the same. I caught a glimpse of the truck turning east on Franklin and told my driver to close in a little. (378: 56)

Occasionally, during moments of tension, Chandler breaks actions into their component movements to heighten expectation. In *The Big Sleep* one watches Marlowe as he carefully drinks whisky which might be laced with cyanide: 'I sniffed my drink delicately. It had the right smell. I rolled it around on my tongue. There was no cyanide in it. I emptied the little glass and put it down beside him and moved away' (378: 181). In *Farewell, My Lovely*, Marlowe observes Mrs Grayle as she pulls a gun on him: 'All she did was take her hand out of her bag, with a gun in it. All she did was point it at me and smile. All I did was nothing' (379: 244). The first example is closer in tone to Hammett's use of this technique than the second. It is purely mechanical; we do not know what Marlowe is thinking as he tastes the whisky. In the second, Chandler has used the repetition of 'All' to imply a reaction on Marlowe's behalf. The repeated use of the word imparts a sarcastic tone. The repetition also heightens the implicit contrast between 'All she did . . .' and 'All I did . . .', effectively underscoring Marlowe's self-restraint. The irregular construction of 'All I did was nothing' further emphasises the contrast. With such subtle alterations, Chandler bends the objective technique to the highly subjective viewpoint of Marlowe.

Chandler also uses the deadpan notation of detail in his descriptions, giving equal treatment to people and things. The discovery of the silenced radio and Jessie Florian's body is related this way:

> He reached around and shoved [the cord] into the plug in the baseboard. The light went on at once. We waited. The thing hummed for a while and then suddenly a heavy volume of sound began to pour out of the speaker. Randall jumped at the cord and yanked it loose again. The sound was snapped off sharp.
>
> When he straightened his eyes were full of light.
>
> We went swiftly into the bedroom. Mrs Jessie Pierce Florian lay diagonally across her bed, in a rumpled cotton house dress, with her head close to one end of the footboard. The corner post of the bed was smeared darkly with something the flies liked.   (379: 183)

The body and the radio are given descriptively equal treatment. The passage has all the hard, non-committal clarity of Hammett's prose. In *The Big Sleep*, when Marlowe is taken to meet General Sternwood for the first time, the eye of the narrator again notes the details of the room and the man with equal care, but here the description is no longer neutral:

> The air was thick, wet, steamy and larded with the cloying smell of tropical orchids in bloom. . . . The plants filled the place, a

forest of them, with nasty meaty leaves and stalks like the newly washed fingers of dead men. They smelled as overpowering as boiling alcohol under a blanket.

The butler did his best to get me through without being smacked in the face by the sodden leaves, and after a while we came to a clearing in the middle of the jungle, under the domed roof. Here, in a space of hexagonal flags, an old red Turkish rug was laid down and on the rug was a wheel chair, and in the wheel chair an old and obviously dying man watched us come with black eyes from which all fire had died long ago, but which still had the coal-black directness of the eyes in the portrait that hung above the mantel in the hall. The rest of his face was a leaden mask, with bloodless lips and the sharp nose and the sunken temples and the outward-turning ear-lobes of approaching dissolution.   (378: 13)

Again, Chandler has shifted subtly away from the objective technique. While it is true that people and plants are equated, it is notable that the comparison endows the plants with eerie life rather than objectifying the man: the man is dying; the plants have 'stalks like the newly washed fingers of dead men'. The descriptive phrases, lavish by the standards of the objective technique, negate the deadpan stance, but heighten the emotional impact of the comparison. The man holds centre-stage, a position emphasised by the process of gradually telescoping in on him, as well as by his physical placement under the dome. What Chandler is doing here is to modify the objective technique to elicit a sentimental response from the reader, an end which a strict use of the objective technique is designed to avoid. By borrowing from the objective technique, Chandler gains impact from the shock produced by the equation. The combination of shock with sentimentality is highly evocative emotionally, producing the heightened response which was Chandler's artistic objective.

Understatement is also employed by Chandler, as when Captain Cronjager tells Bernie Ohls, 'I love private dicks that play murders close to the waistcoat', or when Agnes answers Marlowe's query about whether he has hurt her head much by saying, 'You and every other man I ever met' (378: 106,91). Sometimes Chandler puts a sharp sting in the understatement, as with this descriptive passage: 'She shot him five times in the stomach. The bullets made no more sound than fingers going into a glove' (379: 244–5). The

metaphor is deadly in its understated way, for it implies an inti-
macy with death which most people find shocking. The implicit
equation of the commonplace act of putting on a glove with the
barbarity of sudden death adds to the shock value. One can find
further examples of understatement in Chandler's work, but they
are not a dominant element of his style.

Although Chandler uses all the stratagems of the objective technique, these are not as definitive as they are with Hammett. While
presenting the perfect vehicle for Hammett's philosophy, these
devices are not entirely appropriate to Chandler's sentimentality.
It is hardly surprising that Chandler sets out to soften the edges
of the objective technique while heightening its evocative power.

It is Chandler's poetic descriptions, wisecracks and use of hyperbole which are the hallmarks of his style and which best convey
his particular blend of humour, cynicism and sentimentality.
Chandler is a master at wrapping a vivid scenario in a mood that
makes the description take on a poetic quality. To illustrate this
Philip Durham extracts a passage and breaks it into lines that
give it the appearance of free verse. What gives Chandler's best
passages their poetic quality is his ability to provide the significant
detail that implies the rest of the scene:

> The smell of sage drifted up from a canyon and made me think
> of dead men and a moonless sky. Straggly stucco houses were
> moulded flat to the side of the hill, like bas-reliefs. Then there
> were no more houses, just the still dark foothills with an early
> star or two above them. . . .   (379: 128)

The inability of the houses to provide companionship for Marlowe,
and hence their apparent lifelessness, is underscored by 'like bas-
reliefs'. 'Then there were no more houses', and Marlowe's distance
from humanity and comfort is further emphasised. Chandler's
awareness of pace and sound is keen: there is a predominance of
long (especially *s*) sounds, which gives the passage a slow, almost
lullaby pace, but which also prepare the reader for something
sinister. Chandler's ability to 'write one tenth and imply the rest'
is beautifully illustrated by the two-line summary of Marlowe's
reaction to Anne Riordan's home: 'It was a nice room. It would
be a nice room to wear slippers in' (379: 165).

Chandler does his descriptions of setting so well that the city
and its buildings become an important force within the story. As

Philip Durham has pointed out, the outside of a house introduces the reader to the kind of people he is going to meet inside, while the interior gives him more explicit information about those people. But Chandler's descriptions do more than this: they breathe life into the characters and endow them with an intensity and vitality that is missing from the way the characters themselves are portrayed – perhaps this is a further result of Chandler's misanthropy. In *Farewell, My Lovely*, we are told that Amthor has 'eyes without expression, without soul, eyes that could watch lions tear a man to pieces and never change' (379: 131), but it is Chandler's description of the room in which Amthor works that has not only prepared us for such a man, but also has conveyed the danger he poses and made us shudder at his cold-bloodedness:

> It was octagonal, draped in black velvet from floor to ceiling, with a high remote black ceiling that may have been of velvet too. In the middle of a coal-black lustreless rug stood an octagonal white table, just large enough for two pairs of elbows and in the middle of it a milk-white globe on a black stand. The light came from this. How, I couldn't see. On either side of the table there was a white octagonal stool which was a smaller edition of the table. Over against one wall there was one more such stool. There were no windows. There was nothing else in the room, nothing at all. On the walls there was not even a light fixture. If there were other doors, I didn't see them. I looked back at the one by which I had come in. I couldn't see that either. (379: 130)

The description of the room has made us feel Amthor's impact far more intensely than the description of the man himself. This is also true of the description of the greenhouse quoted earlier: it is the claustrophobic, funebrial aura of the greenhouse which makes the general's approaching dissolution palpable. In both instances, character and setting are linked in an almost Dickensian manner.

Chandler's use of hyperbolic metaphor, another form of condensation, shifts the tone from the delicate blending of mood and scene to a brash humour: 'She was as cute as a washtub' or 'he looked about as inconspicuous as a tarantula on a slice of angel food' (379: 30,7). Sometimes he overdoes it: 'The purring voice was now as false as an usherette's eyelashes and as slippery as a watermelon seed' (378: 170). Here the two similes do not work well together. Often the hyperbole shades off into wisecrack, creating a tough humour that goes a long way toward hiding the sentimentality: 'My God, you big dark handsome brute! I ought to throw a Buick at you', Mrs Reagan tells Marlowe (378: 24). 'It was a blonde', Marlowe says of Mrs Grayle, 'A blonde to make a bishop kick a hole in a stained-glass window' (379: 84).

At his best, Chandler is able to evoke a complex of association and emotion from a simple juxtaposition of 'is' and 'ought' or 'seemed' and 'was': 'I needed a drink, I needed a lot of life insurance, I needed a vacation, I needed a home in the country. What I had was a coat, a hat, and a gun. I put them on and went out of the room' (379: 207). This kind of juxtaposition, with its humorous hyperbole, blends the nostalgia with the tough cynicism. This is essential if Chandler is to wrap his sentimentality in the cloak of realism. Sometimes the sentimentality breaks through, however, as in this passage from *The Big Sleep:* 'There was a problem laid out on the board, a six-mover. I couldn't solve it, like a lot of my problems. I reached down and moved a knight, then pulled my hat and coat off and threw them somewhere' (378: 150–1). The chess metaphor is amplified a page later: 'The move with the knight was wrong. I put it back where I had moved it from. Knights had no meaning in this game. It wasn't a game for knights' (378: 152–3). The nostalgia and romanticism tinged with bitterness are quite plain.

Chandler's style, with its shifts from cynicism to nostalgia, boastfulness to self-castigation, bitterness to resignation, sentimentality to toughness, is essentially the voice of Marlowe. It is the complexity and ambiguities of the style which define Marlowe as an interesting and complex character. This is especially true in the early books. Here the style acts as counterpoint to the action. Marlowe acts like a hard-boiled dick. He talks tough. But the voice of the narrator betrays to us his loneliness, his hopes and fears. In later works, Chandler attempted to develop the character of Marlowe more directly and this balance was lost. As James Whitfield Thomson points out, 'Once Chandler began to place more emphasis on Marlowe's emotional life and the protagonist began to question his own motivations for action, then Marlowe became a much different kind of hero' (420: 157). Chandler began to use the more striking elements of his style with acute self-consciousness, and the subtle balances of tone were lost. In the end, his style descended into self-parody. But, at his best, Chandler is very good indeed.

Bibliography

The following bibliography is divided into eleven sections: 'Dime Novels, Pulps, Magazines'; 'Formula and Popular Culture'; 'Background'; 'The Publishing-Industry and Best-Sellers'; 'The Western'; 'Owen Wister'; 'Zane Grey'; 'Frederick Faust'; 'The Hard-boiled Detective Novel'; 'Dashiell Hammett'; and 'Raymond Chandler'. Works which are primarily of interest in relation to an individual author will be found in the section dealing with that author. More general works of criticism dealing with the Western and hard-boiled detective novel are categorised separately.

DIME NOVELS, PULPS, MAGAZINES

1. Bosworth, Allan R., 'The Golden Age of Pulps', *Atlantic Monthly*, ccviii (July 1961) 57–60.
2. Dredd, Firmin, 'The Extinction of the Dime Novel', *Bookman*, xi (Mar 1900) 46–8.
3. Goulart, Ron, *Cheap Thrills: An Informal History of the Pulp Magazines* (New Rochelle, NY: Arlington House, 1972).
4. Greene, Thomas P., *America's Heroes: The Changing Models of Success in American Magazines* (New York: Oxford University Press, 1970).
5. Gruber, Frank, *The Pulp Jungle* (Los Angeles: Sherbourne Press, 1967).
6. Harvey, Charles M., 'The Dime Novel in American Life', *Atlantic*, c (July 1907) 37–45.
7. Mott, Frank Luther, *A History of American Magazines* (Cambridge, Mass.: Belknap Press of Harvard University Press) iii: *1865–1885* (1957), iv: *1885–1905* (1957) and v: *1905–1930* (1978).
8. Noel, Mary, *Villains Galore . . . The Heyday of the Popular Story Weekly* (New York: Macmillan, 1954).
9. Pearson, Edmund, *Dime Novels or, Following an Old Trail in Popular Literature* (Port Washington, NY: Kennikat Press, 1929).
10. Peterson, Theodore, *Magazines in the Twentieth Century* (Urbana: University of Illinois Press, 1964).
11. Reynolds, Quentin, *The Fiction Factory or From Pulp Row to Quality Street* (New York: Random House, 1955).

FORMULA AND POPULAR CULTURE

12. Austin, James C., 'Popular Literature in America', in James C. Austin and Donald A. Koch (eds), *Popular Literature in America: A Symposium in Honor of Lyon N. Richardson* (Bowling Green, Ohio: Popular Press, 1972).
13. Bigsby, C. W. E. (ed.), *Approaches to Popular Culture* ([London]: Edward Arnold, 1976).
14. Cawelti, John G., *Adventure, Mystery and Romance: Formula Stories as Art and Popular Culture* (Chicago: University of Chicago, 1976).
15. Cawelti, John G., 'The Concept of Formula in the Study of Popular Literature', *Journal of Popular Culture*, III, 3 (Winter 1969) 381–90.
16. Cawelti, John G., 'Notes toward an Aesthetics of Popular Culture', *Journal of Popular Culture*, V, 2 (Fall 1971) 255–67.
17. Feldman, David N., 'Formalism and Popular Culture, or How I Cracked the Case of the Blonde Bonanza', in Michael T. Marsden (comp.), *Proceedings of the Fifth National Convention of the Popular Culture Association*, St Louis, Missouri, 20–2 Mar 1975 (1975) pp. 1244–60.
18. Fine, Gary A., 'Popular Culture as Humor: The Psychology of Cultural Evaluation', in Marsden, *Proceedings of the Fifth National Convention of the Popular Culture Association* [item 17] pp. 302–6.
19. Hall, Stuart and Whannel, Paddy, *The Popular Arts* (London: Hutchinson Educational, 1964).
20. Hamilton, Cynthia S., 'American Dreaming: The American Adventure Formula in the Western and Hard-Boiled Detective Novel, 1890–1940' (unpublished D.Phil. dissertation, University of Sussex, 1984).
21. Inge, M. Thomas, *Handbook of Popular Culture*, I (Westport, Conn.: Greenwood Press, 1978).
22. Kelly, Florence Finch, 'Speeding up the Author', *Bookman*, XLII (Jan 1916) 565–9.
23. Klonsky, Milton, 'Along the Midway of Mass Culture', in William Phillips and Philip Rahv (eds), *The New Partisan Reader, 1945–1953* (New York: Harcourt, Brace 1953) pp. 344–60.
24. Mathews, Brander, 'Writing in Haste and Repenting at Leisure', *Bookman*, XLIII (Apr 1943) 135–9.
25. Madden, David, 'The Necessity for an Aesthetics of Popular Culture', *Journal of Popular Culture*, VII, 1 (Summer 1973) 1–13.
26. Mellard, James M., 'Racism, Formula, and Popular Fiction', *Journal of Popular Culture*, V, 1 (Summer 1971) 10–37.
27. Nye, Russel, *The Unembarrassed Muse: The Popular Arts in America* (New York: Dial Press, 1970).
28. Rosenberg, Bernard and White, David Manning, *Mass Culture: The Popular Arts in America* (London: Collier-Macmillan, 1957).
29. Smertenko, Johan, 'Opiates for the Masses', *Outlook and Independent*, CLIII (27 Nov 1929) 485–7, 516–18.
30. Swingewood, Alan, *The Myth of Mass Culture* (London: Macmillan, 1977).

BACKGROUND

31. Abrahams, Roger D., 'Trickster, the Outrageous Hero', in Tristram Potter Coffin (ed.), *Our Living Traditions: An Introduction to American Folklore* (New York: Basic Books, 1968) pp. 170–8.
32. *Abstract of the Fourteenth Census of the United States, 1920* (Washington, DC: Department of Commerce, Bureau of the Census, 1923).
33. Allen, Frederick Lewis, *Only Yesterday: An Informal History of the 1920's* (New York: Harper and Row, 1931).
34. Allen, Frederick Lewis, *Since Yesterday: The Nineteen Thirties in America* (London: Hamish Hamilton, 1940).
35. Anderson, Jack, 'Frederick Jackson Turner and Urbanization', *Journal of Popular Culture*, ii, 2 (Fall 1968) 292–8.
36. Bridgman, Richard, *The Colloquial Style in America* (New York: Oxford University Press, 1966).
37. Carnegie, Andrew, *The Gospel of Wealth and Other Timely Essays*, ed. Edward C. Kirkland (Cambridge, Mass.: Belknap Press of Harvard University Press, 1962).
38. Chase, Richard, *The American Novel and its Tradition* (Garden City, NY: Doubleday Anchor, 1957).
39. Cawelti, John G., *Apostles of the Self-Made Man* (Chicago: University of Chicago Press, 1965).
40. Dawson, N. P., 'The American Age of Ego', *Forum*, lxvii (Feb 1922) 95–104.
41. Dorsett, Lyle W. (ed.), *The Challenge of the City 1860–1890* (Lexington, Mass.: D. C. Heath, 1968).
42. Fiedler, Leslie A., *Love and Death in the American Novel* (New York: Dell, 1966).
43. Gerould, Katherine Fullerton, 'The Hard-Boiled Era', *Harper's*, clviii (Feb 1929) 265–74.
44. Graham, Hugh Davis, and Gurr, Ted Robert, *The History of Violence in America* (New York: Bantam, 1970).
45. Himmelfarb, Gertrude, 'Varieties of Social Darwinism', in *Victorian Minds* (London: Weidenfeld and Nicolson, 1968) pp. 314–32.
46. Hofstadter, Richard, *The Age of Reform: From Bryan to FDR* (New York: Vintage Books, 1955).
47. Hofstadter, Richard, 'Reflections on Violence in the United States', in Richard Hofstadter and Michael Wallace (eds), *American Violence: A Documentary History* (New York: Alfred A. Knopf, 1970).
48. Hofstadter, Richard, *Social Darwinism in American Thought* (Boston, Mass.: Beacon Press, 1964).
49. Jewett, Robert and John Shelton Lawrence, *The American Monomyth* (Garden City, NY: Anchor Press, 1977).
50. Kelly, Florence Finch, 'American Style in American Fiction', *Bookman*, xli (May 1915) 299–302.
51. Klapp, Orrin, 'The Clever Hero', *Journal of American Folklore*, lxvii (1954) 21–34.

52. Klapp, Orrin, 'The Folk Hero', *Journal of American Folklore*, LXII (1949) 17–25.
53. Leuchtenburg, William E., *The Perils of Prosperity, 1914–1932* (Chicago: University of Chicago Press, 1958).
54. Leuchtenbrug, William E., *Franklin D. Roosevelt and the New Deal: 1932–1940* (New York: Harper and Row, 1963).
55. Levine, Lawrence W., *Black Culture and Black Consciousness: Afro American Folk Thought from Slavery to Freedom* (New York: Oxford University Press, 1977).
56. Levinson, Edward, *I Break Strikes* (New York: Arno/New York Times, 1969).
57. Macpherson, C. B., *The Political Theory of Possessive Individualism: Hobbes to Locke* (London: Oxford University Press, 1962).
58. Mottram, Eric, 'Living Mythically: The Thirties', *Journal of American Studies*, VI, 3 (1972) 267–87.
59. Mencken, H. L., *The American Language: An Inquiry into the Development of English in the United States* (New York: Alfred A. Knopf, 1957).
60. O'Neill, William L., *Everyone was Brave: A History of Feminism in America* (Chicago: Quadrangle Books, 1971).
61. Phillips, Cabell, *From the Crash to the Blitz, 1929–1939* (New York: New York Times, 1969).
62. Shearman, Thomas G., 'The Owners of the United States', *Forum*, VIII (Nov 1889) 262–73.
63. Strong, Josiah, *Our Country*, ed. Jurgen Herbst (Cambridge, Mass.: Belknap Press of Harvard University Press, 1963).
64. Thorp, Margaret Farrand, *America at the Movies* (New Haven, Conn.: Yale University Press, 1939).
65. Weber, Max, *The Protestant Ethic and the Spirit of Capitalism* (New York: Charles Scribner's Sons, 1958).
66. Wiebe, Robert H., *The Search for Order 1877–1920* (London: Macmillan, 1967).
67. White, David Manning, and Abel, Robert H., *The Funnies, An American Idiom* (London: Collier-Macmillan, 1963).
68. Wilkinson, Rupert, 'On the Toughness of the "Tough Guy"', *Encounter*, XLVI, 2 (Feb 1976) 35–42.
69. Wyllie, Irvin G., *The Self-Made Man in America: The Myth of Rags to Riches* (New York: Free Press, 1954).

THE PUBLISHING-INDUSTRY AND BEST-SELLERS

70. Adamic, Lois, 'What the Proletariat Reads', *Saturday Review*, XI, 20 (1 Dec 1934) 321–2.
71. Aley, Maxwell, 'How Large is our Book Reading Public?', *Publishers' Weekly*, CXIX (6 June 1931) 2683–91.
72. Allen, Frederick Lewis, 'Best Sellers 1900–1935', *Saturday Review*, XIII (7 Dec 1935) 3–4, 20, 24, 26.

73. Berelson, Bernard, 'Who Reads What Books and Why?', in Rosenberg and White, *Mass Culture* [item 28] pp. 119–25.
74. 'The Best Seller System', *Publishers' Weekly*, cxxxvi (9 Dec 1939) 2135.
75. Cantwell, Robert, 'What the Working Class Reads', *New Republic*, lxxxiii (17 July 1935) 274–6.
76. Cheney, O. H., *Economic Survey of the Book Industry, 1930–1931* (New York: National Association of Book Publishers, 1931).
77. Ford, Margaret P., 'A Microcosm of Popular Taste: Cleveland, Ohio', in Austin and Koch, *Popular Literature in America* [item 12] pp. 15–29.
78. Greene, Suzanne Ellery, *Books for Pleasure: Popular Fiction 1914–1945* (Bowling Green, Ohio: Popular Press, 1974).
79. Hackett, Alice Payne, *Fifty Years of Best Sellers, 1895–1945* (New York: R. R. Bowker, 1945).
80. Hackett, Alice Payne, *Seventy Years of Best Sellers, 1895–1965* (New York: R. R. Bowker, 1965).
81. Hart, Irving Harlow, 'Best Sellers in Fiction during the First Quarter of the Twentieth Century', *Publishers' Weekly*, cvii (14 Feb 1925) 525–7.
82. Hart, Irving Harlow, 'One Hundred Leading Authors of Best Sellers in Fiction from 1895–1944', *Publishers' Weekly*, cxlix, 3 (19 Jan 1946) 285–90.
83. Hart, James D., *The Popular Book: A History of America's Literary Taste* (New York: Oxford University Press, 1950).
84. Jenkins, Herbert F., 'The Nation's Appetite for Fiction', *Publishers' Weekly*, c (24 Sep 1921) 973–5.
85. Madison, Charles A., *Book Publishing in America* (New York: McGraw-Hill, 1966).
86. Mott, Frank Luther, *Golden Multitudes: The Story of Best Sellers in the United States* (New York: R. R. Bowker, 1960).
87. 'Near Best Sellers', *Publishers' Weekly*, cxxxiii (22 Jan 1938) 310–11.
88. Nelson, James, 'Turn the Book Barometer Upside Down', *Publishers' Weekly*, cxix (3 Jan 1931) 34–5.
89. Ogden, Archibald G., 'The Book Trade in War Time', *Publishers' Weekly*, cxxxvi (8 July 1939) 94–8.
90. Sheehan, Donald, *This was Publishing: A Chronicle of the Book Trade in the Gilded Age* (Bloomington: Indiana University Press, 1952).
91. Smertenko, Johan J., 'What Makes Popularity', *Saturday Review*, v (20 Apr 1929) 918.
92. Stern, Madeleine B., *Books and Book People in Nineteenth Century America* (New York: R. R. Bowker, 1978).
93. Stevens, George, 'Lincoln's Doctor's Dog', *Saturday Review*, xvii (22 Jan 1938) 3–4, 14–19.
94. Tebbel, John, *A History of Book Publishing in the United States* (New York: R. R. Bowker), ii: *The Expansion of an Industry 1865–1919* (1975) and iii: *The Golden Age between the Wars 1920–1940* (1978).
95. Uzzell, Thomas H., 'Mob Reading: Romantic Ingredients of the Super Best Seller', *Saturday Review*, xvii (20 Nov 1937) 3–4, 16, 18.

THE WESTERN

96. Agnew, Seth M., 'Destry Goes on Riding – or – Working the Six-Gun Lode', *Publishers' Weekly*, CLXII (23 Aug 1952) 746–51.
97. Arbuckle, Donald Redmond, 'Popular Western: The History of a Commercial Literary Formula' (unpublished Ph.D. dissertation, University of Pennsylvania, 1977).
98. Barker, Warren J., 'The Stereotyped Western Story', *Psychoanalytic Quarterly*, XXIV (1955) 270–80.
99. Barsness, John Alton, 'The Breaking of the Myth: A Study of Cultural Implications in the Development of the Western Novel in the Twentieth Century' (unpublished Ph.D. dissertation, University of Minnesota, 1966).
100. Boatright, Mody C., 'The Formula in Cowboy Fiction and Drama', *Western Folklore*, XXVIII (Apr 1969) 136–45.
101. Cawelti, John G., 'Promelga to the Western', in Gerald W. Haslam (ed.), *Western Writing: Famous Western Authors Explain their Craft* (Albuquerque: University of New Mexico Press, 1974) pp. 116–28.
102. Cawelti, John G., *The Six-Gun Mystique* (Bowling Green, Ohio: Popular Press, n.d.).
103. Clements, William M., 'Savage, Pastoral, Civilized: An Ecology Typology of American Frontier Heroes', *Journal of Popular Culture*, VIII (Fall 1974) 254–66.
104. Crowell, Chester T., 'Cowboys', *American Mercury*, IX (1926) 162–9.
105. Cunliffe, Marcus, 'The Two or More Worlds of Willa Cather', in Bernice Slote and Virginia Faulkner (eds), *The Art of Willa Cather* (Lincoln, Nebr.: University of Nebraska Press, 1974) pp. 21–42.
106. Cunningham, E., 'Better Westerns', *Writer*, LIII (Apr 1940) 105–8.
107. Davis, David B., 'Ten Gallon Hero', *American Quarterly*, VI (Summer 1954) 111–25.
108. Dessain, Kenneth, 'Once in the Saddle: The Memory and Romance of the Trail Driving Cowboy', *Journal of Popular Culture*, IV, 2 (Fall 1970) 464–96.
109. DeVoto, Bernard, 'Phaethon on Gunsmoke Trail', *Harper's*, CCIX (Dec 1954) 10–11, 14, 16.
110. Dobie, Frank J., 'The Writer and his Region' in Haslam, *Western Writing* [item 101] pp. 16–24.
111. Durham, Philip, 'The Cowboy and the Myth Makers', *Journal of Popular Culture*, I, 1 (Summer 1967) 58–62.
112. Etulain, Richard, 'The Historical Development of the Western', *Journal of Popular Culture*, VII, 3 (Winter 1973) 717–26.
113. Etulain, Richard, 'Origins of the Western', *Journal of Popular Culture*, v, 4 (Spring 1972) 799–805.
114. Fender, Stephen, 'The Western and the Contemporary', *Journal of American Studies*, VI (Apr 1972) 97–108.
115. Fiedler, Leslie, 'Montana; or the End of Jean-Jacques Rousseau', in *An End to Innocence: Essays on Culture and Politics*, 2nd edn (New York: Stein and Day, 1972).

116. Fiedler, Leslie, *The Return of the Vanishing American* (London: Jonathan Cape, 1968).
117. Fisher, Vardis, 'The Novelist and his Background', in Haslam, *Western Writing* [item 101] pp. 59–68.
118. Fishwick, Marshall W., 'The Cowboy: America's Contribution to the World's Mythology', *Western Folklore*, xi (Apr 1952) 77–92.
119. Folsom, James K., *The American Western Novel* (New Haven, Conn.: College and University Press Services, 1966).
120. Fussell, Edwin, *Frontier: American Literature and the American West* (Princeton, NJ: Princeton University Press, 1965).
121. Gardner, Erle Stanley, 'My Stories of the Wild West', *Atlantic*, ccxviii (July 1966) 60–2.
122. Gooden, A. H., 'These Westerns we Write', *Writer*, lix (Nov 1946) 364–6.
123. Hoig, Stan, *The Humor of the American Cowboy* (Caldwell, Ida.: Caxton Press, 1958).
124. Hopkins, T. J., 'Writing the Western', *Writer*, lx (Dec 1947) 436–8.
125. Hutchinson, W. H., 'The "Western Story" as Literature', in Haslam, *Western Writing* [item 101] pp. 109–15.
126. 'Inside Views of Fiction: vi Novels of Western Life', *Bookman*, xxxii (Sep 1910) 20–1.
127. Jordan, Philip D., 'Humor of the Backwoods, 1820–1840', *Mississippi Valley Historical Review*, xxv (1938) 25–38.
128. Ketterer, David, *New Worlds for Old: The Apocalyptic Imagination, Science Fiction, and American Literature* (Garden City, NY: Doubleday Anchor, 1974).
129. Karolides, Nicholas J., *The Pioneer in the American Novel 1900–1950* (Norman: University of Oklahoma Press, 1967).
130. Lavender, David, 'The Petrified West and the Writer', *American Scholar*, xxxvii (1968) 293–306.
131. Lee, Robert Edson, *From West to East: Studies in the Literature of the American West* (Urbana: University of Illinois Press, 1966).
132. Linden, George W., 'The Cowboy: From High Noon to Midnight', in Austin and Koch, *Popular Literature in America* [item 12] pp. 78–89.
133. 'Magazine West', *Atlantic Monthly*, ci (Feb 1908) 279–81.
134. Milton, John R., 'The Novel in the American West', in Haslam, *Western Writings* [item 101] pp. 69–89.
135. Milton, John R., *The Novel of the American West* (Lincoln, Nebr.: University of Nebraska Press, 1980).
136. Munden, Kenneth J., MD, 'A Contribution to the Psychological Understanding of the Cowboy and his Myth', *American Imago*, xv (Summer 1958) 103–48.
137. Norris, Frank, 'A Neglected Epic', in *The Responsibilities of the Novelist* (London: Grant Richards, 1903) pp. 59–66.
138. Norris, Frank, 'The Frontier Gone at Last', in *The Responsibilities of the Novelist* [item 137] pp. 69–81.
139. Nussbaum, Martin, 'Sociological Symbolism of the Adult Western', *Social Forces*, xxxix (Oct 1960) 25–8.

140. 'Our Wild West as a Literary Field', *Literary Digest*, LXXXII (26 July 1924) 47.
141. Schein, Harry, 'The Olympian Cowboy', *American Scholar*, XXIV (1955) 309–20.
142. Schroeder, Fred E. H., 'The Development of the Super-ego on the American Frontier', *Soundings*, LVII, 189–205.
143. Sisk, John P., 'The Western Hero', *Commonwealth*, LXVI (12 July 1957) 367–9.
144. Smith, Henry Nash, *Virgin Land: The American West as Symbol and Myth* (Cambridge, Mass.: Harvard University Press, 1973).
145. Steckmesser, Kent Ladd, *The Western Hero in History and Legend* (Norman: University of Oklahoma Press, 1965).
146. Stegner, Wallace, 'On the Writing of History', in Haslam, *Western Writing* [item 101] pp. 25–39.
147. Stewart, George R., 'The Regional Approach to Literature', in Haslam, *Western Writing* [item 101] pp. 40–8.
148. Taylor, J. Golden, 'The Western Short Story' in Haslam, *Western Writing* [item 101] pp. 90–108.
149. Thompson, T., 'Strong, Silent, Stupid', *Writer*, LXVI (Sep 1953) 305–6.
150. Turner, Frederick Jackson, *The Frontier in American History*, Foreword by Ray Allen Billington (New York: Holt, Rinehart and Winston, 1965).
151. Waldmeir, J. J., 'The Cowboy, Knight, and Popular Taste', *Southern Folklore Quarterly*, XXII (Sep 1958) 113–20.
152. Walker, Don D., 'Notes toward a Literary Criticism of the Western', *Journal of Popular Culture*, VII, 3 (Winter 1973) 728–41.
153. Walle, Alf Howard, III, 'The Frontier Hero: A Static Hero in an Evolving World' (unpublished Ph.D. dissertation, State University of New York at Buffalo, 1976).
154. Webb, Walter Prescott, 'The American West: Perpetual Mirage', *Harper's*, CCXIV (May 1957) 25–31.
155. Westbrook, Max, 'The Practical Spirit: Sacrality and the American West', in Haslam, *Western Writing* [item 101] pp. 129–42.
156. Wildman, John Hazard, 'Hopalong to Heaven', *America*, XCIV (17 Mar 1956) 666–7.
157. Williams, John, 'The Western, Definition of the Myth', *Nation*, CXCIII (18 Nov 1961) 401–6.
158. Wright, Will, *Sixguns and Society: A Structural Study of the Western* (Berkeley, Calif.: University of California Press, 1975).

OWEN WISTER

159. Banks, Nancy Huston, 'Owen Wister: Author of "Red Men and White" ', *Bookman*, II (Dec 1895) 275–7.
160. Barsness, John A., 'Theodore Roosevelt as Cowboy: The Virginian as Jacksonian Man', *American Quarterly*, XXI (Fall 1969) 609–19.
161. Boatright, Mody C., 'The American Myth Rides the Range: Owen

Wister's Man on Horseback', *South West Review*, xxxvi, 3 (Summer 1951) 157–63.
162. Bode, Carl, 'Henry James and Owen Wister', *American Literature*, xxvi (May 1954) 250–2.
163. Boynton, H. W., Review of *The Virginian*, *Atlantic Monthly*, xc (Aug 1902) 277–8.
164. DeVoto, Bernard, 'The Easy Chair: Birth of an Art', *Harper's*, ccxii (Dec 1955) 8–9, 12, 14, 16.
165. Houghton, Donald E., 'Two Heroes in One: Reflections Upon the Popularity of *The Virginian*', *Journal of Popular Culture*, iv, 2 (Fall 1970) 497–506.
166. Lambert, Neal, 'The Western Writings of Owen Wister: The Conflict of East and West' (unpublished Ph.D. dissertation, University of Utah, 1966).
167. Marsh, Edward Clark, 'Representative American Story Tellers', *Bookman*, xxvii (July 1908) 458–66.
168. Mogen, David, 'Owen Wister's Cowboy Heroes', in James K. Folsom (ed.), *The Western: A Collection of Critical Essays* (Englewood Cliffs, NJ: Prentice-Hall, 1979).
169. Mather, F. J., Jr, Review of *The Virginian*, *Forum*, xxxiv (Aug 1902) 323–4.
170. Monroe, Lucy. ' "The Virginian" Wins East and West', *Critic*, xli (Oct 1902) 358–9.
171. Obituary on Owen Wister, *Publishers' Weekly*, cxxxiv (30 July 1938) 299.
172. Review of *Lin McLean*, *Bookman*, vii (May 1898) 254.
173. Review of *Lin McLean*, *Nation*, lxvi (26 May 1898) 407.
174. Review of *The Virginian*, *Dial*, xxxii (1 June 1902) 39.
175. Review of *The Virginian*, *New York Times*, (21 June 1902) p. 426.
176. Review of *The Virginian*, *Sewanee Review*, x (Oct 1902) 504–5.
177. Ritchie, Robert Welles, 'Some Scenes from *The Virginian*', *Bookman*, xliv (Jan 1917) 460–3.
178. Solensten, John M., 'Richard Harding Davis, Owen Wister, and *The Virginian*: Unpublished Letters and a Commentary', *American Literary Realism*, v (Spring 1972) 122–33.
179. Stark, Beverly, Review of *The Virginian*, *Bookman*, xv (Aug 1902) 569.
180. Walker, Don D., 'Wister, Roosevelt, and James: A Note on the Western', *American Quarterly*, xii, 3 (Fall 1960) 358–66.
181. White, G. Edward, *The Eastern Establishment and the Western Experience: The West of Frederic Remington, Theodore Roosevelt, and Owen Wister* (New Haven, Conn.: Yale University Press, 1968).
182. Wister, Fanny Kemble, 'Letters of Owen Wister, Author of *The Virginian*', *The Pennsylvania Magazine of History and Biography*, lxxxiii, 1 (Jan 1959) 3–28.
183. Wister, Fanny Kemble (ed.), *Owen Wister out West: His Journals and Letters* (Chicago: University of Chicago Press, 1958).
184. Wister, Fanny Kemble, 'Owen Wister's West', *Atlantic*, cxcv, 5 (May 1955) 29–35; 6 (June 1955) 55–7.

185. Wister, Owen, 'Ancient Grudge', *American Magazine*, LXXXVI (Nov 1918) 14–15, 88, 90, 92, 94.
186. Wister, Owen, 'Don't Squander the Past', *American Magazine*, XCII (July 1921) 42–3, 126.
187. Wister, Owen, 'The Evolution of the Cowpuncher', *Harper's* XCI (Sep 1894) 602–17.
188. Wister, Owen, 'In Homage to Mark Twain', *Harper's*, C (Oct 1935) 547–56.
189. Wister, Owen, *The Jimmyjohn Boss and Other Stories*, The American Short Stories Series, XXXII (New York: Garrett Press, 1969).
190. Wister, Owen, *Lin McLean* (New York: A. L. Burt, n.d.).
191. Wister, Owen, 'Old Yellowstone Days', *Harper's*, CLXXII (Mar 1936) 471–80.
192. Wister, Owen, 'Quack Novels and Democracy', *Atlantic Monthly*, CXV (June 1915) 721–34.
193. Wister Owen, *Red Men and White* (London: Osgood, McIlvaine, 1896).
194. Wister, Owen, *Roosevelt: The Story of a Friendship 1880–1919* (New York: Macmillan, 1930).
195. Wister, Owen, 'Shall we Let the Cuckoos Crowd us out of our Nests?', *American Magazine*, XCI (Mar 1921) 47.
196. Wister, Owen, 'Strictly Hereditary', *Musical Quarterly*, XXII, 1 (Jan 1936) 1–7.
197. Wister, Owen, *The Virginian: A Horseman of the Plains* (London: Macmillan, 1944).
198. Wister, Owen, *When West was West* (London: Macmillan, 1928).

ZANE GREY

199. Cooper, Frederic Taber, 'The Value of Sincerity and Some Recent Books', *Bookman*, XXXII (Nov 1910) 295.
200. Goble, Danny G., 'Zane Grey's West: An Intellectual Reaction' (unpublished MA thesis, University of Oklahoma, 1969).
201. Grey, Zane, *Betty Zane* (New York: Black's Readers Service, n.d.).
202. Grey, Zane, *The Border Legion* (New York: Black's Readers Service, n.d.).
203. Grey, Zane, 'Breaking Through: The Story of My Own Life', *American Magazine*, XCVIII (July 1924) 11–13, 76, 78, 80.
204. Grey, Zane, *The Code of the West* (New York: Black's Readers Service, n.d.).
205. Grey, Zane, 'Death Valley', *Harper's*, CXL (May 1920) 758–70.
206. Grey, Zane, *The Desert of Wheat* (New York: Black's Readers Service, n.d.).
207. Grey, Zane, *The Heritage of the Desert* (New York: Black's Readers Service, n.d.).
208. Grey, Zane, *Knights of the Range* (New York: Black's Readers Service, n.d.).

209. Grey, Zane, *The Light of the Western Stars* (New York: Black's Readers Service, n.d.).
210. Grey, Zane, *The Lone Star Ranger* (New York: Black's Readers Service, n.d.).
211. Grey, Zane, *Majesty's Rancho* (New York: Black's Readers Service, n.d.).
212. Grey, Zane, *Man of the Forest* (New York: Black's Readers Service, n.d.).
213. Grey, Zane, 'The Man who Influenced me Most', *American Magazine*, cii (Aug 1926) 52–5, 130–6.
214. Grey, Zane, *The Mysterious Rider* (New York: Black's Readers Service, n.d.).
215. Grey,Zane, *The Rainbow Trail* (New York: Black's Readers Service, n.d.).
216. Grey, Zane, *Riders of the Purple Sage* (New York; Black's Readers Service, n.d.).
217. Grey, Zane, *Stairs of Sand* (New York: Black's Readers Service, n.d.).
218. Grey, Zane, *To the Last Man* (New York: Black's Readers Service, n.d.).
219. Grey, Zane, *The Trail Driver* (New York: Black's Readers Service, n.d.).
220. Grey, Zane, *Twin Sombreros* (New York: Black's Readers Service, n.d.).
221. Grey, Zane, *The U. P. Trail* (New York: Black's Readers Service n.d.).
222. Grey, Zane, *Wanderer of the Wasteland* (London: Hodder and Stoughton, 1951).
223. Grey, Zane, *Western Union* (New York: Black's Readers Service, n.d.).
224. Grey, Zane, 'What the Desert Means to Me', *American Magazine*, xcviii (Nov 1924) 5–8, 72, 74, 76, 78.
225. Grey, Zane, *Wildfire* (New York: Black's Readers Service, n.d.).
226. Gruber, Frank, *Zane Grey: A Biography* (New York: World Publishing, 1970).
227. 'Heroes Ride on Forever', *Time*, lv (19 June 1950) 51–3.
228. Jackson, Carlton, *Zane Grey* (New York; Twayne, 1973).
229. Karr, Jean, *Zane Grey: Man of the West* (Kingswood, Surrey: World's Work, 1951).
230. 'New York's Awe at the Best Seller', *Literary Digest*, lxxvi (10 Mar 1923) 30–1.
231. Patrick, Arnold, 'Getting into Six Figures', *Bookman*, lx (Dec 1924) 424–9.
232. Rascoe, Burton, 'Opie Read and Zane Grey', *Saturday Review*, xxi (11 Nov 1939) 8.
233. Rascoe, Burton, Review of *Wanderer of the Wasteland*, *New York Tribune*, 21 Jan 1923, p. 19.
234. Review of *Heritage of the Desert*, *New York Times*, 8 Oct 1910, 558.
235. Review of *Wanderer of the Wasteland*, *New York Times*, Jan 1923, 19.

236. Review of *Wanderer of the Wasteland, Time*; repr. in *Time Capsules –
     1923: A History of the Year Condensed from the Pages of 'Time'* (New
     York: Time, n.d.) p. 212.
237. Ronald, Ann, *Zane Grey*, Boise State University Western Writers
     Series, no. 17 (Boise, Ida., 1975).
238. Schneider, Norris F., *Zane Grey: 'The Man whose Books Made the
     West Famous'* (Zanesville, Ohio: published by author, 1967).
239. Steele, Robert S., and Swinney, Susan V., 'Zane Grey, Carl Jung,
     and the Journey of the Hero', *Journal of Analytical Psychology*, XXIII,
     1 (Jan 1978) 63–89.
240. Topping, Gary, 'Zane Grey's West', *Journal of Popular Culture*, VII
     (Winter 1973) 681–9.
241. Topping, Gary Rex, 'Zane Grey's West: Essays in Intellectual
     History and Criticism' (unpublished Ph. D. dissertation, Univer-
     sity of Utah, 1977).
242. Wheeler, Joseph Lawrence, 'Zane Grey's Impact on American Life
     and Letters: A Study in the Popular Novel' (unpublished Ph. D.
     dissertation, George Peabody College for Teachers, 1975).
243. Whipple, T. K., 'American Sagas', *Saturday Review*, I (7 Feb 1925)
     505–6.
244. *Zane Grey: The Man and his Work* (New York: Harper, 1928).
245. 'Zane Grey' (Obituary), *New York Times*, 24 Oct 1939, p. 23.
246. 'Zane Grey' (Obituary), *Publishers' Weekly*, CXXXVI (28 Oct 1939)
     1698.
247. 'Zane Grey: Portrait', *Bookman*, LX (Nov 1924) 373–4.
248. 'Zane Grey: Portrait', *Publishers' Weekly*, CXVII (17 May 1930) 2535.

                          FREDERICK FAUST

249. Bacon, Leonard, 'Appreciation', *Saturday Review*, XXVII (27 May
     1944) 28–9.
250. Bacon, Martha, 'Destry and Dionysus', *Atlantic Monthly*, CXCVI
     (July 1955) 72–4.
251. Brand, Max, *Border Guns* (London: Hodder and Stoughton, 1958).
252. Brand, Max, *Brothers of the Trail* (London: Panther, 1964).
253. Brand, Max, *Destry Rides Again* (London: Pan, 1956).
254. Brand, Max, *Fire-Brain* (London: Hodder and Stoughton, 1960).
255. Brand, Max, *The Garden of Eden* (London: Hodder and Stoughton,
     1965).
256. Brand, Max, *Gunman's Gold* (London: Panther, 1964).
257. Brand, Max, *Happy Jack* (New York: Warner Paperback Library,
     1974).
258. Brand, Max, *The Happy Valley* (New York: Warner Paperback
     Library, 1972).
259. Brand, Max, *Larramee's Ranch* (London: Hodder and Stoughton,
     1967).
260. Brand, Max, *Marbleface* (New York: Warner Paperback Library,
     1972).

261.   Brand, Max, *Mountain Riders* (New York: Warner Paperback Library, 1972).
262.   Brand, Max, *Singing Guns* (London: Corgi, 1968).
263.   Brand, Max, *South of Rio Grande* (London: White Lion, 1973).
264.   Brand, Max, *Speedy* (London: Hodder and Stoughton, 1962).
265.   Brand, Max, *The Tenderfoot* (London: Remploy Reprint Editions, 1973).
266.   Brand, Max, *Trailin'* (New York: Warner Paperback Library, 1975).
267.   Brand, Max, *Tragedy Trail* (London: Hodder Paperbacks, 1968).
268.   Brand, Max, *The Untamed* (London: G. P. Putnam's Sons, 1925).
269.   Brand, Max, *Valley Vultures* (New York: Warner Paperback Library, 1972).
270.   Dodd, Edward H., 'Twenty-Five Million Words', *Publishers' Weekly*, cxxxiii (26 Mar 1938) 1358–60.
271.   Easton, Robert, *Max Brand: The Big 'Westerner'* (Norman: (University of Oklahoma Press, 1970).
272.   Evans, Evan, *Montana Rides!* (Harmondsworth, Middx: Penguin 1957).
273.   'Frederick Faust, et al.', *Time*, xliii (29 May 1944) 44.
274.   'Greatest Pulpist', *Time*, lx (25 Mar 1952) 78–9.
275.   Richardson, Darrell C., *Max Brand: The Man and his Work* (Los Angeles: Fantasy Publishing, 1952).
276.   Schoolcraft, John (ed.), *The Notebooks and Poems of 'Max Brand'* (New York: Dodd, Mead, 1957).

THE HARD-BOILED DETECTIVE NOVEL

277.   Auden, W. H., 'The Guilty Vicarage', *The Dyer's Hand* (London: Faber and Faber, 1963) pp. 146–58.
278.   Aydelotte, William O., 'The Detective Story as Historical Source', in Francis M. Nevins (ed.), *The Mystery Writer's Art* (Bowling Green, Ohio: Popular Press, 1970) pp. 306–25.
279.   Barzun, Jacques, 'Detection and the Literary Art', *New Republic*, cxliv (24 Apr 1961) 17–20.
280.   Becker, Jens Peter, 'The Mean Streets of Europe: The Influence of the American Hard-Boiled School on European Detective Fiction', in C. W. E. Bigsby (ed.), *Superculture: American Popular Culture and Europe* (London: Paul Elek, 1975) pp. 152–9.
281.   Borneman, Ernest, 'Black Mask', *Go*, Feb–Mar 1952, pp. 63–6.
282.   Byrd, Max, 'The Detective Detected: From Sophocles to Ross MacDonald', *Yale Review*, lxiv (Oct 1974) 72–83.
283.   Calder, Jenni, *There Must Be a Lone Ranger* (London: Hamish Hamilton, 1974).
284.   Charland, Maurice, 'The Private Eye: From Print to Television', *Journal of Popular Culture*, xii, 2 (Fall 1979) 210–16.
285.   Cohen, Ralph, 'Private Eyes and Public Critics', *Partisan Review*, xxiv (Spring 1957) 235–43.

286. Cook, Alistair, 'Epitaph for a Tough Guy', *Atlantic Monthly*, cxcix (May 1957) 31–5.
287. Crider, Allen Billy, 'The Private-Eye Hero: A Study of the Novels of Dashiell Hammett, Raymond Chandler, and Ross MacDonald' (unpublished Ph. D. dissertation, University of Texas at Austin, 1972).
288. Crider, Allen Billy, 'Race Williams – Private Investigator', in Larry N. Landrum, Pat Browne and Ray B. Browne (eds), *Dimensions of Detective Fiction* ([Bowling Green, Ohio]: Popular Press, 1976) pp. 110–13.
289. DeVoto, Bernard, 'The Easy Chair', *Harper's*, cxc (Dec 1944) 34–37.
290. Durham, Philip, 'The Black Mask School', in David Madden (ed.), *Tough Guy Writers of the Thirties* (Carbondale: Southern Illinois University Press; London: Feffer and Simon, 1968) pp. 51–79.
291. Durham, Philip, 'The Objective Treatment of the "Hard-Boiled" Hero in American Fiction: A Study in the Frontier Background of Modern American Literature' (unpublished Ph. D. dissertation, Northwestern University, 1949).
292. Gardner, Erle Stanley, 'The Case of the Early Beginning', in Howard Haycraft (ed.), *The Art of the Mystery Story* (New York: Grossett and Dunlap, 1946) pp. 203–7.
293. Gardner, Erle Stanley, 'Getting away with Murder', *Atlantic Monthly*, ccxv, 1 (Jan 1965) 72–5.
294. Goulart, Ron, Introduction to Goulart (ed.), *The Hard-Boiled Dicks: An Anthology of Detective Fiction from the American Pulp Magazines* (London: T. V. Boardman, 1967).
295. Grebstein, Sheldon Norman, 'The Tough Hemingway and his Hard-Boiled Children', in Madden, *Tough Guy Writers of the Thirties* [item 290] pp. 19–41.
296. Grella, George, 'Murder and the Mean Streets: The Hard-Boiled Detective Novel', *Contempora*, i (Mar 1970) 6–15.
297. Gruber, Frank, 'The Life and Times of the Pulp Story', *Brass Knuckles: The Oliver Quade, Human Encyclopedia Stories* (Los Angeles: Sherbourne Press, 1966).
298. Harper, Ralph, *The World of the Thriller* (Baltimore: John Hopkins University Press, 1974).
299. Holman, C. Hugh, 'Detective Fiction as American Realism', in Austin and Koch, *Popular Literature in America* [item 12] pp. 30–41.
300. Jones, Archie H., 'Cops, Robbers, Heros and Antiheroines: The American Need to Create', *Journal of Popular Culture*, i, 2 (1967) 114–27.
301. Kenny, William Patrick, 'The Dashiell Hammett Tradition and the Modern Detective Novel' (unpublished Ph. D. dissertation, University of Michigan, 1964).
302. Lambert, Gavin, *The Dangerous Edge* (London: Barrie and Jenkins, 1975).
303. Lawrence, D. H., 'Fenimore Cooper's Leatherstocking Novels', *Studies in Classic American Literature* (Harmondsworth, Middx: Penguin, 1977) pp. 52–69.

304. MacDonald, Ross, 'The Writer as Detective Hero', in Nevins, *The Mystery Writer's Art* [item 278] pp. 295–305.
305. Margolies, Edward, 'The American Detective Thriller and the Idea of Society', *Costerus*, VI (1962) 93–8.
306. Murch, A. E., *The Development of the Detective Novel* (London: Peter Owen, 1968).
307. Nye,Russel, 'Murderers and Detectives', in *The Unembarrassed Muse* [item 27] pp. 244–69.
308. O'Brien, Geoffrey, *Hardboiled America: The Lurid Years of Paperbacks* (New York: Van Nostrand Reinhold 1981).
309. Orel, Harold, 'The American Detective Hero', *Journal of Popular Culture*, II, 3 (Winter 1968) 395–403.
310. Palmer, Jerry, *Thrillers: Genesis and Structure of a Popular Genre* (London: Edward Arnold, 1978).
311. Parker, Robert Brown, 'The Violent Hero, Wilderness Heritage and Urban Reality: A Study of the Private-Eye in the Novels of Dashiell Hammett, Raymond Chandler, and Ross MacDonald' (unpublished Ph.D. dissertation, Boston University, 1970).
312. Parkes, Henry Bamford, 'The Metamorphosis of Leatherstocking', in Philip Rahv, *Literature in America* (Cleveland, Ohio: Meridian Books, 1962) pp. 431–45.
313. Paterson, John, 'A Cosmic View of the Private-Eye', *Saturday Review*, XLV (22 Aug 1953) 7–8, 31–3.
314. Ponder, Anne Eleanor, 'The American Detective Form in Novels and Film, 1929–1947' (unpublished Ph. D. dissertation, University of North Carolina at Chapel Hill, 1979).
315. Powers, Richard G., 'J. Edgar Hoover and the Detective Hero', in Landrum *et al.*, *Dimensions of Detective Fiction* [item 288] pp. 203–27.
316. Praz, Mario, 'Hemingway in Italy', *Partisan Review*, XV (Oct 1948) 1086–1100.
317. Reilly, John M., 'The Politics of Tough Guy Mysteries', *University of Dayton Review*, X, 1 (1973) 25–31.
318. Ruehlmann, William, *Saint with a Gun: The Unlawful American Private-Eye* (New York: New York University Press, 1974).
319. Ruhm, Herbert, Introduction to *The Hard-Boiled Detective: Stories from 'Black Mask' Magazine (1920–1951)* (Sevenoaks, Kent: Coronet, 1979).
320. Scott, Mark, 'An Introduction to the Private-Eye Novel', in Don Anderson and Stephen Knight (eds), *Cunning Exiles: Studies of Modern Prose Writers* (Sydney: Angus and Robertson, 1974) pp. 198–217.
321. Seelye, John, 'Buckskin and Ballistics: William Leggett and the American Detective Story', *Journal of Popular Culture*, I, 1 (Summer 1967) 52–7.
322. Shaw, Joseph T., Introduction to *The Hard-boiled Omnibus: Early Stories from 'Black Mask'* (New York: Simon and Schuster, 1946).
323. Shrapnel, Norman, 'The Literature of Violence and Pursuit', *The Times Literary Supplement*, 23 June 1961, pp. i–ii.
324. Sturak, Thomas, 'Horace McCoy, Captain Shaw, and *The Black*

Mask', in Adams, *Mystery and Detection Annual, 1972* [item 328] pp.139–58.

325. Symons, Julian, *Bloody Murder: From the Detective Story to the Crime Novel: A History* (Harmondsworth, Middx: Penguin, 1972).
326. Van Meter, Jan R., 'Sophocles and the Rest of the Boys in the Pulps: Myth and the Detective Novel', in Landrum *et al.*, *Dimensions of Detective Fiction* [item 288] pp. 17–21.
327. Widmer, Kingsley, 'The Way Out: Some Life-Style Sources of the Literary Tough Guy and the Proletarian Hero', in Madden, *Tough Guy Writers of the Thirties* [item 290] pp. 1–18.

DASHIELL HAMMETT

328. Adams, Donald K., 'The First Thin Man', in Adams (ed.), *The Mystery and Detection Annual, 1972* (Beverly Hills, 1972), pp. 160–72.
329. Baselon, David T., 'Dashiell Hammett's "Private Eye"; No Loyalty Beyond the Job', *Commentary* (New York), 7 May 1949, pp. 467–72.
330. Blair, Walter, 'Dashiell Hammett, Themes and Techniques', in Clarence Gohdes (ed.), *Essays on American Literature in Honor of Jay B. Hubbell* (Durham, NC: Duke University Press, 1967) pp. 295–306.
331. 'Dashiell Hammett Has Hard Words for Tough Stuff he Used to Write', *Los Angeles Times*, 7 June 1950, pt II, p. 3.
332. Edenbaum, Robert I., 'The Poetics of the Private Eye: The Novels of Dashiell Hammett' in Madden, *Tough Guy Writers of the Thirties* [item 290] pp. 80–103.
333. Editorial comment on 'The Cleansing of Poisonville', *Black Mask*, Nov 1927, p. 9.
334. Editorial comment on *The Maltese Falcon*, *Black Mask*, Dec 1929, p. 91.
335. Federal Bureau of Investigation, file on Dashiell Hammett (file 100–14499), provided by the United States Department of Justice under the Freedom of Information-Privacy Acts (3 sections, 351pp.).
336. Gardner, Frederick H., 'The Return of the Continental Op', *Nation*, CCIII (31 Oct 1966) 454–6.
337. Hammett, Dashiell, *The Big Knockover and Other Stories*, intro. Lillian Hellman (Harmondsworth, Middx: Penguin, 1977).
338. Hammett, Dashiell, *The Continental Op* (London: Pan, 1977).
339. Hammett, Dashiell, *The Dain Curse* (London: Pan, 1975).
340. Hammett, Dashiell, 'Finger Prints' (in 'Our Readers' Private Corner'), *Black Mask*, June 1925, pp. 127–8.
341. Hammett, Dashiell, 'From the Author of "Afraid of a Gun" ' (in 'Our Readers' Private Corner'), *Black Mask*, 1 Mar 1924, pp. 127–8.
342. Hammett, Dashiell, 'From the Author of "Arson Plus" ' (in 'Our Readers' Private Corner'), *Black Mask*, 1 Oct 1923, p. 127.

343. Hammett, Dashiell, 'From the Author of "Slippery Fingers" ' (in 'Our Readers' Private Corner'), *Black Mask*, 15 Oct 1923, p. 127.
344. Hammett, Dashiell, 'From the Author of "The Vicious Circle" ' (in 'Our Readers' Private Corner'), *Black Mask*, 15 June 1923, pp. 126–7.
345. Hammett, Dashiell, 'From the Author of "Zigzags of Treachery" ' (in 'Our Readers' Private Corner'), *Black Mask*, 1 Mar 1924, p. 127.
346. Hammett, Dashiell, 'From the Memoirs of a Private Detective', in Haycraft, *The Art of the Mystery Story* [item 292] pp. 417–22.
347. Hammett, Dashiell, 'The Girl with Silver Eyes', (in 'Our Readers' Private Corner'), *Black Mask*, June 1924, p. 127.
348. Hammett, Dashiell, *The Glass Key* (London: Pan, 1975).
349. Hammett, Dashiell, Introduction to *The Maltese Falcon* (New York: Modern Library, 1934) pp. vii–ix.
350. Hammett, Dashiell, 'Let's Wait' (in 'Our Readers' Private Corner: Inside Dope from Authors'), *Black Mask*, 15 Mar 1924, pp. 127–8.
351. Hammett, Dashiell, *The Maltese Falcon* (London: Pan, 1975).
352. Hammett, Dashiell, *Red Harvest* (London: Pan, 1975).
353. Hammett, Dashiell, *The Thin Man* (Harmondsworth, Middx: Penguin, 1974).
354. Hellman, Lillian, *An Unfinished Woman* (London: Macmillan, 1969).
355. Hellman, Lillian, *Scoundrel Time* (London: Macmillan, 1976).
356. ' "I am Learning to be a Hypochondriac": Lean Years for the Thin Man', *Times Herald* (date uncertain, 11 Mar 1957 likely), in FBI file 100–14499 [item 335] section 3.
357. Johnson, Diane, *Dashiell Hammett: A Life* (New York: Random House, New York, 1983).
358. Layman, Richard, *Shadow Man: The Life of Dashiell Hammett* (New York: Harcourt Brace Jovanovich, 1981.
359. Malin, Irving, 'Focus on *The Maltese Falcon*: The Metaphysical Falcon', in Madden, *Tough Guy Writers of the Thirties* [item 290] pp. 104–9.
360. Marcus, Steven, 'Dashiell Hammett and the Continental Op', *Partisan Review*, xli (1974) 363–77.
361. Moss, Leonard, 'Hammett's Heroic Operative', *New Republic*, cliv (8 Jan 1966) 32–4.
362. Nolan, William F., *Dashiell Hammett: A Casebook* (Santa Barbara, Calif.: McNally and Loftin, 1969).
363. Nolan, William F., *Dashiell Hammett: A Life at the Edge* (London: Arthur Barker 1983).
364. Occhiogrosso, Frank, 'Murder in the Dark: Dashiell Hammett', *New Republic*, clxxvii (30 July 1977) 28–30.
365. 'Our Own Short Story Course', *Black Mask*, Aug 1924, p. 127.
366. Pattow, Donald J., 'Order and Disorder in *The Maltese Falcon*', *Armchair Detective*, xi, 171.
367. Sanderson, Elizabeth, 'Ex-Detective Hammett', *Bookman*, lxxvi (Jan-Feb 1932) 516–18.
368. Spitzer, E. E., 'A Remembrance: With Corporal Hammett on Adak', *Nation*, ccxviii (5 Jan 1974) 6–9.

369. 'They Stand out from the Crowd', *Literary Digest*, 9 Dec 1933, p. 9.
370. 'Three Favorites', *Black Mask*, Nov 1924, p. 128.
371. Thompson, George J., 'The Problem of Moral Vision in Dashiell Hammett's Detective Novels' (unpublished Ph. D. dissertation, University of Connecticut, 1972).
372. Whitley, John S., 'Stirring Things Up: Dashiell Hammett's Continental Op', *Journal of American Studies*, xiv, 3 (Dec 1980) 443–55.
373. Whitley, John S., *Detectives and Friends: Dashiell Hammett's 'The Glass Key' and Raymond Chandler's 'The Long Goodbye'* (Exeter: University of Exeter American Arts Documentation Centre, 1981).
374. Wolfe, Peter, *Beams Falling: The Art of Dashiell Hammett* (Bowling Green, Ohio: Popular Press, 1980).

RAYMOND CHANDLER

375. Barzun, Jacques, 'The Illusion of the Real', in Miriam Gross (ed.), *The World of Raymond Chandler* (London: Weidenfeld and Nicolson, 1977) pp. 160–3.
376. Beekman, E. M., 'Raymond Chandler and an American Genre', *Massachusetts Review*, xiv (Winter 1973) 149–73.
377. Bruccoli, Matthew J. (ed.), *Chandler before Marlowe: Raymond Chandler's Early Prose and Poetry 1908–1912* (Columbia, SC: University of South Carolina Press, 1973).
378. Chandler, Raymond, *The Big Sleep* (Harmondsworth, Middx: Penguin, 1976).
379. Chandler, Raymond, *Farewell, My Lovely* (Harmondsworth, Middx: Penguin, 1975).
380. Chandler, Raymond, *The High Window* (Harmondsworth, Middx: Penguin, 1971).
381. Chandler, Raymond, 'The Hollywood Bowl', *Atlantic Monthly* clxxix (Jan 1947) 108–9.
382. Chandler, Raymond, *Killer in the Rain* (Harmondsworth, Middx: Penguin, 1976).
383. Chandler, Raymond, *The Lady in the Lake* (London: Pan, 1979).
384. Chandler, Raymond, *The Little Sister* (Harmondsworth, Middx: Penguin, 1969).
385. Chandler, Raymond, *The Long Goodbye* (Harmondsworth, Middx: Penguin, 1961).
386. Chandler, Raymond, 'Oscar Night in Hollywood', *Atlantic Monthly*, clxxxi (Mar 1948) pp. 24–7.
387. Chandler, Raymond, *Pearls are a Nuisance* (Harmondsworth, Middx: Penguin, 1964).
388. Chandler, Raymond, *Playback* (London: Pan, 1980).
389. Chandler, Raymond, 'The Simple Art of Murder', in Haycraft., *The Art of the Mystery Story* [item 292] pp. 222–37.
390. Chandler, Raymond, 'Ten Percent of Your Life', *Atlantic Monthly*, clxxxix (Feb 1952) 48–51.

391.   Chandler, Raymond, *Trouble is my Business* (Harmondsworth, Middx: Penguin, 1967).
392.   Chandler, Raymond, 'Writers in Hollywood', *Atlantic Monthly*, CLXXVI (Nov 1945) 50–54.
393.   Conrad, Peter, 'The Private Dick as Dandy', *Times Literary Supplement*, 20 Jan 1978, p. 60.
394.   Craig, H. A. L., 'The Whiskey of Affliction', *Listener*, 27 Sep 1951, pp. 513–15.
395.   Davies, Russell, 'Omnes Me Impune Lacessunt', in Gross, *The World of Raymond Chandler* [item 375] pp. 32–42.
396.   Durham, Philip, *Down These Mean Streets a Man Must Go: Raymond Chandler's Knight* (Durham, NC: University of North Carolina Press, 1963).
397.   Elliott, George P., 'A Country Full of Blondes', *Nation*, CXC (23 Apr 1960) 354–60.
398.   Flint, R. W., 'A Cato of the Cruelties', *Partisan Review*, XIV (May-June 1947) 328–30.
399.   Gardiner, Dorothy, and Walker, Kathrine Sorley, (eds), *Raymond Chandler Speaking* (London: Hamish Hamilton, 1962).
400.   Homberger, Eric, 'The Man of Letters (1908–1912)', in Gross, *The World of Raymond Chandler* [item 375] pp. 8–18.
401.   Houseman, John, 'Lost Fortnight: "The Blue Dahlia" and How it Grew out of Raymond Chandler's Alcoholic Dash for a Deadline', *Harper's*, CCXXXI (Aug 1965) 55–61.
402.   'Interview with Billy Wilder by Ivan Moffat', in Gross, *The World of Raymond Chandler* [item 375] pp. 44–51.
403.   Jameson, Frederic, 'On Raymond Chandler', *Southern Review*, VI (1970) 624–50.
404.   Knight, Stephen, ' " . . . A Hard-Boiled Gentleman" – Raymond Chandler's Hero', in *Form and Ideology in Crime Fiction* (London: Macmillan, 1980) pp. 135–67.
405.   Lid, R. W., 'Philip Marlowe Speaking', *Kenyon Review*, XXXI, 2 (1969) 153–78.
406.   MacShane, Frank, *The Life of Raymond Chandler* (London: Jonathan Cape, 1976).
407.   MacShane, Frank (ed.), *The Notebooks of Raymond Chandler and 'English Summer', a Gothic Romance by Raymond Chandler* (London: Weidenfeld and Nicolson, 1977).
408.   MacShane, Frank (ed.), *Selected Letters of Raymond Chandler* (London: Jonathan Cape. 1981).
409.   Mason, Michael, 'Marlowe, Men, and Women', in Gross, *The World of Raymond Chandler* [item 375] pp. 90–101.
410.   Partridge, Ralph, 'Detection and Thrillers', *New Statesman and the Nation*, 9 Jan 1954, pp. 47–8.
411.   Powell, Dilys, 'Ray and Cissy', in Gross, *The World of Raymond Chandler* [item 375] pp. 82–7.
412.   Reck, Tom S., 'Raymond Chandler's Los Angeles', *Nation*, CCXXI (20 Dec 1975) 661–3.
413.   Ruhm, Herbert, 'Raymond Chandler: From Bloomsbury to the

Jungle – and Beyond', in Madden, *Tough Guy Writers of the Thirties* [item 290] pp. 171–85.

414. Russell, D. C., 'The Chandler Books', *Atlantic*, CLXXV (Mar 1945) 123–4.
415. Schickel, Richard, 'Raymond Chandler, Private Eye', *Commentary*, XXXV (Feb 1963) 158–61.
416. Smith, David, 'The Public Eye of Raymond Chandler', *Journal of American Studies*, XIV (1980) 423–41.
417. Speir, Jerry, *Raymond Chandler* (New York: Frederick Ungar, 1981).
418. Spender, Natasha, 'His Own Long Goodbye', in Gross, *The World of Raymond Chandler* [item 375] pp. 128–58.
419. Symons, Julian, 'An Aesthete Discovers the Pulps', in Gross, *The World of Raymond Chandler* [item 375] pp. 20–9.
420. Thomson, James Whitfield, 'The Slumming Angel: The Voice and Vision of Raymond Chandler' (unpublished Ph. D. dissertation, University of Pennsylvania, 1977).
421. Whitley, John, 'Raymond Chandler and the Traditions', *London Review*, Autumn 1967, pp. 30–41.

Index